framers

framers

human advantage in an age of technology and turmoil

Kenneth Cukier,

Viktor Mayer-Schönberger,

Francis de Véricourt

DUTTON

An imprint of Penguin Random House LLC
penguinrandomhouse.com

LIBRARY OF CONGRESS CATALOGING-IN-PUBLICATION DATA

Names: Cukier, Kenneth, author. | Mayer-Schönberger, Viktor, author. | Véricourt, Francis de, author.
Title: Framers: human advantage in an age of technology and turmoil / Kenneth Cukier, Viktor Mayer-Schönberger, Francis de Véricourt.
Description: [New York, New York]: Dutton, [2021] | Includes bibliographical references and index.
Identifiers: LCCN 2020051813 (print) | LCCN 2020051814 (ebook) |
ISBN 9780593182598 (hardcover) | ISBN 9780593182604 (ebook)
Subjects: LCSH: Cognitive maps (Psychology) | Frames (Sociology) | Reasoning (Psychology)
Classification: LCC BF314 .C85 2021 (print) | LCC BF314 (ebook) |
DDC 153—dc23
LC record available at https://lccn.loc.gov/2020051813
LC ebook record available at https://lccn.loc.gov/2020051814

ISBN 9780593185049 (export edition)

Printed in the United States of America
1st Printing

Book design by Nancy Resnick

To my wife Heather
K.N.C.

To Hans Kraus
V.M.S.

In memory of Hervé Raynaud
F.d.V.

For there is always light,
if only we're brave enough to see it.
If only we're brave enough to be it.

—Amanda Gorman, January 20, 2021

contents

1. decisions   1

the source of human power is neither muscle nor mind but
models

2. framing   23

mental models infuse everything we do, even if we're
unaware of them

3. causality   49

we are causal-inference engines and often wrong, but this
is good

4. counterfactuals   73

envisioning worlds that do not exist lets us excel in this one

5. constraints   97

our vision needs to be bounded to be effective

6. reframing   123

occasionally we need to switch frames or invent new ones

7. learning   149
  a wide variety of frames is crucial for progress

8. pluralism   173
  a coexistence of frames is essential to humanity's survival

9. vigilance   201
  we must remain on guard not to cede our power

a guide to working with frames   219

notes   222

acknowledgments   249

index   253

about the authors   263

1

decisions

the source of human power is neither muscle nor mind but models

Some threats are sudden and unexpected. Others are slow and smoldering. Both represent cognitive blind spots for which societies are unprepared. Whether pandemics or populism, new weapons or new technologies, global warming or gaping inequalities, how humans respond marks the difference between survival and extinction. And how we act depends on what we see.

Each year, more than 700,000 people around the world die from infections that antibiotics once cured but no longer do. The bacteria have developed resistance. The number of deaths is rising fast. Unless a solution is found, it is on track to hit ten million a year, or one person every three seconds. It makes even the tragedy of Covid-19 pale by comparison. And it is a problem that society itself has produced. Antibiotics work less and less well due to overuse: the very drugs that could once staunch the bacteria have turned them into superbugs.

We take antibiotics for granted, but before penicillin was discovered in 1928 and mass-produced more than a decade later, people

1

routinely died from broken bones or simple scratches. In 1924, the sixteen-year-old son of American president Calvin Coolidge got a blister on his toe while playing tennis on the White House lawn. It became infected, and he died within the week—neither his status nor wealth could save him. Today, almost every aspect of medicine, from a C-section to cosmetic surgery to chemotherapy, relies on antibiotics. If their power were to wane those treatments would become far riskier.

From her colorful, plant-strewn office in Cambridge, Massachusetts, Regina Barzilay, a professor of artificial intelligence at MIT, envisioned a solution. Conventional drug development mostly focuses on finding substances with molecular "fingerprints" similar to ones that work. That generally performs well, but not for antibiotics. Most substances with similar compositions have already been examined, and new antibiotics are so close in structure to existing ones that bacteria quickly develop resistance to them, too. So Barzilay and a diverse team of biologists and computer scientists, led by Jim Collins, a professor of bioengineering at MIT, embraced an alternative approach. What if, instead of looking for structural similarities, they focused on the effect: Did it kill bacteria? They reconceived the problem not as a biological one but an informational one.

Charismatic and confident, Barzilay doesn't come across as a typical nerd. But then, she is accustomed to defying categories. She grew up under communism in what is now Moldova, speaking Russian; was educated in Israel, speaking Hebrew; and attended grad school in America. In 2014, as a new mother in her early forties, she was diagnosed with breast cancer, which she survived after difficult treatments. This ordeal led her to change her research in order to focus on artificial intelligence in medicine. As her research gained attention, a MacArthur "genius grant" followed.

Barzilay and the team got to work. They trained an algorithm on more than 2,300 compounds with antimicrobial properties, to find if any inhibited the growth of *E. coli,* a noxious bacterium. Then the model was applied to around six thousand molecules in the Drug Repurposing Hub and later to more than one hundred million molecules in another database to predict which might work. In early 2020 they struck gold. One molecule stood out. They named it "halicin" after HAL, the renegade computer in *2001: A Space Odyssey.*

The discovery of a superdrug to kill superbugs made headlines around the world. It was hailed as a "video killed the radio star" moment for the superiority of machine over man. "AI Discovers Antibiotics to Treat Drug-Resistant Diseases," boomed a front-page headline in the *Financial Times.*

But that missed the real story. It wasn't a victory for artificial intelligence but a success of human cognition: the ability to rise up to a critical challenge by conceiving of it in a certain way, altering aspects of it, which open up new paths to a solution. Credit does not go to a new technology but to a human ability.

"Humans were the ones who selected the right compounds, who knew what they were doing when they gave the material for the model to learn from," Barzilay explains. People defined the problem, designed the approach, chose the molecules to train the algorithm, and then selected the database of substances to examine. And once some candidates popped up, humans reapplied their biological lens to understand why it worked.

The process of finding halicin is more than an outstanding scientific breakthrough or a major step toward accelerating and lowering the cost of drug development. To succeed, Barzilay and the team needed to harness a form of cognitive freedom. They didn't get the idea from a book, from tradition, or by connecting obvious dots. They got it by embracing a unique cognitive power that all people possess.

Mental Models and the World

Humans think using mental models. These are representations of reality that make the world comprehensible. They allow us to see patterns, predict how things will unfold, and make sense of the circumstances we encounter. Reality would otherwise be a flood of information, a jumble of inchoate experiences and sensations. Mental models bring order. They let us focus on essential things and ignore others—just as, at a cocktail party, we can hear the conversation that we're in while tuning out the chatter around us. We craft a simulation of reality in our minds to anticipate how situations will play out.

We use mental models all the time, even if we are not aware of them. But there are moments when we are acutely conscious of how we size up a situation, and can deliberately maintain or change our perspective. This often happens when we need to make a high-consequence decision, such as whether to switch jobs, become a parent, buy a home, close a factory, or build a skyscraper. In those instances, it can become apparent to us that our decisions are not simply based on the reasoning we apply, but on something more foundational: the particular lens through which we look at the situation—our sense of how the world works. That underlying level of cognition consists of mental models.

The fact that we need to interpret the world in order to exist in it, that how we perceive reality colors how we act within it, is something that people have long known but take for granted. It is what made Regina Barzilay's achievement so impressive. She conceived of the problem in the right way. She applied a mental model, shifting her focus from the structure of the molecule (that is, the mechanism by which it worked) to its function (that is, whether it worked

4

at all). By framing the problem differently, she and the team achieved a discovery that had eluded others.

Barzilay was a framer. By correctly framing the situation, she could unlock new solutions.

The mental models that we choose and apply are frames: they determine how we understand and act in the world. Frames enable us to generalize and make abstractions that apply to other situations. With them, we can handle new situations, rather than having to relearn everything from scratch. Our frames are always operating in the background. But we can stop and deliberately ask ourselves which frame we are applying, and whether it is the best fit for the circumstances. And if it's not, we can choose another frame that is better. Or, we can invent a new frame altogether.

Framing is so fundamental to human cognition that even those who study the workings of the mind rarely focused on it until relatively recently. Its importance was overshadowed by other mental capabilities, such as sensing and memory. But as people have become more aware of the need to improve their decision-making, the role of frames as fundamental to choosing and acting well has moved from the background to center stage. We now know that the right frame applied in the right way opens up a wider range of possibilities, which in turn leads to better choices. The frames we employ affect the options we see, the decisions we make, and the results we attain. By being better at framing, we get better outcomes.

Many of society's thorniest problems involve, at their core, a friction over the way an issue is framed. Should America build a wall with other countries or a bridge? Should Scotland remain within the United Kingdom or declare independence? Should China's "one country, two systems" policy toward Hong Kong emphasize the first or last part of that phrase? People can look at the same situation and see different things because they frame it differently.

When San Francisco 49ers quarterback Colin Kaepernick took a knee during the national anthem in 2016 to call attention to racism and police violence, some saw it as a respectful form of quiet, symbolic protest. After all, he didn't turn his back or raise a fist—or a finger. Others saw it as a grotesque disrespect for the country, an antagonistic publicity stunt by a mediocre player that brought the culture wars to one of the few areas of American life that hadn't yet been spoiled by them. The argument wasn't over what happened but what it meant. It was a Rorschach test: what people saw in it depended on what frame they brought to it.

Each frame lets us see the world from a distinct vantage point. Frames magnify certain elements and minimize others. The capitalist frame shows us commercial opportunity everywhere; the communist frame reduces everything to class struggle. The industrialist looks at a rain forest and sees timber that is valuable today, while the environmentalist sees the "lungs of the planet," vital for long-term survival. Should people be mandated to wear a mask in public amid a pandemic? In the United States those using the health frame stated "yes, absolutely," while those applying the freedom frame cried "hell no!" Same data, different frames, opposite conclusions.

Sometimes our frames don't fit the reality to which we apply them. There is no such thing as a "bad" frame per se (save for one exception that we'll raise later), but there are certainly cases of misframing, where a given frame doesn't fit very well. In fact, the path of human progress is littered with the carcasses of misused frames. Take the fifteenth-century anatomy book *Fasciculus Medicinae*. It associated body parts with zodiac signs—a pleasing symmetry between the heavens above and the organs within. But that frame never cured anyone, and it was cast aside as more useful frames came along.

We make similar mistakes in our own day. In 2008 Nokia led the world in mobile phone sales. When Apple introduced the iPhone, few thought it would take off. The trend was to make handsets smaller and cheaper, but Apple's was bulkier, pricier, and buggier. Nokia's frame came from the conservative telecom industry, valuing practicality and reliability. Apple's frame came from the breathlessly innovative computing industry, valuing ease of use and the extensibility of new features via software. That frame turned out to be a better fit for the needs and wants of consumers—and Apple dominated the market.

Misapplying frames can have horrendous consequences. In the 1930s the Soviet Union followed Lysenkoism, a theory of plant genetics. It was based on Marxist-Leninist ideology, not botany. Among its precepts was that crops can be planted close together because, according to communist theory, members of the same class live in solidarity and do not compete for resources.

Taking a communist frame from economics and applying it to farming was lunacy, but the country's leaders made it the basis of their agriculture policy. Its proponent, Trofim Lysenko, had the favor of Stalin himself. Scientists who questioned his findings were fired, imprisoned, exiled, or executed. The great Russian biologist Nikolai Vavilov criticized Lysenko's science and was sentenced to death. As for the result of Lysenkoism? Although the country increased the area of land under cultivation a hundredfold, yields fell as crops died or rotted. The misapplied frame contributed to tragic famines that cost millions of lives.

If a frame doesn't fit, the good news is that we can use a different one, or invent a new and better one. Some new frames are responsible for world-changing breakthroughs. Darwin's theory of evolution provided an explanation of the origins of life without reliance on religion. Similarly, Newtonian physics explained the movement of physical objects in space for centuries, but over time there were phenomena that it couldn't account for. Einstein reframed physics by showing that time, long considered constant, is actually relative.

It is easiest to see the value of frames in the sciences, where they are (or at least should be) explicit, and where researchers document the mental inputs they use to reach their conclusions. Yet when it comes to the vast challenges that humanity faces today, we often fail to notice which frames we are applying. Understanding the power of framing in all domains is vital. We need to see problems differently in order to solve them. The centerpiece of our response to our most difficult dilemmas—whether at the level of the individual, community, country, or indeed civilization—lies within us: our unique human ability to frame.

But we need to get better at it. This book explains how.

Seeing What Isn't There

Over the past few decades, a revolution in cognitive psychology and decision theory has placed mental models at the center of how people live and think. Framing commonly happens subconsciously. But people who consistently make good decisions, or are in positions where they need to make high-stakes ones, are aware of framing and their ability to reframe. This affects the options they see and the actions they take.

When a venture capitalist scrutinizes an investment, a military officer thinks through an operation, or an engineer approaches a technical problem, they have to frame the issue. Need to decide whether to build a wind park in one location or another, or go with a solar farm instead? The information we gather is only part of the decision-making process. More important, in many respects, is how one sizes up the situation itself: how one frames it.

Yet framing is not only for high-stakes matters. It affects our everyday lives as well. We are continually confronted with questions that require having a model of the world in our mind. How can I get along better with my partner? How can I impress my boss? How can I rearrange my life to be healthier? And wealthier? Framing is just as essential for these types of questions. It undergirds our thoughts, affecting what we perceive and how we think. By making our frames apparent and learning how to deliberately choose and apply them, we can improve our lives and our world.

Put simply: we can turn framing from a basic feature of human cognition into a practical tool we can use to make better decisions.

Our mind uses frames to capture the most salient aspects of the world, and filter out the others—we couldn't comprehend life in all of its intricate complexity otherwise. By mentally modeling the world, we keep it manageable and thus actionable. In this sense, frames simplify reality. But they aren't dumbed-down versions of the world. They concentrate our thinking on the critical parts.

Frames also help us to learn from single experiences and come up with general rules that we can apply to other situations—including ones that have not yet happened. They enable us to know something about the unobserved and even the unobservable; to imagine things for which no data exists. Frames let us see what isn't there. We can ask "What if?" and foresee how different decisions might play out. It is this ability to envision other realities that makes possible individual achievement and societal progress.

Humans have long looked to the sky and wished to fly. We now do so—but not like a bird. Yet no amount of data and processing power could have taken a plethora of bicycle parts and conceived of an airplane, as the Wright brothers did in 1903. A mental model was needed; a frame. Likewise, humans dreamed of seeing inside the body without cutting the skin. And today we do, but with technologies like X-rays, not with our naked eyes. For that too a new conceptualization was required, a frame for how to use the electro-magnetic radiation known as Röntgen rays in 1895.

Some of the things we use every day are the result of changing the way they were initially framed—sometimes comically so. The telephone was first thought about as a way to listen to music re-motely: people would dial in to hear a concert. The phonograph was considered to be a way to communicate messages: a company presi-dent might send audio memos on grooved cylinders to far-flung managers. Only when these uses were flipped around did the tech-nologies catch on. Thomas Edison in the early 1900s believed mo-tion pictures would replace classrooms—a vision only realized a century later when Zoom became the new schoolhouse.

The term *framing* is well established in the social sciences. The psychologists Daniel Kahneman and Amos Tversky eloquently ex-plained how different characterizations of outcomes influence decision-making—which they called the "framing effect," and de-scribed it as a flaw in human reasoning. Though we share the same term, the meaning here is somewhat different: not how something is positioned but a deliberate act of harnessing mental models to elicit options prior to making a decision. Although the misframing of a situation can certainly lead to flawed decisions, framing is a valuable and empowering human capability. It lets us make sense of the world and reshape it. We would not be who we are, as individu-als or as a species, without it.

It may be tempting to understand instances of reframing as a par-adigm shift; that is, a fundamental change in the prevailing concepts and practices in a domain. In 1962 Thomas Kuhn, a philosopher of science, argued that paradigm shifts drive scientific progress. But the comparison is inexact. Every paradigm shift is a reframing, such as when Copernicus's heliocentric view overturned Ptolemy's geocen-tric model of Earth and the sun. But not every reframing is a paradigm shift—reframing happens comparatively frequently. Sometimes it changes society's concept of the world; far more often it leads to some small but significant change in our individual lives. In each case, a successful act of reframing leads to better decisions.

Working with frames may sound complicated and difficult. It does require skill. Yet humans are surprisingly good at it. We have been doing it for tens of thousands of years, even though we don't always realize it.

Frames are more than a person's individual perspective—they are cognitive templates. But the concept of perspective is a useful metaphor. Before the Italian architect Filippo Brunelleschi began drawing with geometric perspective around 1420, artists painted the world as flat and positioned objects relative to their implied importance. Taking their cue from Brunelleschi, artists learned to depict depth and draw scenes as they actually appeared. Comparing pictures from before and after this change is one way to realize the potency of switching to a new frame.

We are all framers. We make predictions, from the mundane to the spectacular. In this way, we constantly perform a sort of mental time-travel. Some of us are better at it than others, and there are ways in which we can all improve. In fact, we must.

Dreaming with Constraints

Frames help to do two tasks really well, which we outline in chapter 2. First, in novel situations or when circumstances change, our ability to choose a frame provides us with new options. Second, and at least as important, in situations that are familiar, frames focus our mind, thereby reducing our cognitive load. It's an incredibly efficient way for us to reach a suitable decision. To do that successfully, three elements are in play: causal thinking, our aptitude to create counterfactuals, and our capacity to constrain and shape our imagination toward a particular goal. Consider each element in turn.

Chapter 3 looks at causality. Humans see the world through the lens of cause and effect. This makes the world understandable. We can predict in advance what a given action will provoke and repeat it to our advantage. Causal reasoning is the foundation of our cognition. Children learn to think causally as they grow up, and thinking in cause and effect has enabled human societies to evolve over time. We are causal-inference engines.

Our causal inferences are often wrong, because the world is complex. It's hard to suss out all the intricacies with the three pounds of spongy fat and protein in our skulls. We now depend on scientific methodology to prevent us from jumping to causal conclusions too quickly—for example, that performing a special dance can cause rain to fall. But our tendency to see causes everywhere has a valuable consequence: it gives us a tool to understand the world and to place it more or less under our control.

The second element of our mental models is counterfactuals, which we examine in chapter 4. These are imagined alternatives to reality; hypotheses of a world in which one or several things are changed. As with causality, we think in counterfactuals all the time. They come naturally to us. Counterfactuals let us escape the cognitive here and now: we are not locked into the reality before us—in our mind's eye we can invent a new one.

Counterfactual thinking is crucial to progress. People can envision what does not exist, as a way to understand the actual world and conceive of how it might be different. We do this by asking what-if questions. Our imaginings need not be meaningless daydreams; they are an essential precursor for action, an element of our preparation to make decisions. Often when we imagine and visualize, we are conjuring and assessing counterfactuals. This is what children do when they engage in pretend play and what scientists do when they devise experiments.

Though we can improve the world through counterfactual thinking, it might be foolish to stray too far into the realm of the unrealistic. Chapter 5 introduces the third element of framing, the role of constraints. The right constraints help us to adjust our imagination so that our counterfactuals remain actionable, showing us actions that are actually possible. Framing isn't an exercise of following flights of fancy, untethered balloons tossed by the wind upward to nowhere. It's dreaming within limits. Our counterfactuals are useful only when they are bounded.

Constraints act as the glue that holds the mental model together, so that we can think *What if?* in a structured and deliberate way. If we have a flat tire and have never changed a tire before, we don't look to Starfleet antigravity to help us; we look at the tools we find in the trunk (say, a car jack and a wrench) and visualize how these could work for us.

These three dimensions of cognition—causality, counterfactuals, and constraints—together form the basis of framing. They are our tools for seeing beyond the obvious and thinking forward.

However, sometimes we need to change frames, especially if the context of a problem has shifted. Chapter 6 looks at our ability to sift through our collection of frames to find one that is better suited to a situation. Or we can repurpose an existing frame from one domain and use it in another—deliberately expanding our range by amending that frame to fit a new context and goal.

As we gain experience, we develop a repertoire of frames and can trot out a suitable one when we need to, much as good pianists have a repertoire of styles that they use. Accomplished musicians can instantly find the underlying key, tempo, rhythm, and harmony in a wide variety of pieces they've never heard before. This is the essence of improvisation. Each genre is very different, with its own set of rules. It is hard for a pianist to switch from lovelorn Chopin to Lady Gaga. But reframing is as possible on the ebony and ivory as it is in life.

Choosing among different frames does have its limits, however. In some cases, the right frame may not exist. What's needed then is an act of invention, to devise a completely new one. We laud those who create entirely new frames, since, when successful, they end up changing the world.

How we can become better framers is explained in chapter 7. Learning this skill depends on embracing a diversity of frames. We offer three strategies to achieve this: expanding our repertoire, developing our curiosity through a process we call "cognitive foraging," and if all else fails, having the courage to leap into the cognitive unknown.

Chapter 8 considers the importance of framing for communities, countries, and civilization writ large. The goal is pluralism: fostering and celebrating differences, instead of aspiring to a homogenous way of seeing the world. We need to promote the "colorful," not believe that we achieve some form of valor by deliberately making ourselves "color-blind."

What we cannot allow are frames that deny the existence of other frames (the sole exception to the idea that there are no bad frames). Uniformity of mental models is what crushes human progress. It makes people no wiser than automata that perpetuate the past because they cannot see beyond the present. If our frames cannot coexist, how can we?

The true heroes of human framing do not live in palaces, manage big companies, or teach at fancy universities. They are all around us—indeed, they are us. As individuals, our framing matters because it shapes our lives. But for humanity, what matters is the richness of the mental models we collectively possess. Pundits often suggest that people must come together and converge on a perspective to meet pressing challenges. But it is quite the opposite: our power lies in the difference of human frames and in our ability to see the world from a myriad of angles. Only if we tap the breadth of human frames can we devise the original solutions we will need to survive as a species.

The Machine and the Mob

Belief in the value and power of framing is under threat. Around the world, people are losing confidence in humanity's cognitive abilities, and turning to solutions that deny the role of mental models. On one side are those who place their faith in the machine, and on the other are those who accept the rough justice and easy answers of the mob.

The hyper-rationalists, who embrace facts and value reason, represent the first side. They believe we can rely exclusively on data and algorithms to solve our myriad problems, and are tempted to bypass human framing for artificial intelligence. They are not just a handful of geeks waiting for the "singularity," the moment when computers are smarter than people. A growing cohort looks to technology to deliver exactly the kind of detached, objective superrational decision-making that people seem to be incapable of. For them, there is no doubt that humans will remain in the seat of power but that everyday judgments will be handled by machines.

Need to drive to Delhi? Fight crime in Berlin? Deliver groceries in Wuhan? There's an algorithm for that. As the technology evolves, many look to AI to remedy social ills that people have shown themselves to be unable to address. This, they hope, will lead humanity out of our current irrational darkness and ensure the victory of reason. Supporters laud AI for its potential to take away decision-making from humans and place it in the computer.

Equally vocal are the emotionalists, who argue the opposite: that humanity has been suffering from too much rationality, too much reliance on data, and cold, merciless, analytical reasoning. They believe that humanity's core problem is not too much passion but too little; that we are suffering because we do not rely enough on our gut and our instincts. They long for collective bonding in communities of similar-minded folks, and for clear distinctions and boundaries with "others" who do not belong. The appeal to emotional roots is a call to accept irrationality as a core quality of humanness.

We see this phenomenon on both the right and the left, in industrialized democracies as well as developing countries. It is associated with right-wing populists, who prefer decisive action over long-standing processes to weigh evidence. Governance is a feeling; leadership is an emotion; decisions are made from an innate sense of the rightness of one's beliefs. Yet it also crops up in the social sphere on the left, when activists wish to silence critics of their worldview or delegitimize others with whom they disagree.

Though the increasing power of AI is new, we have been dealing with this basic struggle for centuries. The tension between reason and emotion, artifice and nature, deliberation and gut instinct has shaped how we order our lives and govern our societies. In the 1600s the French philosopher and mathematician René Descartes advocated for a life of rationality, order, and evidence. Parisian parks that are laid out in perfect symmetry remind us of his influence.

A century later Jean-Jacques Rousseau urged a different approach, one of trust in feelings and intuition, and of looking to the inner self for answers: "All the evil I ever did in my life was the result of reflection," he wrote. "And the little good I have been able to do

16

was the result of impulse." It is a world of inklings, passions, and appetites—wild fits of fury perfectly excusable as expressions of one's humanity. When British and American landscapers make urban parks resemble rambling nature, it is an unwitting nod to Rousseau's outlook.

The same dichotomy played out in twentieth-century business. Frederick Taylor's influential theory of scientific management aimed to quantify every aspect of a company's operations. Managers armed with stopwatches and clipboards paraded the factory floor to ensure productivity. Yet the century ended with the celebrated success of GE's voluble chief executive Jack Welch, whose business autobiography was aptly subtitled *Straight from the Gut.*

There is a certain feeling of authenticity in the rejection of linear, fact-filled rationality for the joyous, human embrace of emotion in decision-making. Not everything can be reduced to a number or a formula in logic. But this ethos cannot solve problems—it can only glorify them. It can tear down but not construct. Over the past half century, psychologists and behavioral economists have amassed a mountain of experimental evidence showing the inferiority, in most cases, of decisions driven by the gut. Relying on instinct may give us a warm feeling of doing what feels right. But it fails to deliver a viable strategy to solve the challenges we face.

Meanwhile AI may make better decisions than people and steal our jobs, but computers and algorithms cannot frame. AI is brilliant at answering what it is asked; framers pose questions never before voiced. Computers work only in a world that exists; humans live in ones they imagine through framing.

Consider the computer's shortcomings in the very arena where it is usually feted for its excellence: board games. Even people who are familiar with this story extract the wrong lesson.

In 2018 Google DeepMind unveiled a system called AlphaZero that learned to win at chess, Go, and shogi purely by playing against itself, with zero human input other than the rules. After just nine hours, during which it played itself in forty-four million games of chess, it was beating the world's best chess program, Stockfish. When grandmasters played against it, they were amazed by its alien approach. For over a century chess experts had a settled consensus on basic concepts and strategies, such as the value of pieces or board position. AlphaZero made radical moves, privileging mobility over position, and feeling no reluctance to make sacrifices. AlphaZero seemed to have conceived of an entirely new strategy for the game.

Only, it hadn't.

An AI system cannot conceive of anything. It cannot concoct mental models. It can neither generalize nor explain. AlphaZero is a black box—for us and for itself. It was people, not AI, who could look at the moves and develop the concepts of "board position" or "sacrifice." Humans frame AlphaZero's actions, making them explainable and applying them generally. Humans become smarter because we can abstract AI's accomplishments. Appreciating and applying the lessons is something that AI cannot do on its own.

Both the rationalists and the emotionalists correctly identify something unique about human cognition. But both lead to dead ends. Neither offers a suitable answer to our civilizational challenges. Nor can we expect much from a synthesis of the two. Amalgamating two approaches built on unsound foundations, at best, will simply maintain a fragile tension without hope of real progress.

The crucial insight is that our choice isn't limited to these two options. We do not have to decide between a dehumanizing singularity or a tsunami of populist terror—nor try to meld them into a suboptimal mix. We have at our disposal another strategy, a different human capacity that until now has been overlooked: framing. Our ability to apply, hone, and reinvent mental models provides us with the means to solve our problems without deferring to the machine or accepting the mob.

That brings us back to Regina Barzilay. We find ourselves at a crossroads. Huge challenges loom. As with antibiotics, many of our vulnerabilities are homegrown, the consequences of decisions we made, alternatives we failed to identify, actions we did not take. We got ourselves into our current troubles. The good news is that we can get ourselves out. But it requires a new mind-set.

What Is Without Starts from Within

There is a project called "Our World in Data" run by a team at the University of Oxford. It takes all aspects of life and, as its name suggests, views them through the lens of information. Infant mortality stats? They're on it. Global GDP? They've got you covered. The material is beloved by Bill Gates, who occasionally retweets its charts and whose foundation supports its work. And to judge from the rainbow-hued lines and bar charts they pump out, we've never had it so good.

It is true that by almost every metric, the world has been inexorably improving. There are fewer wars, less disease, more literacy, cleaner water, richer countries, happier people, longer life spans. Covid-19 will make a dent in some of these trend lines, but only a temporary one—raise our eyes to the more distant future and the dip will surely be smoothed out as time and progress march on.

The evolution of human thinking has played a crucial role in all these improvements. Before there is a change on the ground, there is a transformation in the mind. All that is without starts from within. We frame and reframe our world, and civilization advances.

But this sunny optimism may be misplaced. Its purveyors extrapolate to how things will evolve into the future. But their analyses disguise troubles. There is a pathology of human progress, that the very fruits of our creation risk being the sources of our destruction.

Whether it is a high-tech arms race or a hotter climate or a growing underclass around the world, we need to get better at framing to respond.

Bookshelves sag with tomes extolling the virtues of human progress. But the affluent, immortal brainiac who is predicted in the book *Homo Deus* by Yuval Noah Harari will in time be as ridiculed as the rich, safe, and happy "last man" in Francis Fukuyama's *The End of History*. A more clear-eyed and responsible look at the world suggests that things aren't getting easier but harder. The toughest challenges facing humanity are not behind us but ahead of us.

In the past most of our challenges were a matter of survival for individuals or communities, but not the entire planet. And many of these challenges had obvious solutions. For hunger we hunt and gather. For shelter we build a home. For war we raise an army. Often there was a frame we could readily apply.

But as our framing improved our decision-making, this success created its own weakness: a belief in a single frame of truth. In countless cases, humanity has created and enforced such frames, from the Spanish Inquisition to Soviet collectivism. And we have learned surprisingly little from their failures. We are still susceptible to monolithic thinking, convincing ourselves that past failures of single frames were due to the frame, not because it was singular.

That makes our current moment in history so precarious. The fate of humanity depends on our learning to reconceive our challenges. Crises of nature (from climate change to pandemics) and humanity (from new forms of tribalism to violent oppression) demand not a cognitive leap of faith, but a doubling down on what humans have always done so well: applying imagination under constraints to come up with novel solutions and appreciating their long-term consequences.

Ours is an age of division and paradoxes: grand charities and everyday tyrannies, science and anti-science, facts and fake news. The International Space Station visible from the slum, rockets to colonize other planets, and immigrant children held in cages. The primitive and the transhuman; dogs and gods.

Normally species go extinct because they cannot adapt to their circumstances. Human beings could be the first species that has everything we need to adapt but perishes because we did not use it— not because we have no other choice but because we failed to make the right choices.

Framing offers a way out. Humans can adapt by relying on our cognitive capacity to generate mental models, by better envisioning consequences and choosing alternatives. Yet this requires a degree of cognitive freedom that is being winnowed from every side. We must realize that we have what we need to survive and to thrive— provided we grasp the responsibility, courage, and imagination to accept our role as framers.

2

framing

**mental models infuse everything we do,
even if we're unaware of them**

On Sunday, October 15, 2017, Alyssa Milano was sitting in bed at
home in LA reading the news. The internet was abuzz with revelations about the movie producer Harvey Weinstein. As a child star of
1980s sitcoms now making it as a fortysomething actor, she knew
all the names in the news. Sexual harassment is hardly unheard of
in Hollywood; the proverbial "casting couch" is an ugly institution.
But this felt different. These were not unwanted advances but physical assaults, dozens of them, which were not merely ignored but
actively covered up, stretching back decades.

A message popped up on her phone from a friend suggesting that
if women spoke out on Twitter, the world would see the extent of the
problem. Milano liked the idea. She had always had a deeply moral
streak. As a celebrity at fifteen, she kissed a boy who was HIV positive on a television talk show, to make the point that casual contact
with AIDS victims is safe. In 2013 she "leaked" online what seemed
to be a sex video of herself and her husband, which, rather than show
steamy stuff, focused the camera on a two-minute news segment

explaining the conflict in Syria—clickbait in the service of human-itarianism.

Turning to Twitter made sense. "This is an amazing way to get some idea of the magnitude," Milano recalls thinking, and "a way to get the focus off these horrible men and to put the focus back on the victims and survivors." Milano herself had been assaulted on a film set almost twenty-five years earlier—but she had never mentioned it publicly. She opened a message window on Twitter and typed: "If you've been sexually harassed or assaulted write 'me too' as a reply to this tweet." She turned off the device, looked at her sleeping three-year-old daughter, and went to bed.

When she awoke, she was stunned to see the tweet had thirty-five thousand replies and growing. It spread across the world in a flash. By the end of the day, the #MeToo hashtag was used in more than twelve million posts. Reporters started calling. It became a global phenomenon.

The MeToo movement is many things, but perhaps most power-fully, it is a frame. It transformed how sexual assault is perceived, not as something to be kept private but something that could be made public. The declarations on Twitter became a source of empowerment and liberation. MeToo reversed the stigma: women need not be ashamed, and could bring shame upon the men who assaulted them.

Before MeToo, a woman speaking about an assault might be seen not as a victim but as complacent, complicit, or culpable. (*Why did you go to his apartment? Why did you wear that provocative dress?*) With this new frame, women could bear witness knowing they had strength in numbers, with a ready, global support group.

The new frame didn't merely provide an alternative way of thinking about the issue: it opened up new possibilities for decisions and actions.

Mapping the World

Whether it is the way women respond to sexual harassment or how scientists conceive of the molecular structures in antibiotics, frames make the complexity of the world intelligible. Our minds are filled with them. That's the way we think. Frames can be simple or sophisticated, accurate or imprecise, beautiful or evil. But they all capture some aspect of reality. In so doing, they help us to explain, focus, and decide.

Democracy is a frame, as is monarchism. In business, lean manufacturing is a frame and so is OKR (objectives and key results, the management system popularized by Intel and later Google). Religion is a frame, as is secular humanism (that is, morality without a god). The rule of law is a frame, as is the notion that might makes right. Racial equality is a frame, as is racism.

Frames are as foundational to our reasoning as they are versatile. In recent decades researchers in disciplines as broad as philosophy and neuroscience have studied human framing (though the terms they use to describe it vary, including *templates*, *abstractions*, *representations*, and *schemas*).

Today the idea that humans think by way of mental models is widely accepted in the hard sciences and the social sciences. Yet it is a comparatively recent phenomenon. In the early twentieth century, pondering human thinking was largely left to philosophers. Sigmund Freud and his interest in the mind's mysterious ways was an exception, not the rule. Between the wars, philosophers such as Ernst Cassirer and Ludwig Wittgenstein understood the mind to be based on symbols and the words it manipulates. It was a step toward a more rational view of cognition, but it was all theory, no empirics.

After the Second World War, the empirical sciences turned to the human mind. Research shifted from philosophers to psychologists, especially as the latter began pondering cognitive processes inside the brain. Initially, they likened these to strict logical operations, but empirical studies failed to back up that view. Around the 1970s, the idea of "mental models" gained traction—along with the concept that human reasoning isn't an operation of formal logic but works more like a *simulation of reality*: we assess options for action by imagining what might happen.

This view has now been empirically confirmed in numerous experiments by psychologists and cognitive scientists. Neuroscience has chipped in as well in recent years, thanks to functional MRI scanners that can visualize brain activity of test subjects in real time. Studies have shown, for example, that when we plan for the future we activate brain areas that are associated with spatial cognition and our ability to think in three dimensions. We quite literally engage in a kind of deliberate and purposeful dreaming.

This work has led to a quiet transformation in understanding how people think. It points to mental models as the fundamental building blocks of human cognition. What we see and know, feel and believe, starts with the way we look at the universe. We can understand the world in relation to how we believe it works: why things happen, how they may unfold in the future, and what will happen if we act. Frames are not "imagination" or "creativity" but they enable it.

Most people probably haven't thought much about their mental state when they make decisions. This is because most decisions we make are of low consequence: what shirt to wear, what toppings to put on salad, and so on. But when people make more substantial decisions, their work has been transformed by the concept of mental models. Many of them take great strides in being aware of and deliberate about the frames they hold.

The central importance of frames is not what they are but what they facilitate. Frames *empower* us because they focus our mind. When they work well, they highlight the essential things and let us disregard the rest. That's a feature, not a bug (in the parlance of coders). Frames work as gigantic, efficient cognitive shortcuts, shaping the mental space in which we decide. They make it easier and faster for us to identify options. They simplify, fortify, and amplify how we conceive the world so we can act in it.

Frames also *liberate* us, because we can select them based on what aspects of reality we want to highlight. By deliberately trying out alternative frames, we go far beyond the animal that follows its instincts or the machine that adheres to its instructions. As we see the world from different vantage points, we enrich our understanding and come up with better solutions. In selecting a frame, we choose the path through which we eventually reach a decision. To see what it means in practice, consider maps.

Maps are a physical representation of a mental model. They delineate space and pinpoint location. Like frames, maps cater to specific purposes. And just as we pick frames—depending on the demands we have and the decision we face—the maps we select are a considered choice, with consequences for how we understand the world and act in it. But they also shape what we perceive through them.

We are most familiar with Cartesian maps, with two perpendicular dimensions. Their advantage is their seeming objectivity: all distances are correct relative to each other, and each location has its unique place. With Cartesian maps, we gain a sense of place and we can project ourselves to any location and imagine how the world looks from that vantage point. But they leave aside many other features. To name just one, they are typically flat and cannot easily reflect elevation (we need contour lines or different colors for that).

That makes them valuable at finding where things are but not how long it will take to get to them. Maps, like frames, are good in particular circumstances but not in all.

If you are in a city like London or Tokyo and want to go from one part of town to another, you probably don't want a Cartesian map. You're better off with a transit map. These maps reduce the complexity of a city's territory to a diagram of lines and stations, distinguished by color. They make it easy to identify where individual bus or train lines intersect. Transit maps are masterpieces for what they leave out. They're designed so people can choose the most expedient route. But woe to the person who takes their transit map aboveground to find their way around town!

London's Tube map, for instance, makes a particular virtue of ignoring distance in the interest of readability: two stations abutting each other on the map might actually be a mile apart. And most transit maps do not tell riders how long it will take to reach their destinations. The length of lines between stations is usually not to scale. Transit maps forgo depicting distance in favor of readability.

Even for topographical maps there are dozens of methods for drawing them, since the surface of a sphere can be projected onto a two-dimensional plane in different ways. Each has its strengths and weaknesses. Pick one in which longitude and latitude are projected perpendicular to each other—such as maps that use the common Mercator projection—and the area becomes more distorted the farther you go from the center. This makes Alaska look bigger than Australia even though it's less than a quarter the size. Other maps show correct size for area but distort shape. It's always a trade-off.

Hence the question "What map is best?" is nonsensical in the abstract. The answer depends on the context in which the map is used and the purpose to which it is put. The same is true of frames. There is no right frame per se. It depends on the situation and our intent. Once we pick a frame and apply it, this opens up choices. Without applying a frame, we might endlessly debate but never act. Choosing and applying a frame—becoming "framers"—lays the groundwork for decision and action.

Americans are familiar with the term *framers* from their history lessons. It describes the men (and back then, only men) who drafted the Constitution. They were called framers at the time, because they were designing the "frame of government." The word is well chosen because the US Constitution is a frame that defines and demarcates the institutions and processes of government. It was the result of intense debates between two key camps over different models of government that lasted for months during the summer of 1787.

The Federalists advocated a strong, centralized model of government with a powerful chief executive, firm rule of law, and limited states' rights. Their frame focused attention on what would be needed to build a strong national state that could rise to be a great power. It was "federal" in that power devolved down from the top, not a "confederation" in which power was derived from the component pieces. In contrast, the Anti-Federalists wanted a weak center, a decentralized form of governance, guarantees for individual rights, and more direct democracy. Their frame prioritized building strong local democracies, which could join forces to defend each other against external threats.

As with maps, neither of these two frames is inferior in itself; each has its pros and cons, and either might be appropriate in a particular set of circumstances. To this day, these two distinct mental models have remained central to debates about how to govern democratic republics. Well over two centuries later and across the Atlantic, European nations continue to use similar frames in their debate about whether to envision the European Union as a *demos* (a united people with a strong center), or a *demoi* (a bundle of peoples desiring a more decentralized form of governance).

Multiple, competing frames can lead to useful debates and elicit a variety of diverse options. But when there is more than one possible frame that could apply (and this happens frequently), choosing the right one for the situation is difficult. It requires a careful understanding of the objectives and the context for which the frame is being applied. And much rides on it.

Misframing and Misfortune

The wrong framing can be catastrophic. We can appreciate the importance of choosing the right frame by looking at how experts and decision-makers handled two different pandemics.

When the Ebola virus broke out in West Africa in the spring of 2014, experts were called in to study it and staunch it. The two main organizations working on a response were the World Health Organization (WHO), a UN agency, and Médecins Sans Frontières (MSF), an international aid group. Experts at both organizations knew that their first weapon in the battle was information. But while they had the same data, they drew opposite conclusions. It wasn't that their analyses were flawed. It was that they used different frames to assess the situation, each based on a distinct view of the outbreak's context and future spread.

The WHO's model was based on a historical frame. Looking at the relatively low number of Ebola cases, they reasoned that the 2014 outbreak was very similar to previous ones in the region, all of which had been contained locally. WHO forecast a limited outbreak and advised against drastic international measures. In contrast MSF took a spatial view of the outbreaks. The virus had proliferated across different villages that were far apart from one another and which dotted the borders of three countries. Because of this, MSF concluded that it must have scattered farther than the data indicated. The group pushed for immediate, draconian action.

A different way of conceptualizing the crisis—whether the outbreak was concentrated or dispersed—was at the heart of the tension. The plague risked blowing up into a global catastrophe. Hundreds of people had already died, but potentially hundreds of millions of lives were at stake. Initially, WHO won the argument and only local measures were adopted. But Ebola's fast spread validated MSF's alarmist view. A global panic ensued, dubbed "Fearbola." (Donald Trump, then a property developer turned reality-TV star, called President Barack Obama "psycho" for not canceling flights from West Africa—though direct flights didn't exist—and tweeted "KEEP THEM OUT OF HERE!") Only extraordinary actions from governments were able to control the situation, and in the end, the crisis ebbed.

Now, fast-forward to 2020. When the novel coronavirus blipped onto public health authorities' radar early that year, it wasn't clear what sort of disease the world was dealing with. Seven coronaviruses were then known to affect humans, with a wide range of infection rates and lethality. Some cause the common cold. Others, like SARS (in Asia in 2002 to 2004) and MERS (in the Middle East in 2012), proved to have harsher symptoms, longer incubation periods, and case fatality rates of 10 percent and 35 percent, respectively. Yet the world had endured coronavirus outbreaks before, and they were squelched, just as Ebola had been.

Perhaps for this reason, it wasn't clear to countries how seriously to take the discovery of SARS-CoV-2 and the illness it caused, Covid-19. China closed the city of Wuhan, an unprecedented step that seemed like something only an authoritarian regime could or would do. In Italy, cases mushroomed before they knew what had hit them. Lombardy's hospitals were so overrun that for a period, weeping doctors were forced to give sedatives to the elderly so they could die in less pain, to save limited medical resources for younger sufferers.

All countries were working off the same data, as WHO and MSF had been in 2014. And as in the case of Ebola, the way countries initially framed Covid-19 affected the options they envisioned, the actions they took, and how they fared at the outset of the crisis. The responses of Britain and New Zealand in particular show how different frames lead to different outcomes.

New Zealand framed Covid as being like SARS, and took an "elimination" approach. Though they had not been hit by SARS, the country's officials regularly mingled with their counterparts from places in the region such as Taiwan and South Korea, which had suffered, and had developed robust disease-monitoring systems and policies. Hence, at the very start of the Covid-19 outbreak, health officials in New Zealand went into disaster mode. Prime Minister Jacinda Ardern decided it would be better to overreact than underreact. "We currently have 102 cases—but so did Italy once," she told the nation in March. The country went into lockdown, closed its borders, and committed to contact tracing every case.

Britain, meanwhile, framed Covid as being more like the seasonal flu, and went for a "mitigation" strategy. Health officials assumed that the virus would inevitably spread through the population, eventually creating herd immunity. The government gave up on testing and contact tracing early in the crisis, and was later than its European counterparts to take actions such as banning large public events and closing schools. Officials opted for a national lockdown only after epidemiological models showed that the virus would swamp the National Health Service. In early June, Prime Minister Ardern declared her country Covid-free—while Britain had recorded around 50,000 Covid-related fatalities, one of the highest rates in the world.

Two countries. Same data, same goals—different frames, different actions. And very different outcomes.

Frames help us get where we hope to go, but we have to pick the direction. This is reassuring: it means we are still in command. But it is also daunting. As powerful and versatile as frames are, as valuable and indispensable as they can be, we are ultimately the ones who need to choose.

Envisioning New Worlds

Frames let us envisage what isn't there. This is a superpower that everyone possesses. There may be many reasons why we can't observe something directly. We may not have the time to collect information, or can't make the effort, or we cannot gather the data at all because it eludes us. In all these situations, we don't directly see what's there, but our mental models can fill in the blanks. They extend our ability to reach decisions by harnessing our imagination, letting us transcend the immediate and embrace ideas that are more general and abstract. This empowers us to put our intellect to uses that we could have only dreamed of.

To appreciate how frames can be used to fill in the blanks, consider the moon landings. When the Apollo 11 lunar module touched down on the surface of the moon in the summer of 1969, it was a remarkable achievement. But neither the thundering Saturn V engines nor the novel, rudimentary digital computers got the astronauts to the moon. Rather, in many ways, it was the ability to use frames to "see" what wasn't there.

Nobody knew how to navigate through more than 200,000

miles of empty space between Earth and the moon. Experts at NASA had to imagine it, creating a mental model of space navigation and the tools that would enable it to happen. It wasn't simply that a compass would not work—the whole idea of north and south makes no sense in space. Similarly, engineers had little experience with building motors that would work in the cold, airless vacuum of space—and could be started and restarted at the press of a button. So they constructed the rocket based on mental models of how engines work, not just in our planet's atmosphere but also in space. Testing helped, of course, but mainly to validate what scientists had already conjured up in their minds.

When Neil Armstrong took his "small step" onto the lunar surface, he was startled by its firmness: he had expected to sink down an inch or two. "The surface is fine and powdery," the thirty-eight-year-old captain radioed to his crew and ground control. "I only go in a small fraction of an inch, maybe an eighth of an inch." But that was about the extent of the surprises for Apollo 11. The rest of the humans on Earth, hundreds of thousands of miles away, and months and years earlier, had successfully applied frames to understand what would be needed to bring the astronauts to the moon and back.

Being able to conceive of what we've never experienced doesn't come naturally all the time. The day after the Apollo 11 launch, the *New York Times* ran what might be considered the best newspaper "correction" ever—some forty-nine years after the original article. "On Jan. 13, 1920," the paper explained, it published an article that "dismissed the notion that a rocket could function in a vacuum." The original article teased the scientist who "seems to lack the knowledge ladled out daily in high schools." Now the paper teased itself. "Further investigation and experimentation have confirmed the findings of Isaac Newton in the 17th century and it is now definitely established that a rocket can function in a vacuum as well as in an atmosphere. The Times regrets the error."

Using frames to see what's not there (yet) is common in the sciences. In 1846 scholars predicted the existence of an eighth planet, Neptune, based on their model of planetary motion and data gathered from observing Uranus, its planetary neighbor. When astronomers pointed their telescopes to Neptune's presumed position, they found it—exactly as predicted by the mental model.

Or take the Higgs boson, a tiny elementary particle. In the 1960s physicists using the frames of quantum and particle physics predicted its existence. But it took fifty years and the Large Hadron Collider, which cost $10 billion to build, to gather sufficient data and prove them right. Thanks to their frame, they foresaw what they would discover. And in 2020, scientists were able to apply Einstein's frame of relativity to predict the "dance" of one black hole around another, billions of light-years away heating matter equivalent to a trillion suns almost hour by hour. That's how precise frames can be in describing what is not yet observable.

Seeing what isn't there works in other domains as well. In management, the so-called Blue Ocean Strategy identifies unexplored market spaces—akin to being alone at sea—that companies ought to tap into. It carefully harnesses the qualities of human framing to help managers visualize commercial voids and come up with options and alternatives on markets and products. Conceived by two professors, W. Chan Kim and Renée Mauborgne, who teach at INSEAD business school, Blue Ocean Strategy has proven useful. The Japanese video game company Nintendo employed it to identify the empty market spaces and products that would become the successful Nintendo DS and Wii.

Understanding and explaining the world, seeing what isn't there, eliciting options, and informing our decisions: frames are a cognitive Swiss Army knife, and human framing is a comprehensive and versatile means for us to reach to the stars, literally as well as figuratively. But how do we apply a frame to a situation, and how exactly does a mental model translate into decisions?

Staying Within the Frame

Applying a frame isn't simple, but it isn't rocket science either. To do it well requires the right mix of rigorous thinking and bounded imagination. In the chapters that follow, we look at how to successfully put a frame to work. But first we consider how key features of frames work together and reinforce one another. We'll examine that through a well-known case of momentous innovation: taking flight.

On a cold, windy morning on December 17, 1903, Orville and Wilbur Wright took turns lying on their torsos to steer a two-winged plane made of spruce wood, muslin, and bicycle parts on the beach of Kitty Hawk, North Carolina. Their flights covered less than a thousand feet each; the longest lasted for just fifty-nine seconds. But it started a revolution. By the end of the decade, an aircraft flew the twenty-one miles of the English Channel. A century after the Wright brothers' flight, before Covid-19 depressed air travel, 4.5 billion passengers took to the skies annually.

Orville and Wilbur Wright had been obsessed with flying for years. They ran a bicycle shop in Dayton, Ohio, and had no formal training in physics. But they were methodical and structured. They read all the technical papers they could lay their hands on and studied in detail how birds fly. They understood the basic model of aerodynamic updrift and applied it by constructing and successfully flying gliders. They took detailed notes about how different designs affected their flights. When they discovered inaccuracies in the measurements of the German aviation pioneer Otto Lilienthal, they built their own wind tunnel to redo the performance tests. Hewing strictly to the frame of aerodynamics gave them two essential insights early on.

The first was that stability wasn't critical, control was. They were bicycle experts, after all. Just as a cycle is inherently unstable but can be balanced and controlled by the rider when in motion, so too it was crucial that a plane could be controlled and balanced by a flier in the air. The second insight built on this. Aspiring aviators were launching themselves off ramps or swooning down cliffs to produce uplift for flight. The brothers' rival, Samuel Langley, made a "Great Aerodrome" that needed to be launched by catapult from a houseboat. But it was hard to get enough speed. So the brothers turned the problem around and looked for a place with a strong wind against which to launch their aircraft. In 1900 they consulted National Weather Bureau data on wind speeds by location and settled on Kitty Hawk, with its steady winds of fifteen to twenty miles per hour.

The aerodynamic frame helped them at every step, from the camber of the wings to generate uplift, to their design for turning, based on watching birds, called "wing-warping" (that later was abandoned for better techniques). But at the crux of their success was a third insight: the propeller.

Previous airplane designers based propellers on those used for ships. But water has a million times the density of air. Boat propellers bite into the water to produce momentum. Air, on the other hand, is compressible, and the Wrights realized they needed to rethink how an airplane propeller would work. The aerodynamic frame led them to the answer. As Orville later described their insight: "It was apparent that a propeller was simply an aeroplane [wing] travelling in a spiral course." The blades would need a camber to produce uplift, like the wings.

Modern research pegs the Wright propeller's efficiency at more than 80 percent, many times better than their competitors. The brothers understood that for powered flight, they had to translate engine power into forward motion. That ensures sufficient airspeed over the wings, which translates into updrift and thus flight. It's a chain of cause and effect. Other aviators focused on designing the most powerful or efficient engine. The Wrights understood that the causal chain was longer, with the engine but one element.

They also realized that one could imagine a vast variety of propellers, differing in length, thickness, inclination, and shape. An airplane's propeller does not need to look like one for a boat. It's important to free the mind from preconceived notions that are too limiting. Tapping the imagination greatly increases the options that can be considered, and that in turn may increase the chance to find a solution that's really good.

A lively imagination, however, also has downsides. With so many different designs being possible, the Wrights would have had to spend a long time testing all the variants. In addition to broadening the search space, one needs to find a way to efficiently focus on the options that count. That's exactly what the brothers did, constraining their initial flights of fancy to the most promising types of propellers. These they looked at carefully and tested.

By applying their frame, they had come up with many options that could cause the desired effect, then successfully sorted out the ones that mattered. It was a very efficient process and led them to win the race for the world's first powered flight. They achieved their breakthrough not because they came up with something completely novel but because they masterfully applied the very frame they had identified to be the best fit. They weren't geniuses—they were exemplary framers. They attained success by thinking clearly about cause and effect, by imagining alternatives, and by applying the constraints derived from the laws of physics. These three features—causality, counterfactuals, and constraints—are essential to applying frames.

The story of the Wright brothers also highlights that a frame itself is not a solution, it's just a means to find a solution. Using a frame isn't simply instinctive; it is considered. And it isn't instantaneous and automatic, like flicking a switch. It takes time and determination. Framing is a *process*—a method that guides the human mind toward understanding, imagination, and the evaluation of options.

Values and Worldviews

Frames also help us operationalize our values. By making us evaluate options, they are a means through which we can delineate between good and bad choices. Constraining our imagination based on our objectives is where values enter our assessment. Of course a frame does not substitute for values; only what fits our needs, as we see them, and what doesn't. It is the mechanism through which we judge different options. Without frames, we would have no obvious way to connect our goals and values to possible courses of action.

Frames not only guide us to our goals, they shape our broader worldview. Seeing the world through a particular cognitive lens may gradually turn into a more general dimension of one's reasoning. In a 2010 experiment in Ethiopia, researchers changed people's perspectives so that they could see they had control over their future. The result was that those people saved more and invested in their children's education, suggesting tangible benefits from altering the way one frames things. It also highlights how mental models can have a powerful impact on economic development. Conversely, if one adheres to the frame that the Earth is flat, they will bump up against various scientific frames frequently. Over time, that may convince them to abandon the flat-earth frame—or turn them into a skeptic of science more generally.

We can take this a step further: by shaping our broader view of the world, frames shape the world itself. Option pricing in financial markets offers a case in point. The Black-Scholes theory—a widely used mathematical frame to price options—pushed option prices toward the prices the frame predicted, leading financial institutions to promote the frame's application, which in turn brought the prices even closer to the frame's predictions. There is a self-fulfilling dimension to this: often the more a frame is used, the more it validates its use (up to a point).

It's not just in financial markets. The more that people adhere to a given frame, the more legitimacy that frame gets, whether it is the mental model of human rights, philanthropy, the gold standard, or abhorrent racist views. For example, the racist frame suggests that blacks and whites are different, which led to separate-but-equal rules, apartheid laws, and biased AI systems that further reinforce the frame. Similarly, the human rights frame led countries to set up courts of human rights and teach those rights to schoolchildren, which further reinforces that frame. So too, environmental consciousness prompted antipollution laws and renewable-energy subsidies that entrenched green thinking. However noxious some cases may be, they demonstrate the power of human framing. But they also underscore just how hard it is to rid the world of frames once they've stuck their hooks into society.

Frames do more than make us better decision-makers. They help us inject values as we make our choices. In turn they influence our worldview and even shape reality. Quite obviously, therefore, much hinges on the frame we pick for a particular situation.

Choosing the Right Frame

Applying a frame is a relatively structured process, guided by causality, counterfactuals, and constraints. But choosing the right frame is considerably harder.

If one has a rich repertoire of frames, it's easier to find a good fit for a given situation than if the repertoire is small or full of similar frames. Think of a musician who is good at only one particular genre, such as country music. They'll be tempted to croon a tear-jerker on every occasion, whether or not it's appropriate. Musicians with a rich repertoire are more likely to find a song that's a better fit for the moment.

A rich repertoire, however, isn't sufficient. We also need to understand the qualities of each frame and be aware of its strengths and its weaknesses. Otherwise we can't know which frame is a good fit for our objectives and the context we are in.

Consider a good orator, who not only knows how to express thoughts and emotions in different ways but also has an excellent sense of which way best suits a given situation. People remember Abraham Lincoln's famous Gettysburg Address, Winston Churchill's "Blood, Toil, Tears, and Sweat" speech to a frightened wartime Britain, and Martin Luther King Jr.'s "I Have a Dream" oration because they hit exactly the right tone; they were the right words at the right time. It's very similar with frames: know them and their distinct qualities well, and one will make better use of them.

The first hurdle to choosing the right frame, however, is that we are cognitively biased to stick to the frames we have used before. We are like the proverbial handyman, who while holding a hammer can only see nails. Sticking to a frame we have employed and are intimately familiar with isn't necessarily bad. In fact, sticking to a frame that has proven to work is a smart strategy. It reduces the amount of thinking we have to do and still yields a good outcome. As we keep applying the same frame, we likely get better at it, honing our skills and producing even better results.

Yet hewing to a familiar mental model also curtails our ability to shift our perspective by switching to an alternative one. As the famed venture capitalist Eugene Kleiner once said, "It's difficult to see the picture when you're inside the frame." Circumstances may have changed, perhaps our objectives evolved, or a situation may look familiar to one we have previously encountered but really isn't. In each of these cases our tried-and-trusted frame turns into a less optimal fit. That's the right moment to engage in a more comprehensive examination to identify a better frame. Perhaps we can find it in our own repertoire, if we only take the time, make the effort, and look carefully enough. Or we may need to look further.

Choosing a new frame is a challenging and time-consuming process, and we should only do it when it's really necessary. And to make things even more difficult, it is also a process that we don't get much better at even if we practice, because the answer lies not in trying over and over again, but in trying differently. Finding a better frame is worth it: it takes substantial cognitive investment and there is a risk of failure, but the rewards can be substantial and long-lasting.

Take something as quotidian and familiar as reading. Superficially, reading is just a technique for extracting what has been stored in letters and words. But look closer and you discover that the way we read shapes the consequences of our reading. It becomes obvious when we compare reading silently and reading aloud—two different frames for the same content, but with different objectives.

Until around the year 1000, most reading in Europe was done in monasteries and churches and happened aloud and in groups. The primary aim was to engage in a communal activity to praise God. By the eleventh century, a different frame of reading emerged: reading silently. It facilitated a different objective. Reading was no longer a communal experience: silent reading became an individual, personal one. Readers could retain full control of how fast or slow they read. They could reread passages, or pause and ponder a thought. Unlike communal reading aloud, personal silent reading lets one mull the content. It stimulates the mind and facilitates independent thinking. It encourages new ideas.

Silent reading did not replace reading aloud overnight. Both frames coexisted for centuries, in significant part because of the mechanics of reading. Text in early books and manuscripts had no punctuation at the end of sentences and often no space between words; it was an endless string of letters. That made it very difficult to read at all, and almost impossible to read silently. Reading such texts aloud together was easier, because some in the group likely had read the text before. They might remember how to read and intonate the words, thereby guiding their co-readers. The way books were written created the context in which human readers chose the frame. And mostly, it was reading aloud.

Around the eleventh century, an innovation emerged. Books started to be produced with spaces between the words and rudimentary punctuation. It made reading easier in general, but especially silent reading—one could read a book on one's own, without guidance. This made it possible for readers to switch their frame of reading. The eventual effect was profound.

When Martin Luther translated the Bible in the 1500s from the largely inaccessible Latin to the everyday language that Germans spoke, and advocated a new Christian tradition of reading the holy text individually to think and ponder its meaning oneself, he also gave silent reading a new purpose. It was the means by which believers could now access the Holy Scripture on their own. Spurred by rising demand, Gutenberg's printing press churned out millions of Bibles in vernacular languages with spaces and punctuation for a new generation of silent readers to enjoy. Context and objective had shifted, and so did the frame. It provided a better fit for European

societies. Silent reading facilitated individual thinking and origi-
nality, which reshaped the world.

Not every shift is as monumental, but switching frames is almost
always extraordinary. We don't do it casually. It entails leaving behind known and trusted mental territory. Our impulse tells us to
resist, to hold back. Only infrequently do we plunge ahead.

The Frame Problem

Framing is a central quality of humans that is impossible for machines to emulate. The idea that computers and algorithms can't
frame is not new. In 1969, one of the fathers of AI, John McCarthy
of Stanford University, cowrote a paper modestly titled "Some Philosophical Problems from the Standpoint of Artificial Intelligence."
Among the hiccups the relatively new field of AI was encountering
was what he dubbed "the Frame Problem."

The "frames" he referred to are different from what we describe
in this book, but they are related. McCarthy was writing about the
need to represent a "state of knowledge" at a given time in mathematics, logic, and computer code. Books, conferences, and PhD the-
ses were devoted to the frame problem from the 1970s to the 1990s.

A decade and a half after the paper appeared, the philosopher
and cognitive scientist Daniel Dennett became fascinated by the
idea of cognitive frames in a wider sense, closer to how the idea is
used in decision science and in this book. In an essay called "Cognitive Wheels," he developed the idea by way of three vivid scenarios.

Imagine a robot, Dennett asks, whose only instructions are to
fend for itself. It learns that a bomb is set to go off in a room with
its spare battery. It locates the room and sees the battery on a
wagon. So it formulates a plan to recover the battery by pulling
the wagon out of the room. It does so, but *BOOM!*

44

The bomb was on the wagon. The robot knew this, but it didn't realize that pulling out the wagon with the battery would also pull out the bomb. "Back to the drawing board," Dennett writes.

"'The solution is obvious,' said the designers," in Dennett's essay. "'Our next robot must be made to recognize not just the intended implications of its acts, but also the implications about their side effects, by deducing these implications from the descriptions it uses in formulating its plans.'" And so in the second scenario, when the robot gets to the battery and wagon, it pauses to consider the implications of its plans. It deduces that moving the wagon will not change the color of the room, that moving the wagon will mean the wheels will turn, that moving the wagon . . . *BOOM!*

"'We must teach it the difference between relevant implications and irrelevant implications,' said the designers, 'and teach it to ignore the irrelevant ones,'" writes Dennett. This time, the robot finds itself outside the room with a pensive gaze, Hamlet-like. "'Do something!' they yelled at it. 'I am,' it retorted. 'I'm busily ignoring some thousands of implications I have determined to be irrelevant. Just as soon as I find an irrelevant implication, I put it on the list of those I must ignore, and . . .'" *BOOM!*

Dennett's three scenarios capture the key elements of frames. In the first scenario, the robot failed to see basic causality. In the second, it failed to quickly conjure up the relevant counterfactuals. In the third, it was paralyzed by applying too many constraints. The machine, as Dennett suggests, can do a lot of calculating with an immense amount of formal logic and processing reams of data, but it cannot frame.

Much has changed in AI since Dennett wrote his three scenarios. AI no longer relies on humans feeding abstract rules into machines. Instead, the most popular methods today, such as machine learning and deep learning, involve systems partially self-optimizing from massive amounts of data. But although the process is different, the difficulty hasn't gone away. Even with lots of training data, when a robot encounters a novel situation like a ticking bomb, it can be at an utter loss.

Framing—capturing some essence of reality through a mental model in order to devise an effective course of action—is something humans do and machines cannot.

Always Inside a Box

Self-improvement books frequently call on their readers to "think outside the box" when they want to advocate creative thinking, unencumbered by stifling limitations. It has become a cliché, especially in the world of business and management. The expression comes from a business-psychology experiment called the nine-dot test. It was popularized in the 1960s by the British management scholar John Adair, though the origins go back further. The test was included in a "Cyclopedia of Puzzles" published in 1914 in America and was used in psychological experiments on creativity in the 1930s. It was part of an internal management technique inside the Walt Disney Company. Still today, academic papers are regularly published on it.

The task in the nine-dot test is to connect three rows of three dots using only four straight lines, without lifting the pen. Our mind imagines the dots as forming a square, but the only way to solve the test is to draw beyond the implied border—hence "think outside the box." The general point is that solutions will present themselves more easily if we leave behind our existing mental models.

The nine-dot test may be useful to get people to see options they don't realize exist, but as a metaphor, "thinking outside the box" is fundamentally ill-conceived. As humans, we cannot *not* frame. We can't switch it off; we frame all the time. The only choices we have are what frame we use and how well we use it. Even if we could think outside of frames, it would be of questionable value. Frames impose boundaries—without boundaries we may have vivid fantasies that completely fail to surface effective options. If faced with a ticking bomb, like Dennett's robot, we could hope for divine intervention, the sudden appearance of a bomb-disposal specialist, or the ability to talk the bomb out of exploding. All these options would be "out of the box" but hardly effective.

Human framing is useful precisely because it lets our mind wander in a structured, purposeful, and constrained way. The box is very much the magic.

The nine-dot test itself tells as much. There are, in fact, several possible solutions: wrap it around like a barrel, or fold it, or cut it in pieces. Or just imagine it solved in four-dimensional space. That's not allowed? Who says? Any imposition of a restriction is just another box, which we have been told we should deliberately think beyond. For every test, we can imagine a crazy solution that's completely outside the mental box. But that does not *solve* the problem; it does not provide us with a workable choice, an effective answer.

To get that, we need to constrain our imagination. The "aha moment" that gives us the solution to the nine-dot test—to connect the dots by drawing lines beyond the box that we imagine is formed—requires us to limit our thinking to a two-dimensional sheet of paper, without considering things like folds and scissors. The nine-dot test *necessitates* constraints. It isn't an example of "thinking outside the box" but of human framing. It's an example of the need to consider our mental model, choose our constraints, and with them imagine alternatives. The test is a useful reminder of the importance of choosing the right frame and imagining with the right constraints.

In real life, we constantly feel boxed in. That's why we need frames to open up new possibilities. In one famous instance, framing affected how the United States responded in the heat of the global financial crisis in 2008. The country was lucky to have as its chief economic policymaker a person who had prepared for such a calamity most of his professional life. But at the decisive moment, he was thinking inside an alternative box—and saddled with doubts.

3

causality

we are causal-inference engines and often wrong, but this is good

"I can still stop this," Ben Bernanke remembers thinking. On the evening of Tuesday, September 16, 2008, he paced his office at the Federal Reserve and stopped at a large window. He looked down at the glowing traffic on Constitution Avenue and the dark silhouettes of elm trees on the National Mall. The previous days had been intense. But he sensed that worse was to come.

Bernanke was two years into his tenure as Fed chairman and he was in the midst of a crisis. Just one day earlier, the big investment bank Lehman Brothers had declared bankruptcy, laid low by a toxic sludge of subprime mortgages. Its failure threw markets into a tailspin. Yet that evening an even bigger threat loomed.

An insurance firm that covered Wall Street's mortgage-backed securities, AIG, faced collapse too. The subprime sludge was oozing everywhere. Bernanke spent the entire day with President George W. Bush and Congress explaining why it was vital to bail out AIG—not to rescue the company but to save the economy. As he looked out the window, he took a contemplative moment to rethink his decision to bring the machinery of the Fed directly into the markets.

People have long understood the economy in terms of causality. But the frames they used were at times ill-fitting. In the late 1600s Isaac Newton's principles of inertia and gravity were adapted to explain market competition. In the mid-1700s in France a clique of economists who had initially studied to be physicians called themselves physiocrats. They saw the flow of money through the economy like blood in the body's circulation system. Neither frame captured the complexity of the situation, but they worked a bit.

In the twentieth century, a new generation conceived of the economy with an eye toward mechanical engineering but with mathematical models. One was Ben Bernanke. He devoted his career to studying financial crises and market panics, though it was considered an academic backwater.

One of his chief findings was that the 1929 market crash turned into the Great Depression not because of the crash itself but the central bank's response. It tightened the money supply, which lowered prices and caused deflation. Then it let thousands of small banks across the country fail, which wiped out people's savings. What might have been a recession turned into a decade-long depression. Bernanke realized the exact opposite action was needed: flood the market with capital. He used a cute metaphor to make this point in a 2002 speech—throwing money from a helicopter. The image stuck, earning him the nickname "Helicopter Ben."

Staring out his office window that September evening, Bernanke understood that his concerns were different from those of the policymakers around him. They framed the issue as being about incentives for individual firms—bailing out one, they worried, would only encourage more risky behavior. He didn't see it that way. His mental model was focused on the causal link between the availability of capital, trust in the system, and the health of the economy. The banks' mortgage losses were trifles compared to the financial markets as a whole: a fall of hundreds of billions of dollars only amounted to a bad day on Wall Street. But he knew it undermined confidence in the system—and a lack of trust would prevent banks from providing credit to one another, which could lead to chaos.

It was this arcane, delicate system of interbank lending that haunted Bernanke. If bank confidence failed, the impacts would cascade down to ordinary people and businesses. It was already starting to happen. One of America's biggest McDonald's franchises didn't think it could make its monthly payroll because banks weren't supplying basic credit. There was a serious question whether bank cash machines would dry up.

Recalling his research, Helicopter Ben was focused on a system-wide credit crunch, not the failure of individual firms. That frame gave him an idea. He would buy the toxic-sludge assets from the banks, taking them off their balance sheet. Then, the banks could use those fresh, clean dollars to lend—pumping capital into the system. Between 2008 and 2015, the Fed's balance sheet soared from $900 billion of mostly high-quality Treasury notes to $4.5 trillion of largely risky assets.

And it worked. The financial crisis was painful, but the system did not collapse. Bernanke's framing, imbued with causal understanding, allowed him to see the economy in a way that others did not. Even amid market uncertainty, the system can be understood by human reason, predicted with human foresight, and controlled by human hand. And sometimes those hands throw wads of cash from helicopters.

Templates and Abstractions

We see the world through the lens of cause and effect. This makes it predictable. It gives us confidence in how things work and what the next moment may bring. It lets us plan—whether it is to hunt for food, climb a tree, throw a rock, cross a street, build a bridge, or write a constitution. Among the first things that we learn as babies is causality; it enables us to survive.

We perceive causal relationships everywhere we look. Sometimes they do not truly exist—someone may misperceive that stock prices are linked to solar storms, say, or that drinking detergent cures Covid-19. But without being able to consider possible relationships between actions and outcomes, and explanations for those relationships, we would not know where to start to live in this world. Causality helps us comprehend reality and predict the consequences of our decisions. It is an essential element of framing.

Cause and effect is deeply embedded in all living things. Euglena, the microscopic single-celled organisms that are found in ponds, have crude photo receptors. Photons hitting the receptors trigger a signal that makes the organism move in the direction of the light. For the euglena, it is not a conscious decision: its reaction is encoded in its DNA, and it can't help but follow the light. But there is no question that euglena, like other organisms, reacts to stimuli in its environment, causally linking the stimulus to the response.

Mammals, too, respond seemingly unconsciously to stimuli. Laboratory-born monkeys that have never before seen a real-life reptile show fear when they encounter a fake black rubber snake. They recognize snakes in pictures faster than nonthreatening objects. Preschool children do the same. Humans are born with several such innate, causal models of the world. Even babies expect that a dropped object should fall straight down.

In complex organisms, reactions to perceived causes are not always hard-coded. A dog can learn that if it gives its paw, it receives a treat. So, predicting a treat, it will offer to give its paw. The perceived causal link between the paw and the treat influences the dog's behavior; it shapes its decisions to act.

Humans extract causal connections from experiences too; we do it all the time without much thought. By reacting to perceived causal structures around us—every lion's roar, every burning ember, every compliment from our spouse—we hone our choices. It is smart to be attentive to causality. It helps organisms search for food, avoid predators, and find mating partners.

That is why causation is so pervasive in all living beings, from the tiny euglena in our marshes to the gazelles on the Serengeti to schoolchildren studying for exams (or defying the cold hand of causality and goofing off instead). Living beings whose actions are based on a superior knowledge of how to leverage causal structures in their environment are, more often than not, better off than organisms that care less about cause and effect.

Ben Bernanke's reasoning, similarly, was causal. But there's a fundamental difference between Bernanke's frame and the way most organisms react to causal structures. Most animals, even those closely related to humans, like chimps, focus on directly observable causal links; they have great difficulty imagining causality that's not obvious and immediate. When dogs understand that giving a paw leads to a treat, they cannot reason that other affectionate behavior, like turning in circles too, may lead to a treat. They have to learn such causal links again and again through immediate experience. Dogs, like chimps, can't engage in abstract framing and know that it is friendliness, not the paw, that earned it a treat.

In contrast, humans have acquired the ability to generate abstractions and turn their causal inferences into frames. These mental models offer reusable templates to understand the world causally.

So when we realize that touching a hot coal causes painful burns, we are able to generalize from that and learn not to touch very hot things, whether they are red-hot or white-hot, or any shade in between.

The ability to abstract from the here and now to a more general causal template has huge advantages. Such templates are far more versatile. Because we can apply them to new circumstances they are flexible and fungible. In fact, humans can infer causal links that they have never observed before, say, between butter melting on a hot stove and zinc melting in a hot furnace.

Causal templates are like getting a specific tool and realizing that it can be used in many different ways. Whenever the environment changes or we face novel circumstances, we otherwise would have to start with a blank slate in deducing causes and making predictions. With causal templates, we have an adaptable structure available. They may not work perfectly, but they are certainly better than having to start from scratch.

By speeding up learning, causal frames save crucial time, especially in situations that demand swift decisions. Without templates, we'd lose precious time by having to slowly explore the so-called search space of potential decisions step-by-step—just as Daniel Dennett's bomb-obsessed robot, which we met in the previous chapter, was stuck contemplating every possible causal relationship because it couldn't generalize its knowledge.

Together, the twin advantages of adaptability and speed of learning provide versatility and efficiency. But the most important benefit is the ability for abstraction. It frees us from reacting to only low-order causation, as plants and simple animals do, which would shackle us to the present. Instead, we can go beyond it. Our abstractions let us make a fundamental cognitive leap to free causal thinking from the concrete, the contextual, and the observable.

With frames, we no longer need to "run the experiment," so to speak, to suffer through trial and error each time we face a new situation.

Our ancestors benefited greatly from framing with causal templates. They realized that what worked when hunting for one kind of animal could work with different kinds of animals too. Because they thought in causal templates, they were better at hunting and better at avoiding getting killed. When some of our ancestors developed the capability, it spread through natural selection and cultural communication. Causal reasoning turned into a trait shared by all.

Humans are not wholly unique in this respect. Research has shown that a handful of animals, notably crows, have a limited capacity for abstract causal reasoning. They can plan and trade. And just as in Aesop's famous fable, a study has shown that they can drop pebbles into a pitcher to raise the level of water so they can drink. Crows are special this way: that's why they make the cover of academic journals while other birds end up on dinner plates. But humans' ability to see causation, generalize from it, and communicate the abstractions to others is unparalleled in the animal kingdom. Early humans built small dwellings; modern ones build skyscrapers. Meanwhile, beavers construct wood dams and over thousands of generations they've not produced a single château—to say nothing of monuments to great beavers of days gone by.

Take away people's ability to generalize, to think at higher and higher levels of abstraction, and you would take away ambition and transcendence. We would be stuck like the beaver, doing only what we already know how to do, not striving, not experimenting, and not evolving that knowledge into new planes of thought. Life would be static; there would be no history and no vision of the future.

The Cognitive and the Cultural

How did this crucial evolutionary advantage come about? After all, our brains are not the biggest, nor are our neurons fundamentally different from the neurons of other mammals. The answer is in our cognition, the processes of our thought.

Human brains are good at recognizing patterns, especially visual ones. At its core, pattern recognition is about generalizing from the specific. The aphorism that it is vital to distinguish the forest from the trees resonates, because it is precisely what our brain does with the onslaught of visual stimuli it receives. It constructs a reality in our mind that's beyond what our eyes can see.

In the distant history of humanity, some of our ancestors must have become able to repurpose this capability to abstract from the narrow but useful domain of our senses to something bigger and more conceptual. This resulted in the ability to make a wider and more comprehensive set of tools, and adapt to a wider range of habitats. It also helped in the evolution of human communication. Many animals communicate with one another, as far as we know, about matters purely in the present, such as an imminent threat or the presence of food. But our ability to abstract enabled humans to develop grammatical language, which in turn gave us the ability to coordinate with one another beyond immediate kinship and across space and time.

Groundbreaking research in recent years sheds powerful light on the factors behind the success of frames. The work of two professors in particular underscores the role they play. One is Steven Pinker, the Harvard neuroscientist and polymath whose ideas are as distinctive as his flowing silver hair. The other is Michael Tomasello, a Floridian who teaches at Duke University (and whose own gray hair, for the record, is neat and trim).

In Pinker's view, the most important factors include our ability to use cognitive skills for abstract thinking, the development of grammatical language, and humanity's social tendencies that let us share ideas. He places special emphasis on the role of metaphors to understand, remember, and communicate abstract explanations. Metaphors "reflect an ability of the human mind to readily connect abstract ideas with concrete scenarios," he wrote in an academic paper in 2010 titled "The Cognitive Niche."

Metaphors can be considered expressions of human frames. They reflect causal relationships that capture a concrete situation and can be abstracted to apply to other domains. The fact that we can think and communicate through metaphors hones our skills in framing, and vice versa.

Tomasello, in contrast to Pinker, highlights the importance of the "cultural niche." Our sophisticated, high-order causal thinking, he argues, originated from a need to collaborate effectively. Many millennia ago, ecological pressures forced our ancestors to cooperate in a way that is unique to our species. This form of cooperation required the abstract representation of complex social interactions in order to organize the actions of each group member toward a common goal.

In other words, we need to understand one another's intentions—and, more important, what others expect from us—to be able to work together and to learn from each other. Out of that we established things like language and script, and later perhaps schooling and apprenticeships. Once developed, the faculty to represent abstract relations became central to our causal framing.

Tomasello studied young children, chimps, and great apes to understand what makes humans tick. In a series of studies, he compared chimps with young children around the ages of one and two years old. The chimps could do some of what the toddlers could, but what they were unable to accomplish was social coordination.

Tomasello gave the toddlers and chimps a tube containing a reward that could be extracted only if both ends of the tube were pulled on at the same time. Children as young as eighteen months understood that they needed to cooperate with someone else to release the reward, and were able to direct the attention of a potential collaborator who initially acted as if they did not understand what they had to do. The chimps could not do this: they may have had an inkling of causality, but they failed in abstract causal representations—they could not take the perspective of another chimp and see their role in regard to the other. Tomasello suggests that humans' capacity for causal representations developed from being a part of society.

New studies have shown that the rapid technological change humanity has experienced in the past two centuries cannot be explained solely by either an individual's ability to connect concrete situations to abstract principles (Pinker's "cognitive niche") or our social ability to share knowledge (Tomasello's "cultural niche"). They suggest that humanity has developed by combining the advantages of both.

In one experiment, researchers showed that successive "generations" of individuals were able to optimize the design of a wheel—a fundamental technological advance in human history. Each participant had a few chances to see if they could improve on the performance of a simple wheel that descended a ramp, by adjusting the placement of weights on its spokes. After each person's turn, another individual stepped in to continue the process. Over five generations, the design continually improved, reaching 71 percent of the best possible performance, even though the participants knew nothing about the underlying mechanisms.

That finding supports the notion that human technology is too complex to be the product of individual genius but emerges from the accumulation of improvements across time that are communicated by others (Tomasello's cultural niche). It helps explain how primitive societies, even preliterate ones, can produce complex tools. Yet cultural learning through trial and error is way too slow to account for the astonishing speed of technological change humanity has experienced in the past two centuries. For this, we need Pinker's cognitive niche as well.

Causal reasoning shapes the way humans explore alternatives, at times making the search much more efficient. In the wheel study, for instance, causal reasoning restricted the participants' attention to the most promising trials, which accelerated cultural learning across generations. Humanity would never have moved from the first flight of the Wright brothers to the Apollo program in just sixty years without the help of frames and causal templates about the physical world.

Of course, we don't know what first prompted humans to combine cognitive and cultural dimensions. But our ancestors already used abstract causal reasoning when, about fourteen millennia ago, they began to settle down and farm. They put aside the seeds they had collected each season (for tens of thousands of years) instead of eating them, understanding that the next season they would grow into grains and vegetables. Sowing and harvesting not only marked the beginning of systematic agriculture and the end of nomadic life for many people; it also showed that by this time, humans had developed causal templates. They had become not only farmers, but framers.

And we have been at it ever since. Ancient philosophy, the rise of logic, the age of reason and exploration, the Enlightenment, the scientific revolution, and the massive expansion of knowledge in the twentieth century are all founded on the fact that humans have become sophisticated causal framers. Everywhere we look, everything we do, every idea we think, is accomplished with the help of causal mental models.

The Need for Explainability

The biggest benefit of seeing the world through abstract causal templates is that it makes the world explainable—though we may not always be able to find the right explanation.

At the Vienna General Hospital in Austria in the 1840s, a young obstetrician named Ignaz Semmelweis noticed a strange difference in childbirths. Women in the maternity ward whose babies were delivered by doctors died of puerperal fever at five times the rate of women whose births were handled by midwives. Pregnant women knew about these differences too. They would literally beg hospital staff to be assigned a midwife rather than a doctor, even though the doctors were supposed to be more learned and professional. Semmelweis ignored all that: he cared about the data. So he sought to isolate the differences to identify the cause.

He noted that women gave birth on their sides with midwives but on their backs with doctors, so he had them all deliver on their sides—but there was no difference. He wondered whether the priests who walked the halls ringing a bell upon every death might be terrifying others in the ward. But when the practice was discontinued, it didn't change the death rates. Then one day he learned of the death of a doctor from puerperal fever after pricking his finger during an autopsy. It was a crucial detail for Semmelweis: it suggested that the disease might be contagious. Doctors performed autopsies; midwives didn't. It was the difference he was looking for.

Semmelweis reasoned that the deaths were from "cadaverous particles" on doctors' hands coming in contact with the new mothers. The answer, therefore, was for doctors to wash their hands before deliveries. They did, in chlorinated lime water, and the high incidence of puerperal fever ended. Semmelweis came up with a frame that enabled better decisions and saved lives.

The frame was causal on a number of levels. First, Semmelweis understood that the disease caused the deaths; that it was contagious. Second, he understood that handwashing caused the incidence of puerperal fever to drop. But his reasoning for what *caused* puerperal fever in the first place—"cadaverous particles"—was not only vague but flawed. It wasn't a death particle that caused women to become sick. It was that the bacteria that caused puerperal fever and remained on doctors' hands were passed on to healthy women. Semmelweis's causal frame was faulty, even though his proposed solution, to wash hands, was correct.

The frame failed to catch on *even though it worked.* For Semmelweis, his inability to convince his peers led to tragic consequences. The more that he was laughed at, and the more his technique was effective, the more irritable he became. In 1865 he suffered a nervous breakdown. Several associates coaxed him to an asylum, and when he figured out what was going on, he tried to escape. But guards treated him with the standard of care at the time: they beat him, placed him in a straitjacket, and threw him in a cell. He died two weeks later, at age forty-seven, from an infected wound that he got during the scuffle. His successor at the hospital's maternity clinic discontinued the peculiar handwashing protocol. Deaths again soared.

The same year that Semmelweis was locked in the asylum, a French biologist named Louis Pasteur was called in to investigate the cause of a mysterious illness that afflicted silkworms and threatened France's silk industry. It would lead to the discovery of germs, and the new frame of "germ theory." Around the same time, a gentleman scientist in England named Joseph Lister—baron, doctor, member of the Royal Society, mutton-chop sideburns—had been experimenting with sterilizing the bandages for wounds to reduce infections. Two years later, based on Pasteur's frame, he wrote a long series of articles in the medical journal *The Lancet* on the success of sterilizations and instructed all surgeons to wash their hands. Lister, as a member of the establishment and offering detailed explanations in the scientific literature, succeeded where Semmelweis hadn't. Today, he is considered the "father of modern surgery," and his name is immortalized on the sterilizing mouthwash brand Listerine.

The tragic case of Ignaz Semmelweis highlights that it is not sufficient for a mental frame to improve decision-making. For a frame to catch on, it also has to offer a convincing causal explanation. In that, Semmelweis failed. There may have been multiple reasons for this. His explanation may have sounded too radical. It may have been because he lacked the evidence amassed by Pasteur and Lister, who played by institutional rules of scientific publication. Or, Semmelweis may not have been sufficiently respected, especially as a Hungarian amid the elite physicians of Imperial Austria. But whatever the reasons and their merits (and as institutional radicals ourselves, we can only commiserate with Semmelweis), the case highlights the importance of having a persuasive explanation for the acceptance of a new frame.

Explainability is essential to a causal frame's success; it gives meaning to our existence and to what we experience. When we comprehend a phenomenon—having a sliver of the world become understandable—it is enormously satisfying. It bears noting that Semmelweis too, not just Pasteur and Lister, felt the need to offer an explanation for his ideas. So strong is our urge to create causal explanations that we even invent them when we need to. This is highlighted by the neuroscientist Michael Gazzaniga's experiments on people who had undergone an operation to sever the connection between brain hemispheres, usually to relieve severe epilepsy. Gazzaniga presented the right side of a patient's brain with an instruction, such as "walk."

When asked why he had gotten up and begun to walk, the patient replied, "I wanted to go get a Coke." Because of the disconnect between the right side and the left side of the brain, the left (or reasoning) side had no clue what the other side had seen. But it knew that we do things for a reason, and so the "left-brain interpreter" (in Gazzaniga's words) quickly filled the void. It invented a cause to instill order.

Learning, Agency, and Control

The explainability that is baked into causal frames enables us to do more than generalize: it helps us learn. This is a special feature and a relatively new finding. Normally we learn when we *receive* information: when a teacher instructs, a book describes, an apprentice tinkers. But in the case of causal explanations, the person who *imparts* information, who does the explaining, actually learns as well. This insight is the work of Tania Lombrozo, a psychology professor at Princeton and rising star in the field, who is pioneering a new science of explanation.

As an undergraduate student, Lombrozo noticed that the idea of explanations cropped up everywhere she looked, from psychology to sociology to philosophy. While that might seem obvious, it turns out that fundamental questions around explanations themselves have not received deep academic treatment in the sciences. For example, why do we try to explain certain things but not others? How do explanations lead us to reach goals—and how do they lead people astray? Lombrozo's work is filling the holes in our knowledge around explanations, in both psychology and philosophy.

Her research on "learning by explaining" is a case in point. Lombrozo asked adults to look at illustrations of two categories of robots from an alien planet, called "glorps" and "drents." The robots differed in color, body shape, and foot shape but the subjects in the experiment were not told about the variations. Half the people were asked to *describe*, and the other half to *explain*, what characterized glorps or drents. (The robots were all cute, but color and body shape did not account for why a robot belonged in a category—foot shape did.)

The result? Those asked to *explain* how they classified the robots performed significantly better than those who just described the robots without being asked to explain. Lombrozo has run several experiments with similar results. She has even performed experiments with young children, and yes, kids too are better at their task when they are asked to causally reason about it, when they are asked to explain.

Put in the context of framing: as humans explain the world using causal frames, they are actually learning more about the world they are explaining, generating deeper and more accurate insights. Explaining the world to others leads to understanding it better oneself. The finding has direct application to education and parenting: get kids to explain their reasoning, not just give an answer. (There may be an evolutionary advantage too. By explaining, we are likely to learn more and faster about the world than those who don't bother.)

The advantages transcend the rarified world of glorps or drents. From our earliest days, we have created concepts of order, mapping the forms of gods in the stars and establishing taxonomies of species. Children spend hours sorting and reordering their toy cars, dolls, Lego bricks, and Halloween candy (till their parents gobble it while they sleep). Such categorizing and reclassifying rests on our ability to abstract and generalize.

If we had no way to abstract, then each situation we experienced would present itself as completely novel and would leave us without any general rules to guide our behavior.

Yet explainability based on causal frames has far bigger consequences than just providing order to the world. It is the foundation of human agency, responsibility, and control.

The idea of agency provides that humans have choices and can exercise them. We are subjects, not objects, in the world. We have the capacity to act. Having agency hinges upon our ability to frame causally. This is not to say that "free will" exists objectively, nor that human choices aren't influenced by social structures. Yet only if our actions have consequences—only if we can predict how our choices will shape reality—can we actually choose.

Experiments have shown that notions of causality and agency are intimately related. In the 1980s, Koichi Ono, a psychology professor at Komazawa University in Tokyo, presented people with a machine with levers they could pull in different ways. They might get a reward—but they didn't realize that the reward was given at random. Instead, they conjured up complex explanations for how their actions "caused" the reward and then stuck to that behavior in the hope of getting rewarded again. The study powerfully shows that people not only have a strong need to explain using causality, but that their causal understanding is directly connected to their agency and actions.

As frames give us agency, they also assign responsibility. Because we can choose our actions, because we decide, we also can be blamed. Accountability comes with choice. Being forced at gunpoint to hand over money doesn't make us culpable, but robbing a bank does. Crossing a street while sleepwalking will not lead to punishment, but deliberately running over a pedestrian will. Responsibility is the flip side of agency; it's part and parcel of making choices.

Yet agency and responsibility do not happen in a vacuum. If a person can influence another's decision, one can exercise control beyond one's self. Perhaps counterintuitive at first, the assertion that humans have some sense of agency (and therefore responsibility) is a key precondition for thinking about and exerting control over them. For example, some governments have "nudge units" to influence people's actions, such as saving electricity by showing them their usage compared with that of their neighbors. Because people have both agency and responsibility, others can impose some influence on them. If humans had no agency, it would be truly senseless to try to shape somebody else's views.

Social structures shape individual agency, but social structures (themselves being human-made) are also shaped by agency. Hence, our frames influence the sorts of social structures we inhabit. This explains why frames are so foundational for how we understand not just the world, but ourselves.

Skepticism and Wisdom

Causal thinking is a requisite for human progress. It lets us bend reality to our will. But the value of these templates is surprising when one considers how often our causal inferences are wrong. When we were kids our parents hounded us to wear hats and mittens on wintery days, lest we catch a cold. But is the seasonal flu virus really deterred by yarn? Semmelweis and the subjects of Ono's experiment with the reward-giving machine, too, were victims of misplaced causal connections. And it happens frequently. Perhaps we think we uncovered a cause when it is just a coincidence that we notice. Or perhaps some other underlying mechanism is responsible for what we see as effect and cause. Does the arrow of causality fly in the opposite direction?

For example, we notice each morning that as a rooster crows, the sun rises. Over time, we might take the specific incident (the crowing) and make a causal connection to establish a general rule (it causes the sun to rise). As an association, it is not wrong. In fact, the connection has never failed for as long as we've lived on the farm. But then the sad day comes when the rooster's spirit leaves this dusty world and goes to the big henhouse in the sky. And the next morning the sun rises with nary a cock-a-doodle-doo. Clearly something else had been going on.

We should not be surprised that some of our causal frames are flawed. For starters, we simply don't know all there is to know; how causes and effects are actually linked. For instance, before the first steam-engine railway trains began operating in the 1820s, experts feared that passengers might suffocate when traveling at high speeds such as fifteen miles per hour, and that people's eyes would be harmed by the blur from the speed.

Passengers, as we now know, did fine. The causal model that prompted the predictions was too primitive, lacking important elements of science and an understanding of how the human body would adjust. But as reality exposed the model's flaw and we learned more about air and eyesight, we substituted the model with a more appropriate one when assessing the impact of speed, much like we substituted our model of the rooster causing the sun to rise with one in which the sun rises every day as Earth turns. The need for humans to learn about the world and thus adjust their mental models is no indictment of the idea of frames, only encouragement to improve the practice of framing.

Much of life is revising what we thought we knew but really didn't. The whole scientific method presumes that there is never an end point of knowledge and that we must regularly cast away one set of understandings for better ones. In other words, our causal frames are always being shown to be imperfect. That's a bit depressing: framers are never allowed to pop champagne corks having reached a victorious end point, like professional athletes after winning a championship.

The repeated and frequent failures of causal framing have prompted many people to suggest that the whole project of causal reasoning is futile. They seemingly have David Hume on their side. The apparent flaws of causal thinking were articulated by the Scottish philosopher in the 1700s. An empiricist, Hume believed that all knowledge derives only from experience. He argued that causation cannot be justified rationally and that our inductive reasoning misleads us: just because the sun has always risen doesn't mean it will rise tomorrow.

In the same vein, traditional statisticians, driven by a well-meaning sense of caution, did much to prevent people from drawing causal inferences from data. They long insisted that we can only regard events as correlated or coincidental. "Correlation is not causation" was their battle cry—and the dogma they taught students on the very first day of class. On causality, they were mute. "They declared those questions off-limits," explains Judea Pearl, the modern father of the "causal revolution" in computer science.

The causal skepticism ascribed to Hume rests, at least in part, on a misunderstanding. He wasn't against what we call framing at all. Quite likely he would have approved of it for obvious pragmatic reasons: framing has improved our lot, and people are good at it, so it makes sense to continue doing it. Hume simply noted that causal reasoning is human, and as such we have no way to prove causation objectively, outside our own mind. And a new generation of statisticians and quantitative social scientists is softening their stance, accepting Pearl's "causal revolution" in their work.

But there is another kind of criticism against the causal enterprise, coming not from a rejection of causality per se but a dismissal of human frames as the primary source of causal explanation. This comes from the two extreme positions that we described in chapter 1, from the ultra-emotionalists and the uber-rationalists.

The emotionalists reject causal framing, seeing it not only as difficult to ascertain but also as not even needed: things are actually easier to know than they seem to the eggheads. Decisions can be made without all the navel-gazing or faffing about. The rightness of one's views is its own source of strength; certainty is solidity. The gut speaks truth where the brain is cloudy.

There is some truth to it. Gut decisions combine feelings and intuition, and in the right circumstances can be useful. But in terms of outcome, the emotionalist approach only goes so far. Relying on intuition and emotions cuts us off from tapping our ability for causal framing. It is like having a race car whose body is aerodynamic but lacks an engine. Dismissing causal frames and instead embracing emotions may feel good, but it entails amputating humanity's most powerful cognitive abilities.

On the other side, the hyper-rationalists abandon causal thinking from the opposite starting point: it is too important to be left to humans, who aren't very good at it anyway. The answer, in their view, is to hand the whole matter to the machines. So police forces use algorithms to organize patrols; courts use them to set bail; prisons use them to determine parole; schools use them to report grades; merchants use them to detect fraud. The promise is that AI can identify causation better than humans and eliminate bias to boot.

There is what appears to be good evidence that AI can "grok" causal connections and work with causal templates. To see how, look to games—but not the classic board games of chess or Go, where AI has famously beaten the world's best human players. Instead, turn to the more complex environment of e-sports.

Defense of the Ancients, or *Dota*, is a multiplayer online video game where teams of five players vie to destroy a large structure in the other team's base (and slaughter one's enemies in violent battle).

It requires complex strategic decisions, long-term planning, and cooperation among players. And it's a global phenomenon, with international tournaments and talk of adding it as an official Olympic sport. The annual prize money for the top teams reaches a pixel-popping $40 million.

In 2019 OpenAI, an AI research organization in San Francisco, built a system that stunned the *Dota* universe by crushing the best human players at *Dota 2*. On the surface, it seems that the system could divine causation, generalize from experience, and, with those abstractions, apply causal templates to new circumstances. But a closer look reveals that there's a human under the hood, just as the Wizard of Oz was a man behind the curtain.

The system uses "deep reinforcement learning." By playing against itself millions of times, through trial and error it identifies the best sets of actions—and gives itself a statistical "reward" to reinforce the behavior. Yet in its most critical areas what constitutes a reward isn't learned by the system itself: it needed to be coded manually.

For example, the OpenAI developers learned from *Dota 2* geeks that players conceive of battles in three phases, so the concept was encoded. This enabled the reward function to prioritize different strategies depending on the stage of the game. Next, the developers realized they would need to create "team spirit" among the bots, who otherwise battled selfishly. By manually tuning this "hyper-parameter," as they called it, the bots learned to play as one unit. The AI system performed well, so to speak: the bots butchered the humans. But people had to peck at a keyboard to input causal frames for it to work.

Causal framing can't be rejected by people vaunting extreme rationalism. Even when they build systems that outperform humans, the technology works only because the human element of causal frames has been injected. Likewise, those who urge a return to a more emotive way of seeing the world harm themselves by narrowing the range of their options for decisions. A different way is to not give up developing mental models with causal templates but to embrace them.

Order and Decision

As we explain the world through causal frames, we accept that there is a force larger than ourselves that governs all that is under the sun—if not a divine entity, then at least something that obeys the laws of physics.

The opposite would be a universe without pattern or meaning, in which every moment would entail random happenings: a world, as in T. S. Eliot's epic poem *The Waste Land*, where one "can connect nothing with nothing." But that is not how the universe works. Cause, comprehension, and cohesion exist. Early astronomers looked at celestial bodies sailing above and saw regularity: the term *kosmos* means "order" in ancient Greek.

So how can people become better at thinking in causal templates? Part of the answer is by at least being aware of them and actively harnessing them as we think through problems. We can pause and ask ourselves, "What is the reason why this is happening? What is the silent assumption or explanation that I'm making, that may or may not be true?"

That is what Ben Bernanke did the evening of September 16, 2008, when he paused in front of his office window and mulled his decision to flood the market with capital. And it is what enabled the NASA scientists to apply the principles of thrust to the void of space, where no man had gone before, using a causal template based on the physics on Earth.

Our causal thinking is sometimes wrong, occasionally terribly so, but over the millennia, framing has provided us with a superior way of understanding and deciding. If we suppress it, we desecrate a powerful cognitive mechanism that makes us human. But in order to fulfill the potential of frames, another cognitive human trait is needed: our ability to imagine an alternative reality. And the unlikely place where that is most needed is with the models by which we try to make sense of global warming.

4

counterfactuals

envisioning worlds that do not exist lets us excel in this one

On the morning of August 23, 1856, in Albany, New York, eminent scientists gathered for the eighth annual meeting of the American Association for the Advancement of Science. The halls were buzzing with the latest discoveries from across the thirty-one states in the union. The big news was the opening of the nearby Dudley Observatory, which aimed to sell "time service" to banks, companies, and railroads, for whom knowing the correct hour, minute, and second was essential.

But one paper at the conference—presented by a male scientist instead of its female author—marks the event as a landmark moment.

"Science," began Joseph Henry of the Smithsonian Institution, is of "no country and of no sex. The sphere of woman embraces not only the beautiful and the useful, but the true." When his short preamble was finished—which he meant as respectful though today rings comically sexist—he got down to describing the experiments performed by Eunice Foote, in a short paper titled "Circumstances Affecting the Heat of the Sun's Rays."

Foote had compared the temperature of different sorts of air, such as moist versus dry, when heated up by the sun or placed in the shade. Damp air heated up faster, as would be expected. However, when she compared "common air" with "carbonic acid gas" the effect was stunning: the latter, similar to carbon dioxide, heated up more and took longer to cool. The paper concluded: "An atmosphere of that gas would give to our earth a high temperature." In the midst of the Industrial Revolution, as American and European cities choked on belching gray factory smoke, Foote was ringing alarm bells about global warming.

Foote's study is the paragon of nineteenth-century science and the quest for causality. (And she did it years before the scientist credited in the history books with linking carbon dioxide and climate change, John Tyndall of Britain's Royal Society.) Since then, the scholarship on how the climate works has only become more robust, the data more comprehensive. So why can there still be climate deniers in the twenty-first century?

The answer is because showing the causal link between carbon in the atmosphere and warming temperatures is not enough. The crucial question is whether humans are responsible. And the data is actually of limited help. The hockey-stick graph doesn't answer the question. For that, we need something else. We need a mental model that is imbued with a counterfactual.

This lets us compare what is with what isn't there: the planet with humans and without them. But because there's only one Earth, we can't run an experiment. Instead, we imagine it. By employing a model of how the climate works, we build a counterfactual scenario and calculate temperatures for that imagined world. Then we can compare this data to the information we do possess.

And the celebrated moment of climate modeling happened one summer 132 years after Eunice Foote *didn't* present her paper. This time, the scene was a meeting of the US Senate Committee on

Energy and Natural Resources. On June 23, 1988—a day when the temperature in Washington, DC, sizzled past 100 degrees Fahrenheit, or 38 degrees Celsius—James Hansen, a NASA scientist, laid out three scenarios: if greenhouse gases stayed level, increased moderately, or grew a lot. All three scenarios were dire.

"Global warming is now large enough that we can ascribe with a high degree of confidence a cause and effect relationship to the greenhouse effect," he told the rapt audience of sweltering senators. "Our computer climate simulations indicate that the greenhouse effect is already large enough to begin to affect the probability of extreme events." There had been climate models before, but nothing with this rigor. Or impact. It made news around the world. "Global Warming Has Begun," blared the headline of the normally taciturn *New York Times*.

Hansen's research group included some of the world's foremost climate scientists and applied mathematicians. Among them was a math whiz responsible for the critical modeling, the paper's second author: Inez Fung. She is perhaps Eunice Foote's spiritual successor.

Like Foote, Fung was somewhat of an outsider to the field. Her specialty was mathematics, not meteorology. She was the lone woman on the team of the 1988 climate model. She was from Hong Kong and spoke with a slight Cantonese accent. Fung got into MIT after blurting out that school bored her, when asked during the interview why her grades weren't better.

As part of Hansen's group in 1979 to analyze climate change, she knew that data wasn't enough. What was required were models that depended on counterfactuals—not the world as it is, but as it might be.

"Temperature and carbon dioxide do not tell of cause and effect," Fung, now a professor of climate science at Berkeley, explains in an interview. "Both ice cream sales and murder rates in New York

City increase in the summer," she quips, suggesting a correlation without causation. "Models represent our best approximation of the real system. They allow us to identify the processes that are responsible, as well as processes that are not responsible," she explains. "Models are the only way to project what would happen if the carbon dioxide emission trajectory changes."

By crafting a model, Fung and her colleagues created an imagined world like ours, but without the extra carbon dioxide attributed to humans. No data or technology alone can make us "see" this alternative world directly. Only our careful imagination can. But this process of envisioning can be a powerful tool: it enables us to calculate the climate and compare. And that comparison, as Hansen revealed on a hot June day in 1988 using Fung's counterfactual models, showed that human activity was responsible for global warming.

Fung went on to have even broader reach, doing groundbreaking research on the carbon cycles and the concept of "carbon sinks"— where landmass and oceans pull carbon out of the air. And again, it took counterfactuals, not just data, to see it.

Imagining Alternative Realities

In our thoughts, we frequently run through a myriad of possibilities of how the world might be different, playing the game of life several moves ahead. Counterfactuals are a way to see beyond the reality that surrounds us. Without this ability to imagine "what could have been," "what has been," and "what could be," we would be forever stuck in the "what is" of the here and now.

Counterfactual thinking is the second element of framing. It is different from freewheeling fantasizing. It is not intellectual buffoonery. Unlike random stream-of-consciousness thoughts and free associations, counterfactuals are focused and goal-oriented. We use them to understand the world and prepare for action. Counterfactuals rely on the understanding of cause and effect that is embedded in our frames. This allows us to project forward or backward in time in our imagination, or take something that happened in one context and imagine it happening in another.

Thinking in counterfactuals comes naturally to us, even though it can actually be quite a complex process. It enables us to "fill in the blanks" of how the world might play out—imagining the information we do not have while making sense of the information we do have. Take the sentences: "John wanted to become king. He went to get some arsenic." For a moment, they seem unconnected. Then we apply counterfactual thinking to fill in the connection—and as we play out a mental simulation, perhaps a wry smile fills our face.

Counterfactuals enable us to imagine how situations might unfold differently in different circumstances. When the French soccer team scored against Croatia in the eighteenth minute of the 2018 World Cup final, the referee did not attribute the goal to the French striker Antoine Griezmann, though Griezmann took the twenty-seven-meter free kick and his shot was on target. Instead, it is officially recorded as an "own goal" from the Croatian defender Mario Mandžukić. The ball skimmed the top of the defender's head, which changed its trajectory, causing it to soar just out of the goalie's reach and into the net.

To make the call, the ref had to imagine what would have happened had Mandžukić's head not touched the ball. He needed to mentally construct a fictional alternative trajectory and rely on his general causal knowledge of how speed and spin affect a ball's movement. This imaginary trajectory let him predict that Croatia's goalkeeper would have certainly caught the ball—an easy save. If instead the referee had concluded that the ball was nevertheless on course to elude the goalie's grasp, he would have awarded the goal to Griezmann. The person whose name went on the scoresheet depended on the referee's counterfactual thinking—to the dismay of poor Mandžukić.

Using counterfactuals to inform causal reasoning is commonplace. In a set of experiments in 2017 researchers from MIT and elsewhere showed billiard balls ricocheting across a pool table. One ball hitting another caused it to either pass through a narrow gate or miss. The researchers tracked people's eye movements as they observed the action. They found that people rapidly shifted their focus to visually imagine the possible trajectories of the ball. In other words, they applied counterfactual reasoning to anticipate what might happen.

Recall that NASA's engineers were able to predict (almost) everything that would happen during the Apollo 11 moon landing, despite never having been on the moon. They were following the footsteps of generations of scientists before them. Galileo is famously said to have let two objects fall from the Tower of Pisa to refute a theory advanced by the ancient Greeks that heavier things fall faster than lighter ones. Yet scholars today believe that Galileo never actually dropped the objects but only did so mentally, applying counterfactual reasoning.

Newton's apple, Einstein's clocks, Schrödinger's cat: the annals of science are full of imagined alternative realities that enabled their creators to reach insights that have shaped our view of the world, from gravity to relativity to quantum theory. And it isn't limited to the sciences.

In *The Republic*, Plato mentally invents the city-state he calls Kallipolis to envision and evaluate how the ideal form of justice could work. The mind's eye can imagine possibilities where the physical eye can but see the present. The genre of "counterfactual history" tries to deepen our understanding of the effect of human actions by probing what might have happened if a hinge of history had swung a different way: Japan didn't attack Pearl Harbor; America didn't drop the atom bomb. Historians are divided on its value, whether it is serious insight or mere entertainment. However, mental examinations of alternatives open up our imagination, allowing us to conceive a reality different from what exists.

When we dream up alternative realities, we actually do serious cognitive work, requiring a wide spectrum of skills. Counterfactual thinking requires our minds to be fully engaged. We know this because humans with brain disorders, such as Parkinson's disease, are more impaired in thinking counterfactually than for other cognitive tasks. They may have no difficulties speaking and reasoning, but they find it hard to envision alternatives to what exists.

Imagining alternative realities enables us to make causal reasoning actionable. We can test potential causes for their particular effects. But both elements, counterfactual thinking and causal reasoning, reinforce each other. Without causality we would drown in a sea of happenings devoid of meaning; without counterfactuals we would be prisoners of what is, devoid of choices.

In his book *Sapiens*, Yuval Noah Harari explained the importance of humans' unique ability to cooperate and communicate shared, "intersubjective" ideas like religion. As he memorably put it: "You could never convince a monkey to give you a banana by promising him limitless bananas after death in monkey heaven."

And that's true: the ability to communicate values is a human trait. But there is a bigger point that is more fundamental: only humans can imagine scenarios that never happened—be it bananas that don't really exist or the reaction of monkeys. That is the power of counterfactuals.

The World of Pretend Play

Imagining alternative realities is something people do from early childhood. In fact, the long period of childhood, known as "protected immaturity" in psychology, may be specifically for this purpose. But it usually goes by the rather untechnical term of *play*. Infants and toddlers spend most of their time exploring the world and trying to figure out how things work.

Though young animals are also known to play, their play entails imitating activities they will perform as mature species—it is a low-risk environment in which to practice fighting, hunting, and the like. Human young also use play to mimic skills they will use as adults, but it goes far beyond the real world into the universe of their imagination. "Pretend play" hones our ability to imagine alternative realities.

The mental capabilities of very young children were not always celebrated. Rousseau in the mid-1700s called the baby "a perfect idiot." In the late 1800s the American psychologist William James characterized a baby's mentality as "one great blooming, buzzing confusion." Sigmund Freud believed young children were amoral, selfish, and unable to tell the difference between reality and fantasy, and the psychologist Jean Piaget described them as "pre-causal." In 2009 the satirical newspaper *The Onion* encapsulated the thinking of exasperated parents with the headline: "New Study Reveals Most Children Unrepentant Sociopaths."

Over the past few decades, our understanding of the cognitive ability of infants has undergone a significant change. As we now know, children have an acute sense of causality and counterfactuals. One of the world's leading experts investigating this is Alison Gopnik, a professor of psychology at the University of California, Berkeley.

In many respects, Gopnik never left the world of childhood. The eldest of six, she grew up in a "polymath atmosphere," as she describes it, and was often the one to keep an eye on her siblings (who are now famous writers and intellectuals themselves). Home life, in Philadelphia's public housing with academic parents, was poor in income but rich in literature, music, and art. As preschoolers, she and her brother Adam went trick-or-treating dressed as Hamlet and Ophelia. At age fifteen she began attending graduate-level university courses. By twenty-two, she was expecting a child of her own while earning a doctorate at Oxford. She specialized in developmental psychology and kept a playpen in her office.

Today Gopnik is the leader in a field of psychology known as "theory theory." The idea is that very young children use the same form of causal and counterfactual reasoning, and develop mental models, as scientists use when performing experiments (i.e., it is the theory that babies think theoretically). When scientists reason in this way, it's referred to as "research"; for toddlers, we call it "getting into everything," she explains.

Gopnik hails children as "the Scientist in the Crib" and "the Philosophical Baby" (titles of her bestselling books) for their use of counterfactuals and causal models. Her research lab devised several clever experiments that show that children as young as three years old have a grasp of causal mechanisms and alternative realities. One is the "zando test." (A zando is a colorful, funny-shaped object invented for the experiment.)

In the first phase of the test, kids playfully learn a causal association: that placing a zando on top of a machine plays a song to surprise a doll named Monkey, who is celebrating its birthday. In the key phase of the experiment, the focus is on "pretense" or pretend play. A colleague enters the room and explains she needs to borrow the machine and zando, and takes them away. The experimenter expresses disappointment that they hadn't yet surprised Monkey—but then has an idea.

She brings out a box and two blocks of different colors and says, "I thought we could *pretend* this box is my machine. And this block *is* a zando, and that block *is not* a zando. Then we could still surprise Monkey!"

Then she asks: "Which of these should we use to pretend to make the machine play music?" After this, she reverses the roles of the blocks and asks the question again.

By this time, the phraseology might seem so convoluted that an adult would need to parse it carefully to figure out what it means—but for a small child prodded to imagine alternative realities, it's simple. Children use this ability to better interact with and shape the world around them. And Monkey gets a "Happy Birthday" song.

Such pretend play prepares humans to think in counterfactuals. In fact, Gopnik found that "children who were better at pretending could reason better about counterfactuals," she said in describing the study. It is only partly tongue-in-cheek that she calls babies and young children the "research and development" division of the human species, while adults are relegated to the more mundane "manufacturing and marketing."

Mental Rehearsals

This imagining does not stop with childhood. We practice our ability to construct counterfactual realities throughout our lives. Consider literature and art. We are transfixed by stories of daring feats, dangerous threats, and desperate ordeals. They can be long or short, comic or tragic, extraordinary or artfully banal. But we love telling stories and listening to them.

Stories are evolutionarily useful because they help us hone our reasoning with counterfactuals. They are springboards to thinking vividly and imaginatively. Epic adventures are a feature of many cultures and eras, from the stories that comprise the holy texts of religious traditions to the Harry Potter series that delights Muggles everywhere. Salt and sugar light up the human appetite in a primal way; stories do the same thing for our minds. They are a platform to contemplate scenarios of alternative realities and how humans act within them. They help us evaluate options and prepare decisions. In this way, they expand and improve our framing skills.

As we create or listen to stories of alternative worlds, we use our imagination to act them out in our minds. We think about what follows in a particular situation, about what to do, or not do. When we say that a story "pulls us in," we really mean it: our mind is absorbed by the imagery of an alternative world, sensing it almost as if it were reality itself. Just a few sentences can conjure up a rich mental image. Consider a few snippets from literature.

The opening lines of Patrick Süskind's novel *Perfume*, describing eighteenth century France:

> *In the period of which we speak, there reigned in the cities a stench barely conceivable to us modern men and women. The streets stank of manure, the courtyards of urine, the stairwells stank of moldering wood and rat droppings, the kitchens of spoiled cabbage and mutton fat. . . . People stank of sweat and unwashed clothes; from their mouths came the stench of rotting teeth.*

Erich Maria Remarque's antiwar novel *All Quiet on the Western Front*, about the First World War:

> *We see men go on living with the top of their skulls missing; we see soldiers go on running when both their feet have been shot*

away—they stumble on their splintering stumps to the next shell hole. . . . We see soldiers with their mouths missing, with their lower jaws missing, with their faces missing; we find someone who has gripped the main artery in his arm between his teeth for two hours so that he doesn't bleed to death.

A steamy scene from Chimamanda Ngozi Adichie's novel *Americanah*:

She leaned in and kissed him, and at first he was slow in his response, and then he was pulling up her blouse, pushing down her bra cups to free her breasts. She remembered clearly the firmness of his embrace, and yet there was, also, a newness to their union; their bodies remembered and did not remember. . . . Lying next to him afterwards, both of them smiling, sometimes laughing, her body suffused with peace, she thought how apt it was, that expression "making love."

The imagery is vivid. Whether it appeals to the sense of smell, the agony of war, or the sensuality of sex, the deeper point is that we become captive in the universe of the author's creation. Once in that world, we begin to imagine the situation, imbue it with possibilities of what may happen.

What works for stories told or read, works even better for stories that we act out. Theater exists in vastly different societies, in significant part because acting out a counterfactual, experiencing other lives, can absorb us and stimulate us to ponder options. The chorus in Greek drama knew how the play would end and implored the audience to think how they might have acted differently to avoid the tragic fate of the hero. In *Poetics*, Aristotle declares the role of tragedy is to purge the emotions, to produce "catharsis." We put ourselves in the skin of the character and imagine what we might do differently; we wrestle with alternatives.

From the earliest days of cinema, films presented other worlds. The first short movies captured "actualities"—scenes from everyday life; in effect, the first documentaries. But soon movie creators began to experiment with technical tricks. They made people appear or disappear, elongated human extremities, and created other "unreal" situations. After huge initial success, the novelty wore off and was replaced with movies that, much like theater and literature, told stories. These apparently offered a more comprehensive, thickly woven, and sustainable alternative reality.

Literature, paintings and sculptures, theater, movies, and radio and television all let us experience alternative realities, but not interact with them. We can act them out in our minds—or with others, through role-playing games or anime cosplay—but we cannot directly manipulate them. One relatively new medium though is changing this.

In her classic 1993 book, *Computers as Theatre*, the video game designer Brenda Laurel suggests that the essential quality of computer games is that they let users influence alternative realities. We've come a long way since then, from Mario jumping on magic mushrooms to *World of Warcraft*, *Fortnite*, *Among Us*, and of course *Dota* players slaying their friends. These games borrow some elements of the world we know but introduce ones that are novel and different. It is the combination of the familiar and the new, and the ability to manipulate these elements, that makes such games so compelling.

Monument Valley is a case in point. On the surface, the game is about navigating a little figure named Ida through an Escherian world of three-dimensional geometric landscapes to arrive at a specific place. But how one gets there is a mystery: What part of the environment can be manipulated? And how?

Anyone who has ever seen or played the game has been mesmerized by the sumptuous elegance of the imaginary world, at once minimalist, intricate, and elaborate. When one starts interacting with the stairs, stones, buttons, dials, and other graphical items, they turn out to be forms that cannot exist in real space but can be used in the virtual world. The cognitive dissonance between the reality we know and the virtual world we navigate is what makes *Monument Valley* so appealing. Humans are suckers for counterfactuals.

Whether reading a book, playing a video game, or losing oneself in a daydream, these mental activities are not cognitive idling. Even a couch potato does more than just sit on the couch like a potato. As we experience and manipulate alternative realities—evaluating the universe of counterfactuals that we mentally construct—we ponder options and perhaps improve our judgment. We are training our mind and honing our skills as framers.

Thinking in counterfactuals is also a cornerstone of professional education. This is exemplified by the case method. It is most closely associated with business schools—and its origins, like so many dubious things, began at Harvard. But as the name hints, it started with lawyers, not managers. In 1870 the newly appointed dean of Harvard Law School, Christopher Columbus Langdell, was frustrated by the state of legal education. Students were force-fed the legal code on one side and highly abstract ideas on the other. It failed students and arguably failed society too.

Langdell came up with a novel solution: find a representative legal situation and examine it in depth, having students debate the various arguments. It was an open invitation to think through counterfactuals. One day, instead of giving a standard lecture, he surprised students by insisting they "state the case!" and then challenged them with hypotheticals—carefully crafted alternative realities to engage the students in elaborate discussions of "what if."

It was a radical way to teach: rather than conveying rules, the case method helped budding lawyers reconsider situations in alternative ways. And it worked. Harvard became a buzz of smart classroom discussion, as students assessed legal arguments and considered the law through counterfactuals, not passively ingesting what their professors said. Legal education almost everywhere adopted it and was forever changed.

Fast-forward five decades. In 1919 Wallace Donham was named the second dean of Harvard Business School, which had been founded eleven years earlier. A graduate of the law school, Donham knew the case method well. He wanted to apply it to business education. But there are no "cases" in business as there are legal cases. So he commissioned a professor to produce a book of short articles describing classic business decisions, with data for students to mull. Two years later, the first case—called "The General Shoe Company" and labeled "Confidential" on the top left corner—was handed out to students.

The format puts students in the role of an executive facing a problem with reams of information (some of it irrelevant and always incomplete, as in real life). It forces them to come up with options, evaluate them, make a decision, and justify it. Should the company invest in a radical new product under development, or incrementally improve existing products and boost marketing? What if they make a bid to acquire the biggest competitor in a market, rather than compete against it? Should they bundle some of their products rather than sell them separately? Within the numerous limitations of a seemingly real-world situation, the professor guides the discussion as students propose counterfactuals and challenge one another (and vie to score brownie points without making it too obvious).

The case study method, spurring students to actively think in counterfactuals, is now used in many domains. In medical school, aspiring doctors are prompted to think through what is called "differential diagnosis," the idea of collecting and then eliminating alternative explanations—distinct variations of reality. Professional athletes have "film study": sessions to review game situations to tease out all the what-ifs, hoping this might give them an edge. The celebrated NFL quarterback Peyton Manning swore by it.

Taking time to engage in such alternative worlds is a particularly human trait. Ospreys don't go to operas, nor monkeys to movies. When a medical student unwinds by playing *Dota* after a hard day at school, it may seem like these are very different activities, but both involve mentally rehearsing through a continuous stream of what-ifs, honing a human skill that enables us to maintain and expand our framing capabilities.

From Abstractions to Alternatives

Counterfactuals do more than help us imagine what isn't there. They offer powerful additional benefits.

First, they act as a counterbalance to "causal determinism," the idea that there is only a set path to follow. The causal reasoning that is part of framing makes us focus on a particular causal dynamic. That is good, because it helps us understand a situation swiftly. If we have saved a final chocolate-chip cookie, only to find the jar empty, our causal-inference engine goes into overdrive and we may quickly blame our child. But what if we are wrong? What if it was our partner, in a sudden craving, who looted the cookie jar?

That's where counterfactuals shine. As we dream up alternative realities, we also imagine different causes. They are the antidote to jumping to a particular causal conclusion too quickly (and save our cherub from an unnecessary scolding). They remind us that things may be different than first thought. They make us more open-minded to see a world beyond our first causal hypothesis.

During the Cuban missile crisis, President John F. Kennedy put counterfactuals to work in this way. On the morning of October 16, 1962, the president and his advisers were presented with aerial photographs that showed the Soviet Union was placing nuclear missiles in Cuba, just ninety miles off Florida. The military immediately urged a massive strike to knock out the installations. But Kennedy resisted. He had been burned before.

A year and a half earlier—and only three months into his presidency—he had agreed to a covert plan for an invasion by exiles at the Bay of Pigs in Cuba to install a new government. But it failed disastrously. The lack of diverse views and alternative thinking when vetting the plan popularized a new term in decision-making: groupthink. The young president was not going to let that happen again.

This time, confronted with an even more serious challenge, he encouraged his advisers to present him with a wide variety of alternative ways to see the situation, leading to a myriad of potential solutions that went far beyond the bombing campaign that the generals instinctively put on the table. In other words, JFK actively solicited imaginings to resist the temptation for one-track thinking.

And it worked. The team around him narrowed down the options to two plans that they openly and earnestly argued over, regardless of rank or the part of government they represented. In the end they chose to blockade rather than bomb, and offer the removal of US missiles from Turkey. This provided a way for the Soviets to save face if they removed their weapons from Cuba. The Soviet

Union backed down—and a potential nuclear war was averted. JFK had avoided the groupthink that had led to the Bay of Pigs catastrophe eighteen months earlier, and prevented causal determinism by introducing counterfactual thinking.

This leads to the second benefit, that counterfactuals make us better causal thinkers. In experiments, people improve their causal reasoning after engaging in counterfactual thinking than the other way around. Cognitive scientists, notably Ruth Byrne at Trinity College Dublin, suggest that counterfactuals are so helpful because they remind us of options, broadening rather than deepening our focus. As we think about options, we also ponder cause and effect; in contrast, when we just focus on a single cause, we are not stimulating our imagination. That's why imagining alternative realities is such a central element for successful framing.

A third advantage of counterfactuals is that we interact with them in ways that make them useful to apply. When we imagine a situation and play it out in our minds, we can experience it almost like a bystander watching an alternative reality as it unfolds. Rather than having to painstakingly conceptualize how a situation might play out, we can simply watch our dreams. That is less belabored and more visual; it's easier for us to envisage something that doesn't exist than to think it through in purely conceptual terms. As Daniel Kahneman, the renowned psychologist, has put it, "The most important aspect . . . of mental simulation is that it is experienced as an act of observation, not as an act of construction." It is "the sense that the outcome is observed, not contrived."

The fourth benefit of counterfactuals is that they tap into our implicit knowledge. By imagining alternative ways in which a situation might play out, we activate a lot of our knowledge about how the world works, including causal insights that we would otherwise find difficult to articulate.

The way that counterfactuals reach into our implicit knowledge was the leitmotif of the American television show *MacGyver*, which aired in the 1980s and 1990s. The central character was a half geek, half jock working at a secretive think tank who didn't carry a gun or resort to violence. To get out of sticky situations, he had to rely on his wits—and whatever everyday items were lying around. Thus, two candlesticks, a microphone cord, and a rubber mat became a defibrillator. When he was bound up in rope, he used his feet to fashion a catapult to launch a bottle of sulfuric acid onto a nearby beam—to burn away the cords that secured him. And to defuse a missile, he needed to rewire a circuit: so he bent a paper clip—his signature tool—for that purpose.

The creative solutions were based on counterfactuals that tapped the items' properties beyond their obvious uses. MacGyver relied on abstractions about how things *work*, not what they *were*—just as MIT's Regina Barzilay cared about the antibacterial compounds' function, not their molecular structure.

The fifth and final benefit is that counterfactuals give people a sense of purpose. They expose and express our notion of action and agency. Looking at a particular causal connection helps us understand why things happened, but imagining an alternative reality helps us to act because it creates a choice. As we imagine through alternative realities how different choices would unfold, we gain a sense of predictability and control. Human agency is the key value that causal framing fundamentally enables. Our human decisions matter because through counterfactuals we can see options and have choices. They shift our focus from understanding to acting, from comprehending to deciding.

And this really is a human phenomenon—it's not only ospreys and monkeys who haven't mastered counterfactuals. Machines spend significant time and effort processing real-world data to improve their output, but they aren't following in humanity's footsteps yet.

Vehicles of the Vicarious

By all accounts, it was an ordinary road that bent to the left, and all that was necessary was a gentle, leftward turn. But something was going horribly wrong. The car was too far to the right and dangerously approaching the curb. It was barely turning at all. A collision was imminent. The car braked hard and decelerated quickly—but not before it slammed into the boundary and was poised to go off the road. In the end, it came to a rest . . . on a thin, purple line of pixels on the screen.

The minor accident was a digital simulation. It happened only in the computer servers of Waymo, Google's self-driving-car company. The simulation is designed to overcome a serious shortcoming of all autonomous vehicles: a lack of data on rare events because they are, well, rare. For well over a decade, the industry has been collecting real-world road data to train the AI models that power the self-driving systems. Fleets of cars with sophisticated sensors and video cameras have cruised the streets collecting zillions of data points every second. The companies have been mining reality to capture the essence of driving.

And it worked. At least a bit. The cars certainly could drive. But what they couldn't do was handle uncommon situations, since there aren't enough of them in the data to train the machine-learning algorithms under the hood. Think, a plastic bag fluttering in the wind just as a car hits black ice, or a mattress lying in the middle of the road. Waymo hit a wall (metaphorically speaking). It found that adding more real-world data didn't improve the system much because it was a preponderance of ordinary driving conditions.

So the company invented an alternative reality that was full of rare situations. The system to generate simulated data is called Carcraft, a nod to the video game *World of Warcraft*. It offers twenty thousand base scenarios, including extremely rare but eventful situations imagined by humans—"spicy," in the words of Waymo gearheads. Every day, Waymo's twenty-five thousand virtual vehicles drive ten million miles, akin to going to the moon and back fifteen times. As Waymo put it in an academic paper, the aim is "to simulate the bad rather than just imitate the good."

These base scenarios are counterfactuals that are slightly varied through a process called "fuzzing": changing another car's speed or distance; playing it out at night or in rain; adding a jogger darting across the street. It's a universe of what-ifs. For each scenario, Carcraft produces a plethora of different responses, which then are used to train the system. By 2020, Waymo had improved its performance to well over thirty thousand miles between human interventions, far better than rivals.

Just as AI lacks the causal frames to win at *Dota 2* and needs them encoded by people, so too computers can't generate counterfactuals on their own but require people to supply them. Carcraft's rare scenarios were not the result of a machine dreaming alternative worlds, or randomly generating extreme events. Rather, humans came up with them. The hyper-rationalists in Silicon Valley and elsewhere would like to hand over driving, and much else, to the machine. But that's an oversimplification of what's actually happening. People pull AI's strings in the background like a marionette's puppet master.

Counterfactuals represent our cognitive capability to grasp situations we haven't encountered before and to use them to improve our understanding to inform our decisions. We evolve physically across generations through the exploitation of our outward traits, but we improve mentally as a species because of our framing, of which counterfactual thinking is a central element.

We can get better at it too. There are ways that people can improve their dreaming up of alternative realities. For example, we can look at problems not in terms of what needs to change but by what must remain constant. And like JFK, we can deliberately empower people and institutions to advance novel and diverse views, so as to increase the chances that a useful alternative way of thinking will emerge. Then there is the approach of many high-performance athletes and executives who practice "visualizations": developing a realistic mental image of a situation (whether a ski jump or a board meeting) and simulating within that world the diverse actions and responses that might work, much like Carcraft does for autonomous vehicles.

Imagining alternative realities makes causal frames actionable. But it requires more than imagination. The trick, as toddlers quickly learn, is not to conceive of just any alternative reality but to construct one carefully that can help us achieve our goal. Counterfactuals are functional; their effectiveness depends on how well they are shaped given the goals we have and the context in which we intend to use them. They can't be helter-skelter, hither-thither ideas. To be truly valuable, counterfactuals require boundaries.

Counterfactuals are a form of dreaming—but wisely channeled, deliberately focused. When Kennedy asked his team to come up with a range of solutions, they of course had to be military or diplomatic ones, not the kind of phantasmagoric thoughts that might occur in an actual dream, like sending a musical troupe to entertain the leaders in Moscow. When Inez Fung developed her climate model, it was based on accepting the laws of physics but deferring to a model that represented Earth without humans. Even flashy MacGyver operates under limitations on what he can make happen.

Envisioning alternatives to reality enables us to shape the future, to control events rather than be controlled by them. It was just this trait of human cognition that was decisive for one of the most astounding commando raids of all time. Amid the crack of gunfire, the operation's success was not so much due to the soldiers and planners thinking with counterfactuals—but the degree by which they chose to loosen or tighten the counterfactuals' constraints.

5

constraints

our vision needs to be bounded
to be effective

On the afternoon of June 30, 1976, Brigadier General Dan Shomron was summoned to meet the army's head of operations at the Israeli Defense Force's headquarters in Tel Aviv. An audacious but workable rescue mission was needed. The situation looked bleak.

Three days earlier, an Air France flight between Tel Aviv and Paris had been hijacked by terrorists and flown to Entebbe airport in Uganda, in the heart of East Africa. The hostages were placed in a disused, old terminal that the terrorists claimed was packed with explosives. After releasing the non-Israeli passengers, the terrorists threatened to kill the 106 hostages one by one unless scores of Palestinian prisoners were freed.

Israel had a policy of not negotiating with terrorists, fearing it would invite more terror. But now it stalled for time to weigh its options. A rescue operation seemed crazy. Uganda was more than 2,500 miles, or 4,000 kilometers, from Israel. How could a force get there undetected? How could it free the hostages—especially if the building were wired to blow? Uganda's dictator, Idi Amin, might be allied with the hijackers: Would the Israelis need to battle Ugandan troops too? Even if all that worked out, how would everyone get back? It stretched the limits of "counterfactual thinking."

Shomron, at age thirty-nine, led the Infantry Corps and Paratroopers Brigade. He heard the outlines of the plans being floated and saw their flaws. One was to airlift one thousand soldiers to Entebbe. That was useless: the terrorists would see it coming and kill the hostages. Another was to fly in posing as freed Palestinian prisoners. That too seemed unlikely to work: the hijackers would quickly spot the ruse and blow up the terminal.

A more promising idea was to parachute a dozen commandos with inflatable rafts into nearby Lake Victoria at night, paddle to land, and storm the terminal. That kept the element of surprise. But the lake was filled with giant Nile crocodiles: the soldiers would be eaten alive before they reached the shore. Moreover, the plan missed an essential detail. After eliminating the terrorists, how would the soldiers and passengers return?

It's a dud, Shomron thought.

In planning a military operation, like anything else, there are hard constraints that can't be moved and others that can. For example, the size of the force wasn't what mattered most, nor whether it landed at day or night. Those were adjustable. But a hard requirement was the element of surprise. Using that as the foundation, Shomron and several officers outlined a plan: a commando team would land surreptitiously at night in a transport plane loaded with vehicles typical of an airport, drive to the terminal undetected, eliminate the terrorists, free the hostages, and fly them back.

But there were lots of missing details. What was the layout of the terminal, and where were the hostages kept? How many terrorists were there, and how were they armed? They needed to build a mental model of how the hostage rescue could unfold. That meant getting information so they could engage their counterfactual thinking. Mossad agents flew to Paris to interview the released hostages. Intelligence about the terminal was critical. By luck, it had been built by an Israeli construction company. The blueprints were delivered.

A scale model of the terminal was made of poles and tarps at an airbase where the soldiers trained. The men practiced what to do at every moment, took notes, discussed and iterated their actions.

"The first rehearsal didn't work well. It was too messy—the flow wasn't good enough," recalls Noam Tamir, a commando on the team. Every detail of the operation—every action and every second—was choreographed, analyzed, reconsidered, adjusted, and optimized.

The requirement of surprise restricted certain aspects of the operation—but invited creativity too. For example, to fit in with the setting, the team would fly in with a black Mercedes-Benz with Ugandan flags on the hood and Land Rovers—vehicles favored by Ugandan generals. They had Ugandan army uniforms made, so they would look the part. With all the eventualities considered, the operation commenced.

Just before midnight on July 3, the clouds over Lake Victoria cleared to reveal the Entebbe landing strip. The first of four Hercules transport planes quietly swooped down. An assault unit of twenty-nine commandos drove down the plane's ramp and toward the old terminal a mile away, as rehearsed. But some things can't be foreseen: an entrance guard raised his rifle. Was he waving the motorcade past or ordering it to stop? Amid the uncertainty, the Israelis fired, breaking the night's silence. Building lights flicked on. The group sped to the terminal even faster.

When the first commando arrived, a hail of bullets shattered the window in front of him. Remarkably he wasn't struck but saw the shooter and squeezed off a spurt of rounds that hit. Soon gunfire was echoing throughout the building. Several Israelis stormed in to find more terrorists, just as they had prepared for. Shomron oversaw it all via radio from the planes.

Operation Thunderbolt lasted just ninety minutes: ten minutes to eliminate the terrorists, and the rest of the time to get the hostages onto the planes, count them—recount them when the numbers didn't add up—and go. When they arrived in Israel the next morning, 102 hostages had been rescued, three were killed in the fighting, five soldiers were wounded, and one died, the commander Jonathan "Yoni" Netanyahu (whose younger brother, Benjamin, would later become prime minister).

Looking back today, Tamir credits the planners with the success. "They were the heroes," he says. "We were on the ground; we were trained to do these types of things." But Shomron and the planners were the ones adjusting all the elements of the mission to ensure it would work—not a process of execution but an act of origination.

"It's like chess," Tamir says. "It is the difference between just moving the pieces and planning the moves."

But chess masters do not simply imagine their actions; they apply constraints to limit the number of moves they assess. Similarly, for the Entebbe raid planners, it was not just the vast spectrum of ideas that mattered. It was also how they curtailed them by identifying the most essential requirements. The key was not only the counterfactual thinking that was applied but also the way they wisely tightened and relaxed a mix of constraints.

Binding the Boundless

Constraints are the third ingredient, after causality and counterfactuals, for framing to work. Without constraints, we might imagine an enormous range of alternative realities that are so ill-connected to the causal mental model that they fail to inform our actions. We need the right boundaries for our imagination to elicit the choices we have.

Constraints are rules and restrictions that shape our counterfactual thinking in a particular way. We can play with them—by loosening or tightening them, and by adding new ones or removing old ones. With constraints, framing goes from the purview of cognition to the basis of actions *that matter.* That's seen in how the Israeli military took efforts to build a model of Entebbe's old terminal for the soldiers to train. Or recall Ben Bernanke at America's Federal Reserve in September 2008. As he loosened the ideological constraint that the government doesn't get involved in markets, it allowed him to conjure up the counterfactual of helicopter money and put it into action. Constraints not only help us explain what is happening, they also point us in the right direction for how to respond.

People who are exceptional at framing understand that their imagination needs bounds—cognitive curbs, mental manacles—not to interdict their vision but to guide it. Restraints can free creativity rather than curtail it, providing a zone of permissibility to take mental risks.

Some innovators actively welcome constraints to help shape their creativity. This was what Theodor Seuss Geisel (a.k.a. Dr. Seuss), one of the most popular children's authors, did when he wrote his masterful and surreal rhyming story *Green Eggs and Ham* in 1960. Seuss's friend and publisher, Bennett Cerf, bet the author fifty dollars that he could not write a book with just fifty different words of one syllable each. In books to help young children learn to read, it is a selling point to have a limited vocabulary—but this artificial limit was extreme. Still, with his pride on the line, Seuss couldn't resist proving it possible. (He won the bet using forty-nine one-syllable words and a fiftieth word: *anywhere*.) *Green Eggs and Ham* went on to become one of the bestselling children's books of all time. You can read it on a boat, you can read it with a goat.

The American choreographer Martha Graham developed modern dance by removing some constraints and imposing others, albeit in a way that may not be obvious to audiences mesmerized by her works. When she started choreographing in the 1920s, female dance mostly consisted of classical forms like ballet. Women wore corsets that restricted their movement and, most of all, their breathing. By removing the tight garments from her dancers' torsos, Graham freed their ability to move and allowed them to have more stamina and more style. The freedom also had symbolic value—a breath of fresh air from the stifling social restrictions placed on women at the time.

Yet to prevent a free-for-all, she had to reintroduce a new set of constraints. The so-called Graham technique is the foundation of modern dance. It relies on a breathing cycle of "opposition" between contraction and release. She also imposed other kinds of constraints, most literally in her most famous work, *Lamentation*, in 1930, in which the dancer is contained in a fabric tube. And the Graham technique imposes restrictions in ways that other dance companies may not expect: it is a registered trademark.

As in the cases of Dr. Seuss and Martha Graham, boundaries need not be confining but serve as an opportunity. The architect Frank Gehry believes that the very secret to his creative successes is the limitations he must work through. "As an artist, I got constraints. Gravity is one of them," he adds with a chortle. "But within all those constraints, I have fifteen percent of freedom to make my art." Gehry said his most difficult assignment was when he was asked to build a home for a wealthy patron with *no constraints*. He felt paralyzed. Complete openness was emptiness.

In this very sense, constraints—by providing curbs on the open canvas of our dreams—can actually be more liberating than limiting. But the constraints themselves are not what is most important; it is what we do with them. By changing constraints, we are shaping the alternative realities we come up with. What matters is the *act of constraining* our imagination. Loosening or tightening constraints is like operating valves in complex machinery: one needs to adjust the right combination to produce valuable results.

Think of photography. When taking a photo, most people want the camera to take a shot that's sharp and crisp. But there are actually a number of factors that constrain what image will be captured, like focus, exposure time, aperture, sensitivity. Modern cameras can be switched to automatic, so all these factors will be selected by the camera. But professionals often choose which factors to hold and which others to forgo—say, what to place in sharp focus and what to intentionally blur—to deliberately shape the final result.

The magic is in thoughtfully modifying constraints to produce the suitable counterfactuals. But what are the right ones to ease? After all, not all constraints matter. Martha Graham freed dancers' torsos but did not remove their tutus. Likewise, Dr. Seuss accepted the limitation on the number of words but didn't try to write a book without using the letter *e* (as the French novelist Georges Perec did in the 1960s). If we focus on the wrong constraints, we don't capture what's needed. But focusing on all of them doesn't help either. Select too few constraints and we lose focus on what matters; choose too many and we may miss something important.

As a first step, we must appreciate that for each frame some constraints are soft and some are hard. Soft ones are malleable or amenable, can be adjusted or bent even if only with substantial effort. Hard ones are fixed, impermeable, inviolable. Hard constraints capture the central tenet of a mental model; neglecting them means giving up on the very model itself. So, when the frame is financial accounting, not accepting the constraint of basic arithmetic—that two plus two equals four—is dumping a hard constraint. By discarding it, one essentially discards the frame itself. Similarly, when Christian theologians use counterfactuals to ponder alternative interpretations of the Bible, a hard constraint is their belief in God. Discarding that is to abandon the very mental frame they are in.

As we choose the constraints for dreaming up counterfactuals, we need to ensure we adhere to the most essential ones, the hard ones. Then we'll add other, soft constraints and see where this gets us as we iterate through them. Choosing wisely among these soft constraints is more art than science. But three principles guide the selection: mutability, minimal change, and consistency. Mutability means picking constraints that are open to modification. Minimal change posits that constraints should be adjusted gently, not radically. Consistency means that modifying a constraint cannot contradict another constraint. Consider each in practice.

The Principle of Mutability

When conjuring up an alternative reality, people focus on aspects that they believe they can alter. If running late for a meeting in the city, we might imagine several alternative ways to get where we need to go. Do we take the subway train and risk waiting on the platform but then zooming downtown? Or do we jump into a cab and get on our way immediately, but risk being stuck in traffic closer to the destination? Or do we forgo transportation altogether—not putting our fate in things outside our control—and briskly trot to our destination?

Deciding involves numerous probabilities and trade-offs; it forces us to mentally time-travel as we weigh the options and choose what we believe to be the quickest way. Yet when doing this, we rely neither on teleportation nor on all the traffic lights staying green. Instead, we assume the world as it is (although we may hold out hope); it is the mode of transport that is changeable.

One company that applied the mutability principle well is SpaceX, founded by the entrepreneur Elon Musk. It pioneered the development of reusable rockets. The idea had long been a dream of aeronautical engineers and a staple of science fiction. But when NASA scientists contemplated reusability in the 1960s and 1970s, they imagined a rocket with wings that could land like an airplane after returning to Earth. Their assumed constraint was that the returning rocket's recovery needs to rest on aerodynamic updrift. This gave birth to the plane-like space shuttle. (It also begat the hang glider, which was invented around 1960 by a NASA engineer, Francis Rogallo, initially as a potential way to bring space capsules back to Earth.)

But wings are heavy and bulky, and the amount of aerodynamic updrift they generate is a function of their size. Bigger wings mean more lift but also more weight, bulk, and drag at launch. Given all these constraints, the final shuttle system was a problematic compromise. It included a huge external tank that would burn up each time and a main body that had terrible gliding capabilities. By constraining on aerodynamic updrift, NASA could only imagine wings and parachutes, with all the drawbacks that these options entailed.

In contrast, thanks to innovative breakthroughs, especially on sensors and computing power, SpaceX was able to loosen the constraint for aerodynamic updrift. Like NASA, it aimed to slow the fall of the rocket, but it now could focus on ways to reignite the motors of the rocket's first stage to land it upright. The thinking was: screw aerodynamic updrift and bank on rocket power. It was audacious, because it required relighting the engine, keeping enough fuel to slow the rocket's fall (but not too much since fuel is heavy), and having a control system to stabilize the rocket in order to land it. Where the shuttle required a complex physical structure, the first stage of SpaceX's Falcon had a fairly simple physical structure but a far more complex control system. But because of technological advances, such control was now feasible.

The magic lies in understanding which constraints are mutable. SpaceX accepted that a rocket falling back to Earth needed to be slowed down, but it chose to use the built-in rocket engine instead of a wing to do it. Precisely because the SpaceX engineers were able to relax one set of now mutable constraints, they were able to see new possibilities and to develop the Falcon's reusable rockets.

Technological change, like SpaceX's rocket control system, transforms which constraints are mutable and which aren't (though technology itself is an outcome of framing). When we are choosing which constraints to modify, the principle of mutability suggests that we should single out elements that we can influence. We should not loosen ones that our dreaming ought to adhere to—like a budget if you're a manager, or cooking time if you're a chef—if we want a counterfactual that's effective. Instead, we should look to alter constraints that reflect human behavior or human choices, because it's far more likely that this will yield a useful dream.

The principle of mutability isn't perfect. We may believe in certain things being mutable when in fact they aren't, and vice versa. But using mutability has a big advantage: it focuses our reasoning on things that we can influence, change, or shape. It helps us see choices and act on them. In the context of running late for a meeting across town, it focuses our attention on a choice between subway and taxi rather than sci-fi levitation. In the context of SpaceX, the company focused on alternative engineering solutions to arrest the fall. For the Entebbe raid, Brigadier General Shomron prepared to fight Ugandan troops, not to try to change their allegiances in the heat of the moment.

We often regard human action as mutable, because our causal cognitive lens empowers us to believe in human agency and links that agency to control. For this reason, we also believe human behavior can change and that we can shape the behavior and actions of others. This attention to human actions is not a drawback but a benefit of human framing. Similarly, focusing on the constraints that people have some control over (as the mutability principle suggests) helps us identify the most useful constraints to alter and play with.

In experiments, researchers have identified an interesting wrinkle. We may believe that human activity is quite mutable, but in our counterfactuals, we prefer imagining behavioral changes that fall within widely accepted social norms. While waiting in a taxi line when late for a meeting, for instance, we may think about jumping on our phone to call an Uber. But we less frequently think of jumping the queue.

Of course, social norms are mutable, at least in principle, and they do evolve over time. But in our mental laboratory of constraining counterfactuals, we tend to see norms as fixed and unchangeable. This may be the result of humans being social: we understand that fitting in necessitates limiting our imagination to behavior that won't ostracize us. Hence, we wait in the taxi line.

The Minimal-Change Principle

When selecting which constraints to loosen or tighten, we should aim for the fewest, not the most, modifications. We should aspire to minimal change. With alternative realities in our mind, our imaginings need to stick closer to, rather than further from, the one we inhabit. That way, we reduce the risk of simply conjuring up impractical possibilities. Reality needs to shine through what we envisage.

This principle is in line with the idea of Occam's razor, a rule of thumb in problem-solving that recommends a preference for simplicity. When choosing between alternative explanations or solutions to a problem, embrace the less complicated: it will probably be more accurate than an intricate or elaborate answer with lots of parts. The idea was set forth (in a somewhat different form) by the English friar William of Ockham in the fourteenth century; the "razor" is to shave away the unnecessary to focus on the essential.

To see how the minimal-change principle works in action, consider a scandal in Europe in the 1980s, when wine merchants were accused of pouring "antifreeze" into bottles. For decades, the vineyards along the Danube River in Lower Austria produced high volumes of relatively low-quality wine. To make it taste more full-bodied, and thus command a higher price, a handful of sellers began to add diethylene glycol to sweeten it. (Though toxic in large quantities, it is not the main chemical in antifreeze, which is ethylene glycol—but the media couldn't resist the dramatic term.)

When the practice was discovered, authorities in Europe and America immediately banned the sale of Austrian wine. A staggering thirty-six million bottles had to be dumped in West Germany alone. A well-known winemaker implicated in the scandal took his life. Exports of Austrian wine plummeted by 90 percent. Even *The Simpsons* had an episode based on it.

Within two months of the revelations, new laws were enacted in Austria. They imposed tight controls, transparent labeling, and harsh fines. Every bottle needed to be numbered. Faced with this new reality, the traditional business of high volume and low quality was no longer economically feasible. Some vintners couldn't re-imagine a way out of the crisis and gave up. But others, particularly a younger generation of growers, identified one.

Their solution wasn't to give up winemaking and grow apples or apricots instead. Rather, they made just a small but decisive adjust-ment to their business model. They continued to grow grapes and make wine but transformed the product to emphasize quality over quantity. This entailed tradition-breaking activities like using only the best grapes instead of the full harvest, investing heavily in brands, and building architecturally spectacular wine-tasting centers alongside the fields to encourage a new business of wine tourism.

It was a painful transition. But it was successful. Volumes were much smaller initially, but because of the better quality, prices were also substantially higher. Two decades later, wines from the region achieved top marks by the international wine taster Robert Parker. The change also paid off quite literally: by 2019 exports had about doubled in volume compared to before the scandal, but the value had skyrocketed to six times higher. Applying just a relatively min-imal change—making wine a luxury product, not switching the crop grown—enabled the success. As one of the new generation of vintners, Erich Polz, admitted: "Frankly, it was the best thing that ever happened to Austrian wine."

The minimal-change principle pushes us in a particular direc-tion when picking counterfactuals: we tend to omit rather than add. It is easier for us to imagine a world without some features of reality than to introduce ones that do not yet exist. If you are asked to imagine a color you haven't seen before, you likely will fail.

Combining the minimal-change principle with the mutability principle helps explain why people are more able to imagine a counterfactual in which an activity is absent than if it occurs: a murder that was *not* committed, a driver who did *not* crash the car, a relationship that was *not* ended. Ruth Byrne of Trinity College Dublin believes that "cognitive effort" is responsible. Experiments have shown that omitting a mutable human action from a counterfactual requires less mental work than adding an action from the countless possibilities. As she succinctly put it: "There are more things to keep in mind when someone does something than when they do nothing."

When we apply a frame, we prefer what we can process efficiently to what takes more energy and time. Even though this sometimes may lead us astray, privileging human *inaction* has the advantage not only of a lower mental load to imagine but also of something that's likely easier to achieve. It's often simpler to stop others from acting than to motivate them to act when they had no intention of doing so.

The Consistency Principle

The third principle for choosing constraints is perhaps the most obvious: consistency. Constraints should not be placed in direct contradiction to one another. As we envisage alternative realities, one constraint cannot go against another one; otherwise our counterfactuals would keep running into contradictions. Thus, if the counterfactual world without humans has to comply with the laws of physics, it cannot also have a constraint that depends on divine intervention. That would violate the consistency principle—like the hapless defense attorney who argues that his client wasn't at the scene of the crime but did it in self-defense.

If mutability and minimal change concern how we alter and iterate through individual constraints, consistency looks at the relations among them. This is particularly challenging if there are many constraints that have to be considered. The larger the number of constraints, the more difficult it is to come up with consistent imagined alternative realities.

A lesson on the care needed for consistent constraints comes from how Steven Spielberg invented the imaginary world in his movie *Minority Report* in 2002. The film is based on a 1956 story by Philip K. Dick that is so short that there is no setting, no description of time and place. Spielberg needed one. So he turned to a childhood acquaintance, Peter Schwartz, one of the foremost thinkers in technology and forecasting.

Schwartz had run the renowned "scenario planning" division at Shell in the 1980s, helping the oil company prepare for long-term trends like global warming. His team famously envisaged a collapse in oil prices and the breakup of the Soviet Union years before they happened. Governments around the world called on his services once word slipped out that South Africa's leaders had used scenario planning to imagine a stable postapartheid future, which led to the system's dismantling. Now Schwartz was asked to assemble the smartest people in tech to describe the world of 2050 with the same intellectual rigor. "Steven wanted people to be able to say years later, 'That's just like in *Minority Report*,'" recounts Schwartz.

Hollywood production crews have long included the position of "continuity editor" to ensure that every aspect of a film, from shots to subplots, is perfectly consistent. But Spielberg raised this to another level. In 1999 a dozen experts gathered for a three-day "ideas summit" in a conference room of the posh Shutters hotel beside the beach in Santa Monica, California. The pioneer of virtual reality Jaron Lanier was there, describing a prototype of a glove to enable gestures as the interface to computers—seen at the start of the film as Tom Cruise gracefully waves around virtual screens like an orchestra conductor. The Gen X writer Douglas Coupland was there, typing the ideas into a book for the production director to use, that later was called "the bible." The film's designers and scriptwriters were in the room listening and occasionally pushing back.

"Steven would set various requirements that we would have to invent," explains Schwartz. "For example, he said, 'I don't want any traffic jams in my future—this is a future where we've actually solved the transport problem.' So, we have to figure it out and said, 'Well you can't go any more sideways, all we can go is up.' And if you've seen the film, you'll know that the buildings and roads systems are integrated and you ride up the building to your apartment on the outside."

Making the vehicle an extended form of the room of Tom Cruise's apartment was the musician Peter Gabriel's idea. (He wasn't at the meeting; Schwartz was hanging out with him a few days earlier, talking about the project. Such is the life of a scenario planner. . . .)

However, what made the process successful was not the futuristic imaginings they concocted but the constraints they imposed. For example, the studio's set designers brought in elaborate drawings of Washington, DC, where the story takes place, with intimidating, monolithic, black granite sixty-story buildings. The geeks howled.

"Planning restrictions!" jeered the dean of MIT's school of architecture.

"Why should that matter? It's the future," the designers innocently queried.

"Building codes never change," and "National capitals are preserved, not modernized," the chorus of nerds fired back.

"A city has 'time depth,'" Schwartz patiently explained. "It doesn't get born all in one stroke—parts of it will be one hundred years old and parts of it will be two years old. Structures from different eras coexist."

Still, some scriptwriters grumbled.

"It felt less dramatic but more realistic. Steven opted every time for realism," Schwartz recalls. But there were two notable exceptions.

The first was Tom Cruise's sleek aerial car.

It needs a dashboard, Spielberg stated.

The group answered: it's voice-activated and self-driving. But Spielberg was adamant: the character needs somewhere to look, and the camera needs somewhere to point—we're making a film.

The second exception was settled just as quickly, on the matter of jet packs.

"I said, 'Steven, physics isn't going to give you jet packs.' And he said, 'My cops will have jet packs.' And if you're Steven Spielberg, your cops get jet packs," Schwartz recounts with a broad smile.

The work of creating the setting for *Minority Report* stresses the extremes to which the group went to ensure it was a consistent alternative world. When the film came out in 2002, it made a splash in large part because the setting felt futuristic yet familiar. Once the gadgets, buildings, car dashboard, and personalized ads via retina scans were imagined, the eighty-page bible was regularly consulted by the writers, editors, and set designers to maintain continuity.

The counterfactual world worked not simply because it was constrained but because those constraints were coherent. Today, the production designer for *Minority Report*, Alex McDowell, runs a business in LA that applies the process, which he calls "world building," to give companies a glimpse of plausible future scenarios. Clients include Nike, Ford, Boeing, and others. Consistency is at the heart of the constraints.

Simplicity and Simulations

Mutability, minimal change, and consistency are principles to apply when iterating the constraints we place on counterfactuals. It's tempting to think of this as a gigantic process of trial and error: relax one constraint, dream up a suitable counterfactual and assess it, then relax a different constraint, imagine a different counterfactual, and evaluate it. That way, lots of alternative realities are created, which leads to lots of options—and, hopefully, one may be good. However, this misses the point.

Applying constraints is *not* about maximizing the number of counterfactuals we create. It's about swiftly identifying a manageable number of the most effective options: the goal is to shrink the search space. Dennett's robot in chapter 2 couldn't do that, with explosive consequences.

At the core of any frame lies a trade-off. The fewer constraints, the more counterfactuals a frame can generate. This gives a decision-maker more options, but it also means that many impractical ones have to be weeded out. The more constraints, the fewer options a frame elicits. This helps keep the decision-maker focused, but runs the risk of missing out on better choices.

Figuring out which constraints to adjust means choosing certain aspects of our alternative worlds that we envisage while disregarding others. It's a shortcut of sorts, but a useful and efficient one. Constraints are filters for our choices. We use them because our brain, while extremely capable in many ways, can't efficiently assess all the options we dream up. It's too time-consuming and tiring.

Constraints are the "building codes," so to speak, for effectively shaping counterfactuals. Sometimes the construction is not just in our minds but in physical space. To support our mental models, we build real models. As with the training model of Entebbe airport, the physical limitations of the model simulate the cognitive constraints that we need to adhere to. Think of architectural models and children's traffic parks, for instance, or climbing walls. They "materialize" the constraints that are deliberately chosen to put users in a particular alternative reality.

The benefit of models is that they let us mentally and physically practice, prepare, and probe possibilities with little consequence. Just as children use pretend play to figure out causality and gain experience in counterfactual reasoning, so too models and simulations enable adults to hone their thinking for specific tasks. We externalize elements of the mental model when they become too complex or when we want to make sure we stick to them.

When a constraint is mental, we can break it (although we don't do so lightly). But in a simulator, the constraints are built into the design and are much less flexible. Airplane flight simulators are a perfect illustration. They range from playful versions on computers and phones to sophisticated machines for professional training. They all embody the laws of aerodynamics and the flight controls work like those in a real plane. Rather than re-create any action, the simulators are realistic precisely because they constrain. This centers our attention on a limited number of inputs and potential responses. It helps teach flying skills and improve pilots' decisions by focusing the mind on what seems to matter most.

The emphasis is on "what *seems* to matter most." Such focus also has drawbacks. The flight simulator is a representation, not reality, just as a map is not territory. It focuses on certain aspects of flying, and in so doing, it ignores others. Rudimentary flight simulators, for example, do not include other aircraft, so they fail to prepare pilots to fly the busy skies around New York City. For that, more sophisticated systems are needed that include the constraints of air traffic.

Even more constrained than flight simulators are models that are entirely material. They are less modifiable than ones built in software, but being physical, they emphasize inviolable, hard constraints. Like all models, the purpose is to make it easier for our minds to focus on just the essential bits. A model's value is in the information that is ignored as much as included.

An example is a remarkable bit of history not widely known. In 1952, a nuclear reactor in Ontario, Canada, had a power surge, the fuel rods overheated, and it suffered a partial meltdown. The reactor was just a few hours' drive from the New York state border and was used to enrich plutonium for American weapons. So a team from the US Navy's nuclear-submarine program was called in to quickly and quietly sort out the mess—led by a twenty-eight-year-old lieutenant named Jimmy Carter, later the thirty-ninth president of the United States.

They needed to go deep into the reactor to stabilize it. But the radiation was so intense that the team could only spend ninety seconds at a time in the core. So they started by building a physical model of the reactor on a nearby tennis court and used it to train. "When it was our time to work, a team of three of us practiced several times on the mock-up, to be sure we had the correct tools and knew exactly how to use them," Carter wrote about the assignment.

"Finally, outfitted with white protective clothes, we descended into the reactor and worked frantically for our allotted time," he explained. "Each time our men managed to remove a bolt or fitting from the core, the equivalent piece was removed on the mock-up." The physical model was not an exact replica—all they needed was the essential features so they could practice and build a mental representation of what to do.

In a similar vein, but with far more delicate handling, health care is adopting models. At the pediatric Simulator Program at Boston Children's Hospital and Harvard Medical School, Dr. Peter Weinstock wants to bring the concept of simulation to surgery, notably for rare or complicated operations. So Weinstock and his team of doctors, nurses, computer designers, and even Hollywood special-effects artists produced bio-anatomically accurate mannequins.

This lets surgeons practice operations in realistic conditions dozens of times before they do the real thing and have only one chance to get it right. "Operate twice, cut once," is Weinstock's unofficial motto for the program. What makes the model and simulated surgery useful are the constraints. It doesn't re-create the entire body or all the biological or physiological conditions and reactions—just those that are essential for the surgical team to have in mind before they perform the real operation. The genius of the system is what is left out as much as what is kept in. Its strength is in the focus.

Empowering, Not Imprisoning

With suitable constraints, people can identify viable options for decisions. That helps us as individuals, but there is a wider societal benefit too. As we become more effective at shaping our choices, we achieve our goals and have an impact on the world, therefore changing reality for others. Thomas Edison, for example, didn't simply find a good filament for the lightbulb to produce illumination for himself: we all benefited when he succeeded. The more that people impose wise constraints to improve their frames, the better off all of us become.

Our frames give us the ability to understand (thanks to causal reasoning) and act (through counterfactuals), but they also ensure those actions actually matter (grace of constraints). By dreaming with constraints, we make sure that we have a bias toward impact, a bias toward effectiveness. What we achieve in our lives leaves footprints that others can follow—frames that others can adopt, adapt, and apply.

This does not hold true for machine-made decisions. We have seen that computers cannot consider causality and cannot concoct counterfactuals. They also cannot conjure up constraints. Algorithms on their own are unable to impose boundaries and limitations. This is actually surprising. After all, with the vast computing capabilities available, machines can evaluate a much larger decision space far more efficiently and quickly than people in the available time.

But the problem isn't a lack of processing power or the ability of AI to mechanistically create options. It is that a far larger number of options will still require boundary conditions, choices that the machine should not evaluate in the interest of time. Without such boundary conditions, the machine faces an unconstrained decision space and will fail to offer the best solutions in time. The fact that human framing can deal with these challenges underscores the primacy of people in the age of the machine.

Take music. Researchers have been trying to get computers to compose music for decades, and AI-generated music has become so good in recent years that it is often indistinguishable from human-made melodies. But a closer inspection reveals that these systems are dependent on human frames and the constraints they impose. For example, Coconet, a popular AI music-generator developed by Cheng-Zhi Anna Huang and other researchers at Google, was trained on a data set of 306 Johann Sebastian Bach four-voice chorale harmonies.

Coconet produces music that is just beautiful to the ear. But don't thank AI, thank Bach. The concise structure of his melodic lines and rich harmony made for ideal training data. The system works by randomly removing notes so that the model can predict which tones fit best. The result produces complete harmonic melodies with smooth transitions from just a few notes as inputs. Yet the AI system only works because it contains the limitations in the choice of the 306 scores. And the data itself is Bach's music from the 1700s, which is an expression of his mental models that embody his deliberate, "well-tempered" constraints.

Computers calculate, but minds imagine. People can make their mental wanderings hew to reality and envision new realities by the degree to which they adapt constraints. In so doing, we can improve the world—not accept what is, but create what can be.

Causality, Counterfactuals, and Constraints

Often it is where counterfactuals meet constraints that frames are honed. Our alternative realities only become relevant as we tighten and loosen the limitations that we consider most relevant to a situation. That produces the new options that matter most.

Take the Indian internet start-up Flipkart, the biggest competitor to Amazon in the country. It captured almost 40 percent of the e-commerce market, a feat so impressive that Walmart bought a controlling stake in it in 2018. Flipkart's achievement was not a radical new frame for selling goods online, but the careful loosening of a constraint in the standard e-commerce frame: customers can pay cash-on-delivery, perfect for a country where few people have debit cards.

Someone who successfully came up with a new counterfactual

by creatively adjusting constraints is will.i.am, the front man of the band Black Eyed Peas. The standard practice in music publishing is to pay the artist a small advance and secure most of the rights to the music. The idea is that musicians are financially desperate while the publisher is taking a risk and might never recoup the investment.

"I saw how much money I made selling records versus how much money I made being lucky to have made a song for Dr Pepper," the soft drink. "I moved my mom out of the ghetto with a thirty-second song," he said. "Meanwhile, the two albums that I made, that were, like, two hours' worth of music: I had twenty thousand dollars in my bank. That's when I realized there was a different world."

Will.i.am figured he could change the constraints of the business model: sell to companies the rights to use his upcoming tracks in their marketing, but retain all the other rights to the song, which he could monetize. Loaded with funds *before* he walked into the recording studio, he could use the money to make the best possible songs, so they had a chance to become hits, he explains with a wide grin. It was an unprecedented way to reimagine the business of producing music, but he pulled it off.

Whether it is Indian e-commerce sites or monetizing singles like "Don't Phunk with My Heart," the cases demonstrate the versatility created by the combination of playing with counterfactuals and constraints. From every frame, innovative and powerful new options can emerge as we shape-shift boundaries.

We can improve how we apply constraints. The first step is to be aware that all mental models need them, and they are not binary but on a gradient. Mutability, minimal change, and consistency let us craft the boundaries on our reflections and what-ifs. To improve the simulations we envisage, we can also externalize constraints, be it in the form of physical models or digital software. Architects, surgeons, and soldiers do it; why not more students, businesspeople, and policymakers?

Our frames affect how we live our lives. With causation we get understanding, with counterfactuals we get agency, and with constraints our frames become actionable. But what if our frames aren't enough? Sometimes what is called for is reframing.

6

reframing

occasionally we need to switch frames or invent new ones

Peter Habeler was gasping for air. A few minutes earlier he had been crawling on all fours. Now, on ground less steep, he stood and took careful steps forward. The wind blew hard and pushed away clouds, creating small patches of visibility. A few yards in front of him stood Reinhold Messner, and to his right, an aluminum tripod that marked the summit. It was just after one o'clock on the afternoon of May 8, 1978, and the two men had reached the top of Everest, the world's highest mountain. And they did it without supplemental oxygen.

It was a momentous moment—and it reshaped what was then known about human performance. In 1953, Sir Edmund Hillary and Tenzing Norgay reached the top of Everest for the first time. In the twenty-five years after that achievement, only a handful of climbers ascended to the peak, all with the help of bottled oxygen and all using what is called "expedition-style" climbing. The medical consensus was that people risked death, or at least severe brain damage, at heights greater than twenty-seven thousand feet above sea level without regular oxygen. The air was too thin to sustain human life. Everest's peak surpasses twenty-nine thousand feet.

The only way to climb it, so the thinking went, was to bring canisters of oxygen and to pitch base camps along the way. It meant a vast logistical operation, a kind of human pyramid of dozens of participants to get a small team of climbers to the top. Hillary's expedition in 1953 consisted of some four hundred men, mainly porters.

Habeler and Messner had a very different idea. Both grew up in the eastern Alps: Messner an Italian from South Tyrol, Habeler from Austria. In their teens and twenties, they pioneered a novel form of climbing called "Alpine style," where speed is key. If one goes fast, one can go light. No tents, sleeping bags, food, extra clothing, or other provisions are necessary. They had shown the superiority of this approach four years earlier, when they raced up the infamous north face of the Eiger, an almost six-thousand-foot wall of rock. Where even the best and most experienced climbers took three days or more to reach the top (if they got there at all), Habeler and Messner did it in ten hours, overtaking three other climbing parties on the way. It was a new record. But, more important, it demonstrated the validity of the Alpine climbing frame.

Now, as experienced climbers in their early thirties, Habeler and Messner fixed their sights on the highest peak on Earth, Everest. As more climbers reached more peaks, medical experts came to realize that humans can survive at very high altitudes for short periods of time. The challenge wasn't the altitude itself, but the duration of exposure. Habeler and Messner saw in this an opportunity. If conventional expeditions were boxed in by the need for oxygen and provisions, the alternative Alpine style meant that they could dispense with all the heavy stuff and race up Everest.

"We knew we had to be fast, and we wanted to try," Habeler said. In the spring of 1978 they got their chance.

The day before their final ascent, Habeler and Messner reached Camp 4, ice-cold at twenty-six thousand feet. Early the next morning they began climbing. They soon felt the oxygen deprivation. Their minds were weakening. Every step was painful. The snow was deep. They walked in thick fog, and when they reached the cloud line, the wind began to blow hard. A storm was coming. They pushed on, crawling on all fours, gasping, until they realized there was nowhere else to go. They were standing at the top of the world.

Embracing and crying in their delirium and joy, they absorbed the moment and snapped photos. Then, they applied their Alpine frame once more and dashed down to Camp 4. It had taken just over nine hours to reach the summit and return. Even with oxygen, this would have been a feat.

The mountaineering world was stunned. To be sure, the duo had benefited from the fruits of technical progress since the Everest summit expedition in the 1950s: ropes were lighter, material more compact, clothes warmer. Their most important equipment advantage was their boots. Conventional ones made of leather soak up moisture, freeze, and turn stiff, cold, and heavy. So Habeler and Messner had boots custom-made of molded plastic that were not only warmer and lighter, but provided better control.

Today in his seventies, living in a valley of the Austrian Alps, Habeler thinks back to the achievement and believes the crucial difference wasn't the gear or the psychological preparation, though those certainly helped. Instead, it was the shift in mind-set.

"It was 'the new'—not necessarily success—that we were after," he said in an interview from his home, putting deep emphasis on the German *das Neue*.

Previous groups had accepted the expedition frame as the only valid one. And once one has adopted a frame, it's hard to abandon it. In fact, teams of climbers not only never challenged the expedition-style frame, they optimized within it, thereby further entrenching and perpetuating it.

But Messner and Habeler came to Everest with a different frame in mind. For them, Everest was essentially the eastern Alps, just taller. By summiting it Alpine-style, they affirmed a new frame of mountaineering, and proved it was doable, even in thin air. They showed that climbing the highest peaks, rather than being a logistical accomplishment, could be a sport—an extreme one, to be sure—and a mark of personal achievement. Among the top climbers the expedition-style frame was on its way out. High-altitude climbing was no longer simply a pastime of adventurers and gentlemen explorers after people saw what was possible and adopted the new frame.

Brave New Frame

Sometimes the mental model we use isn't the right one. By sticking to a frame, we might miss the best options because the frame we use fails to capture what matters. In those cases, we need to reframe our thinking in order to advance. That is, we need to switch frames from the one we have and adopt another. It doesn't happen that often. But when and where reframing succeeds, it offers a novel way of understanding and provides us with a new set of options.

Reframing is special because we normally stay within a frame.

This suits our needs: by playing with constraints within a causal frame, we can imagine valuable counterfactuals and solve the challenges we face. It improves mental efficiency because we do not have to reinvent the wheel but can rely on a previous template. Adhering to a well-honed mental model is often the default strategy for success, not the consequence of cognitive inertia. It is not a flaw but a feature of human cognition.

In some ways, reframing appears similar to modifying constraints. But that's not so. Within a given frame, constraints may seem immutable, excluding more radical options. Staying within a frame comes with mental baggage. In contrast, switching to an alternative frame affords the opportunity to start anew. That is risky, but powerful when it works.

Habeler and Messner's reframing might look like a mere tinkering of constraints, but it was something much more. They succeeded only because they were able to bring a new frame to the challenge that emphasized speed. Had they been steeped in the frame of ponderous expedition mountaineering, they could not have imagined scaling Everest without supplemental oxygen. Only as we resist an existing frame do we have the mental freedom to uncover new openings—and generate new constraints. (We return to the interplay between reframing and constraints at the end of this chapter.)

We often celebrate successful reframers because what they achieve is so uncommon. Though it is difficult to do, we all have the capacity to reframe. It is a deliberate process, just as working within a frame is deliberate. But unlike framing, we don't improve our reframing abilities by doing it frequently. Especially when compared with reasoning within a frame, switching frames is more about a stroke of insight than a methodical process. Still, there are several elements to help us successfully reframe.

Repertoire, Repurpose, Reinvent

There are three general ways to reframe. We can choose a different frame from the variety we already possess. Or, we can apply one that exists from another context. And if that doesn't work, we need to invent a new frame altogether. These three forms of reframing—think of them as "repertoire," "repurposing," and "reinvention"—basically correspond to the order in how frequently they happen. We occasionally choose a new frame from the many we possess; we rarely take one from another domain and apply it; and it is a truly extraordinary moment when a new frame is established.

These distinctions aren't razor sharp. Sometimes we may believe we've invented an entirely new frame when in fact it's been lingering in the recesses of our mind. Or, we may feel we're repurposing a frame when we've used it before so it's already in our repertoire. The point isn't to delineate the strategies perfectly but to appreciate that there are multiple ways to reframe—and that if we have difficulties using one strategy, we can try a different one.

Repertoire, the easiest solution, is to mentally riffle through our individual stock of frames and see whether we already have an alternative that will fit. Think of it like switching between different maps to navigate, from chapter 2, whether we're down in a subway or dodging traffic on Broadway. Or think of Ben Bernanke, who applied the mental model of the Great Depression from his armory of templates, at a time when some people felt that what happened on Wall Street didn't matter much to Main Street.

When using our repertoire of frames, knowing the qualities of each frame we possess is crucial to identifying a good fit. But it is equally important to have a wide selection of frames at our disposal.

Like a copious buffet, well-stocked library, or broad music collection, the more varied one's mental catalog, the better the chances of switching to a superior frame. Charlie Munger, the business partner of famed investor Warren Buffett, refers to the need to carry a "latticework of models" around in one's head for just that reason. Peering first into one's internal inventory is a smart strategy because it requires less cognitive energy to trot out the right frame when needed.

Now, consider the second form of reframing, the idea of repurposing a frame from elsewhere. We do this when we need to reframe but have no ready alternative at our disposal, so we look to other domains for an existing frame that could be adjusted to our current circumstances. It won't be a ready template and so may require substantial cognitive work to shape it appropriately, but at least having something to play with can get us started. That sort of reframing lies at the origin of the furniture giant IKEA.

When Ingvar Kamprad began selling flat-pack home furnishings in the 1950s in Sweden, furniture was generally purchased "for the ages," a hefty investment to be passed on to the next generation. But Kamprad spotted a different wave in postwar consumerism, in which furniture could be made cheaply and treated like clothing, which is only used for a limited time. Since IKEA products were inexpensive, people could replace them rather than stick with them because they once belonged to Grandpa. Today customers around the world can frequently restyle their homes for modest sums with Ikea furniture, provided they are willing to assemble it themselves (and possess the dexterity of da Vinci).

The key to IKEA's initial success was its use of an alternative mental frame of what furniture represents and is used for: not timeless but timely. Yet that frame wasn't entirely new. It had been in the air. Other sectors were undergoing a transition from the durable to the disposable. Luckily for IKEA's founder, the furniture sector had not yet, so his repurposed frame gave IKEA an edge.

Another example of reframing via repurposing has been proposed recently in the field of economics. The classical models of supply and demand and price elasticity rely on the concept of equilibrium. In fact, the foundation of economics was developed by philosophers in the late 1700s and early 1800s before there were such terms as *scientist* or *economist*. Their theories of how the money supply expanded or how terms of trade were counted didn't emerge airy-fairy but were based on the data they were collecting. But as we know, data never exists on its own; it can only exist in a model—a mental model.

The frame that economics adopted without much introspection was from classical physics (following Newton and the physiocrats that we examined in chapter 3). Indeed, the very terms *dynamic equilibrium* and *liquidity* are directly borrowed from physics, and then applied to describe the phenomenon of supply and demand, the flow of capital, and how prices change and settle over time. But this perhaps isn't the right model, particularly for the modern economy, which has become far more complex than when the physics frame was embraced.

The economist Andrew Lo at MIT believes it is time to transform economics from its frame of physics and its emphasis on equilibrium to the frame of biology with a focus on evolution and growth. It seems sensible. The economy resembles more a complex, adaptive organism that responds to changes than a slab of iron that has predictable properties of density or the diffusion of heat. And by changing the frame, a host of new possibilities opens up. The regulation of finance, companies, and markets changes if we're dealing with an entity that evolves versus one with set characteristics that we're constantly trying to pin down.

Switching to a frame outside of our own ready repertoire—one that has already been used successfully elsewhere—amounts to standing on the shoulders of others. It's harder than using a frame we already know but easier than having to reinvent one from whole cloth. It requires skills and capabilities, notably being open-minded and curious about people, places, and experiences far afield from one's own.

Repurposing is efficient too. Ideally one would already possess these models and be familiar with their benefits and shortcomings, with when and how they best apply. But it's not possible to stock-pile frames for every eventuality. So repurposing is the next best thing.

Whether we choose a frame from our repertoire or repurpose one from further afield, we are switching to a new frame that in some form already exists. However, sometimes even that won't work. A novel situation will cry out for a unique way to look at and understand it. If reframing by dint of repertoire or repurposing fails, we need to devise a new frame altogether, an act of reinvention.

This is exemplified by Charles Darwin. He is popularly associated with the idea of survival of the fittest. But the frame he invented is more fundamental: that all species of life have descended over time from common ancestors. That basic concept—literally a diagram of the tree of life—transformed how humans understood the origin of life on Earth and how species evolved. In this way, the reframing was not a matter of applying a new frame from one's repertoire or finding and adapting a new frame from another context to a new problem. Rather, it can be seen as inventing a new frame altogether. Reframing by dint of reinvention is the stuff we celebrate and remember in history.

Many reinventions turn into historical milestones. Einstein's theory of special relativity in 1905 was a new frame for physics, complementing Newton's. Once it was articulated, physicists could see it explained the world better and they could build on top of it.

Rousseau's idea of the "social contract" (the title of his book in 1762) was a frame that neatly explained how the public and those in power could mutually derive their status from each other: one gets certain rights by giving up other rights. The Internet Protocol reframed communications from circuit-switched voice traffic to packet-switched data traffic. The open-source software movement reframed how code is developed and monetized.

In all these cases, the innovation was an intangible, intellectual one before it was instantiated in equations, laws, routers, or software. One's whole mental model had to change. It is going beyond what one knows.

Masters of a New Frame

Whatever strategy we choose though, reframing remains an endeavor fraught with failure. The path to reframing has no reliable signposts, no straightforward cognitive processes, no dependable schedules. A new frame may crop up in a sudden rush or after years of plodding. And there is no guarantee of success at all. In the end, a new frame may be conceived—and it could be wrong. In the 1950s, many researchers were trying to identify the structure of DNA. In 1953 the brilliant biochemist Linus Pauling was widely applauded for his landmark work with a colleague describing its *triple* helix form. Two months later James Watson and Francis Crick presented a slightly sparser model that fit reality better.

At times, people make monumental discoveries that lead to a fundamental reframing—but fail to realize it. In 1938 the German chemists Otto Hahn and Fritz Strassmann were considered among the world's best. Their research looked at nuclear decay. In experiments, they bombarded uranium with neutrons, which resulted in what seemed to be barium and energy. But to the two eminent chemists, this did not seem to make sense; it failed to fit their frame of how chemical reactions unfold.

Hahn wrote about the puzzling results to his longtime collaborator, the physicist Lise Meitner. A rarity as a female scientist at the time, and Jewish, she had fled the Nazis for Sweden. At first Meitner and a fellow physicist, Otto Frisch, her nephew, were also perplexed. But then they formed a different mental model based on the data and known physics. It pointed to Hahn and Strassmann having broken up the nucleus of atoms. They called it "fission" in an article in *Nature*, coining the term.

By that act of reframing, Meitner not only explained what happened in Hahn's lab in Berlin, but she revolutionized humanity's understanding of nuclear energy. On reading Meitner's explanation, Hahn realized the enormity of the discovery he had produced and observed—but had failed to conceptualize.

Even when reframers are aware of what they accomplish, they may not grasp its magnitude. "We just have these mysterious electromagnetic waves that we cannot see with the naked eye," Heinrich Hertz is reputed to have said. "It's of no use whatsoever." The radio was just around the corner.

That should not surprise us. New frames are revolutionary. They are hard to grasp initially. And they often take time to catch on. The rest of the world may not understand reframing, since it is an affront to the standard way of thinking. For example, until the mid-2010s many senior executives in traditional companies cackled that Amazon's business still showed no profits. They felt it was a low-margin activity propped up by a hyperinflated share price. And within their traditional way of understanding corporate performance, they were right.

But seen through a different frame, they were utterly wrong. Jeff

Bezos had reframed the idea of commercial growth, away from producing annual returns for shareholders (and handing about a third of the profits to governments in the form of tax) and toward reinvesting every penny of net income to establish adjacent business lines, from Kindle books to cloud services. People see it plain as day in hindsight, but the new frame was incomprehensible to many in the moment.

In some cases, the new frame is so much better that it renders other ones practically obsolete. In other cases, new frames peacefully coexist with the old. Einsteinian and Newtonian physics both have their place in explaining motion, just as proprietary software and open-source code can flourish. Places like Britain, Belgium, Bhutan, and Thailand can meld democracy and monarchy. Central banks manage fiat currencies but people still barter or use Bitcoin.

Yet in all cases, reframing an issue allows us to see it from a new perspective, which reveals alternatives that we might not otherwise have imagined. That, in turn, helps us make good decisions and achieve better outcomes. A place where a useful reframing took place was the city of Camden in southern New Jersey. It did something that most people thought audacious and impossible: it fired its entire police force and created a new one. Behind the radical move was a reframing of the role of law enforcement, from regarding citizens as criminals to community-oriented policing.

Camden was rough. The city of seventy-five thousand people crammed into nine square miles had one of the highest crime and murder rates in the country. Parts were desolate. "There are more than fifteen hundred derelict, gutted row houses. The empty shells of windowless brick factories, warehouses, and abandoned gas stations surround the city. There are overgrown vacant lots filled with garbage . . . and boarded-up storefronts. There are perhaps a hundred open-air drug markets," wrote Chris Hedges and Joe Sacco in the book *Days of Destruction, Days of Revolt* in 2012. The stained- glass windows of the Community Baptist Church on Mount Ephraim Avenue were riddled with bullet holes.

Though crime was bad, the police arguably made it worse. Officers routinely planted evidence, fabricated reports, and were accused of brutality. Courts had to overturn the convictions of scores of people. Many residents were as scared of the police as they were of the gangs. The police union, for its part, resisted change. By 2012 the situation had become so bad, and reforms so ineffective, that local leaders didn't know what to do.

The director of the county government, Louis Cappelli Jr., realized that fixing specific problems was not enough; the whole system needed overhauling. But how? Working with community leaders, residents, and like-minded policymakers, he imagined a different mental model—one that was shared by Mayor Dana Redd and a senior police officer, Scott Thomson.

Camden disbanded its 141-year-old police department and 260 officers lost their jobs. In 2013, when the new force began under entirely new contracts, it had not only new faces, new rules, and new training—but, most important, a new mind-set. Fewer than one hundred officers of the former department were rehired. When people looked at it, stuck in their own mental models, they saw either the dissolution of a police force or the breaking of a union stranglehold. But Camden's leaders' mental model was far broader.

"It really started with being able to build culture as opposed to change culture, and we were able to create an organization wherein the identity of the officer was that of a guardian and not a warrior," explained Thomson, who would lead the new force. Camden reframed the task of a police force to standing with the community—helping, assisting, and guarding it—rather than only arresting people and writing tickets.

"I would have traded ten cops for another Boys and Girls Club," Thomson said.

With the new frame in mind, patrols changed. The job of officers was now to knock on the doors and introduce themselves; talk about citizens' concerns and offer to help. The police began pop-up neighborhood parties, where they'd rock up with Mister Softee ice-cream trucks, grill hot dogs, play basketball with kids, and get to know the residents.

Seven years later, when American cities were up in flames, literally, over the murder of George Floyd by a Minneapolis police officer and protesters chanted "Defund the police," Camden was cited as a success story. Murders were down 60 percent, crime had almost halved, and complaints of excessive force by police had fallen by a stunning 95 percent. The reframing had worked.

A symbolic moment came in June 2020. A new Camden police chief, Joseph Wysocki, not only authorized a big Black Lives Matter street protest—he asked the organizers if he could join them at the head of the procession. It made national news. The television cameras framed an indelible image of what a new mental model of policing can look like.

A New Way of Seeing the World

Whether they plunder their repertoire, repurpose a frame from elsewhere, or reinvent an entirely new frame, all successful reframers share certain things in common. It isn't a clever mind, quick memory, or deep experience. What's needed is a willingness to risk new thoughts and forge new cognitive paths. It requires a mind that is comfortable with the unfamiliar, that can gently let go of preconceptions and presumptions, and can see and seize new possibilities.

Where others may only spot an unexpected shadow in an image or an odd reading from an instrument, successful reframers see something different. And when they do, they often experience a real aha moment. Sometimes this moment is so monumental that it produces overwhelming emotions.

An example of this is the case of gene editing, based on the work of two remarkable scientists, Emmanuelle Charpentier in France and Jennifer Doudna in America.

In the 1980s, researchers found that simple cells like bacteria have their own molecular-size immune systems. In fact, they are able to "remember," identify, and destroy genetic information that is not part of the cell. Researchers called this system CRISPR (for "clustered regularly interspaced short palindromic repeats").

In 2012 Charpentier and Doudna—two female scientists in a testosterone-infused domain—were investigating a specific area of the cell's CRISPR system when a lab researcher noticed that there was a way to cut into a specific area of the DNA. Charpentier and Doudna realized these molecular scissors could be turned into a versatile and powerful tool to edit genetic information. Doudna later said that at the moment of realization, the hair literally stood up at the back of her neck. She was immediately hit by the new mental model that emerged in her mind. "Those insightful moments don't come along so often," she explained, "which is why we cherish them as scientists."

The British mathematician Andrew Wiles, whose reframing cracked Fermat's Last Theorem, a mathematical conjecture that had remained unsolved for centuries, likens the process to "entering a house in the dark and bumping into the furniture, until one finds a switch for the light and you can finally see where you are." Reframing was such an extraordinary moment for him that when recounting it on television years later, the otherwise stoic Brit became so flushed with emotion that he asked to stop the interview.

We have come to cherish reframers who show us how to see the world from a new, more useful perspective—even if we first resist their new frames, as the Viennese medical community did to Semmelweis's ideas on hand sanitation. We also idolize cognitive trailblazers because they are so exceptional: framing comes naturally but reframing is hard and rare. When it works, it feels special. And we all wish to be special ourselves, the next Emmanuelle Charpentier and Jennifer Doudna, who were recognized with a Nobel Prize in 2020.

There is a risk, however, that just because someone has reframed successfully, they believe they can do it again and again. There can be a vainglory attached to reframers, who wear their achievement like a golden crown and reapply the new frame where it does not fit. The best innovators are aware of this and work to minimize it. Steve Jobs of Apple, Jeff Bezos of Amazon, and Larry Page of Google all enjoyed reputations for stubbornness but at the same time actively sought out alternative views that contradicted their own. They understood the shortcoming of relying on a single frame and the value of being exposed to alternative ones.

One of the most notorious examples of a successful reframer becoming too attached to a frame is Albert Einstein. In 1905, at the age of twenty-six, he reframed modern physics by dint of the special theory of relativity. Explaining the vagaries of natural phenomena is a frame—one of an orderly universe in which all physical reality can be explained by principles, qualities, and quantities. When quantum mechanics emerged as a serious theory, he resisted it. That frame, of fundamental randomness in the world, felt too strange, too far from the reasonable. "God does not play dice," he often quipped, summing up his disapproval.

But he was wrong: the ideas behind quantum mechanics have held in the physics community. As much as we treasure Einstein for his successful reframing, we need to also be aware of his failures. It is hard to reframe once, but it's even harder to do it again. Sometimes, our initial success shapes our thinking so much that we can't let go of it when the frame doesn't fit, or we resist accepting new frames. If even Einstein can make that lapse, what hope is there for the rest of us?

There is an important lesson here. In reframing, the celebrated stock-prospectus disclaimer applies: "past performance is no guarantee of future returns." Much as we admire successful reframers such as Jennifer Doudna and Elon Musk, we should not necessarily pin our hopes on their next insights being equally important. The next crucial reframe could come from any one of us.

When Mentality Meets the Moment

And we all can get better at reframing. The starting point is to understand the sources of difficulty we face when attempting to switch frames. There are four in particular: the cognitive energy required to create a novel frame; the need to step away from the familiar; the necessity of identifying a frame that fits the circumstances; and wise timing to recognize the right moment to reframe.

The first is the effort necessary to harness a new mental model. As framers, we have practiced and are good at applying them. But we aren't so well versed in choosing mental models. It demands substantial cognitive effort, and with unclear prospects for success. As reframers, we often have to embrace a mental unknown; "cognitive terra incognita," so to speak. The "unthought" daunts us as much as the unencountered. The idea of going beyond the known is inconceivable for many.

The challenge is exacerbated by our difficulty in diverting from the familiar, the second difficulty we face. When reframing, we must actively push aside an existing frame to free up the cognitive space for something new. It is similar to landscapers, who when laying out a new path, must undo the existing one lest people stick with the route they are familiar with: the well-worn groove in the earth where they have trod so many times before. It's a kind of unlearning that needs to take place as we conjure up something different.

Unlearning isn't something we know how to do. Human forgetting is an automatic process, not one that we easily control. Yet unlearn we must, if we wish to reframe. This is especially the case when the new frame is seemingly at odds with the old one, when the new frame needs to overcome the cognitive dissonance that it causes.

Such cognitive dissonance may happen in one's mind, but it can also happen in a community, making it difficult to adopt a new frame. Switching frames in such a situation may require many people to refocus on an alternative frame. That may necessitate discussions, negotiations, and persuasion, which are time-consuming endeavors. Habeler and Messner may not have needed to push aside the expedition-style frame in their minds, since it was never the basis of their climbing style, but they had to convince the expedition community that they had made their final ascent with their Alpine-style frame—and that took effort. Reframers are the vanguard and are often made to feel it.

The third factor is how well the frame fits the circumstances— that is, the goal one aims to achieve in a given situation. Identifying the frame with a suitable fit does not necessarily mean that tighter is better. Whether a frame needs to be snug or loose depends on the situation. In a narrow frame, many of the constraints are quite transparent and hence easier to keep in mind. But narrower frames no longer work well when some of the conditions change. Broader frames, on the other hand, may stay useful for longer but demand more thoughtful adjustments of constraints when playing with counterfactuals. Think of it like clothing: tight attire brings out the best in our honed shape, but looser-fitting garments allow us more freedom if conditions change.

Importantly, it's not just the circumstances that count when choosing a tighter or looser frame. What also matters is whether the constraints are mutable. If they can't be usefully loosened, this reduces the options we can see and the decisions we can make. A frame with few mutable constraints may fit closely, but it produces few useful options. That not only limits our choices, it also reduces the sense of agency. Such frames make us feel we understand a situation, but can't do much about it. Hence, all else being equal, it is better to choose a frame with more mutable constraints, even if it fits more loosely. The disadvantage of looseness is compensated by the additional choices it lets us generate, and the sense of empowerment and agency it provides.

Finally, it is difficult to recognize the right moment to reframe. In the abstract, timing is straightforward. An existing frame needs to be replaced if circumstances have changed substantially. In such cases, no amount of adjusting constraints to elicit new counterfactuals within the existing frame will suffice. This may happen when the original goals have changed and the new goals cannot be achieved in the existing frame. Or it may be that the conditions and the context have changed fundamentally, even though the goals remain. In short, reframing is about switching frames when circumstances change, not sooner, and certainly not much later. But it's hard to get the timing right when one is deeply invested in a mental model.

There is a lesson in the history of green innovation. In 1900 a third of all automobiles were electric. But because of the rapid evolution of internal-combustion engines, electric cars quickly fell behind. For over a century, the mental model of a car was synonymous with a gas-powered motor. A slew of inventors and businesses tried to revive electric vehicles, but they flopped. They had poor acceleration, speed, and range. Fine for carnival bumper cars and golf carts, but not the open road, went the thinking.

Then Tesla revived the electric car frame. This time, the timing was right: electric motors had become highly efficient, battery technology had improved, and computers had advanced enough to manage an electric vehicle. Moreover, public perception of gasoline-powered cars had changed. If the latter half of the twentieth century had equated the car with personal freedom, at the start of the twenty-first century cars were seen as contributors to environmental degradation. The shift in context established the perfect conditions for Elon Musk's reframing: cars didn't need to be petrol-powered, they could be green and look cool.

But in Germany, the country's proud automakers, such as Daimler, BMW, and VW, resisted this reframing. Steeped in the conventional frame, they argued that only gasoline cars were real cars, and they delighted in pointing out electric cars' shortcomings. Their CEOs declared that the gas engine had a long and prosperous future. While other traditional car manufacturers around the world reframed, in Wolfsburg, Stuttgart, and Munich the auto engineers held on to the familiar. Isn't German engineering most visible in the beauty and efficiency of an internal-combustion engine? Hadn't this frame brought about prosperity for decades?

It was a delusion. By the time the companies finally came around and embraced the electric frame, it was almost too late. Important time had been lost. They had focused for too long on what was now the wrong kind of engine, because they stuck to what had become an outdated frame. That necessitated expensive programs to get the country's auto champions to reimagine their business, redesign their vehicles, restructure their operations, and refresh their engineering workforce. Timing matters, and it is harder to reframe the more mentally invested one is in an existing frame.

For successful reframing, we need to overcome these hurdles. Fortunately, there are useful strategies to make surmounting them easier. For example, switching to a new frame is needed when circumstances have fundamentally changed. To assess if that is so, one needs to understand the context and goals and qualities of the existing frame. Spending time considering one's mental models and circumstances is useful because it makes one a better reframer.

Also, we know that switching to an alternative frame within our repertoire is easiest, followed by looking to repurpose an existing frame from another field. Hence, it makes sense to start reframing by searching one's repertoire or adjusting another mental model rather than trying to develop a new frame from scratch. That lowers the cognitive load and increases the chances for success.

Counterintuitively, it is also better to reframe infrequently. There is a temptation to reframe swiftly and repeatedly. It's the idea that if a reframe doesn't work, one can quickly rectify the problem by reframing again, jumping from frame to frame until the right one is found. Yet that is a fallacy. Each act of reframing is costly. It requires extra cognitive energy to abandon something one knows well, to come up with something new, and to understand it so well that it can be applied successfully. As a consequence, one cannot continually switch frames. It's like changing directions: do it too often and it leaves you disoriented.

Reframing Reframing

Switching frames takes effort and is risky. But as it offers a different perspective, it points us toward options we might not have otherwise considered. Switching frames provides the potential for breakthroughs, but because humans aren't so adept at it, we may never fully realize that potential. In contrast, by staying within a frame, and carefully constraining counterfactual thinking, one can swiftly and efficiently identify suitable options for decisions. This helps us act in time, and thanks to practice, it's something that people tend to be good at.

This suggests a clear division between the two aspects of framing: use counterfactual reasoning to work within a frame if efficiency is essential, and switch frames when a fundamental rethink is necessary.

In practice, however, the differences between the two are not always so stark. For example, a broad frame provides some wiggle room to play with constraints and come up with a wide range of counterfactuals. This is not too distant from switching to a relatively similar frame. With a broad enough frame, one need not reframe when conditions change: it may be sufficient to use the flexibility of loosening constraints to produce more appropriate counterfactuals.

To see how this might work in practice, consider the miraculous transformation of Singapore's economy over the past four decades—and the strategy behind it. In the 1980s, the Asian city-state turned itself into a leading port between Europe and Asia. It was remarkably successful. Yet when conditions changed, Singapore needed a new plan, and in the 1990s it became a manufacturing base for the electronics industry. In the early 2000s it changed focus to become a hub for finance, professional services, and information-economy jobs. In recent years it transformed again, becoming a tourist and gambling destination with the world's two biggest casino resorts, capitalizing on wealthy visitors from nearby China and Indonesia.

Singapore's numerous changes could be seen as continually reframing its national economy. Each strategy seems to reflect a distinct mental model, offering a tight fit for the specific goals and conditions of the particular period. But another way to see it is that Singapore's strategic frame never changed because it was broad enough for policymakers to shift the counterfactuals they imagined and the constraints they imposed.

In other words, Singapore may have stuck to a frame and played with its components. The country's broad frame was flexible enough to seize competitive advantages based on the few resources it possessed: geographic position, well-educated labor, political stability, and a free-market ethos. It was the same blueprint adapted to new realities.

Singapore's experience shows that when circumstances change but the existing frame is sufficiently broad, we have a choice. We can either work within the frame or choose to switch to a different one. Staying within a broad frame may be cognitively simpler, but coming up with appropriate counterfactuals takes significant time, because of the large search space that a broad frame entails. Switching to a different frame may be swifter, but is far riskier—one may end up with the wrong frame and no suitable options at all.

What's important is that we realize in many, but far from all, situations we can choose the strategy we want to employ depending on context (e.g., how fast a decision is needed, how broad our existing frame is) and individual preferences (e.g., how risk-taking we are).

This plays out in business with powerful effects. In 2008 a Swedish start-up company launched an online music-streaming platform. Until then, the online music market was dominated by Apple's iTunes, which sold individual songs. But the start-up, Spotify, let users listen to anything they wanted by either paying a small subscription fee or enduring a short audio advertisement. By 2020 Spotify had more than three hundred million users worldwide. We could look at Spotify and say that it reframed music from something owned to something streamed.

But we could also understand Spotify's actions through the lens of a broader frame, and see it as Spotify and Apple both working within the frame of music as *experience*. Spotify used the wiggle room of the experience frame to come up with a different counterfactual. From this conceptual vantage point, Spotify did not reframe access to music but relaxed the limitation that music is something we own, control, and manage on our devices, to an experience of music that is shared, remote, ubiquitous, and unlimited.

Seeing Spotify less as a reframer and more as an expert at adjusting and applying a broad frame of music-as-experience also implies that it did not have to choose the riskier reframing path but instead could stick to its broad frame. That may have made the effort of framing less daunting, even if it meant ignoring some of the more radical alternatives.

Having a strategic choice between radical reframing and the more limited working within a broad frame adds yet another instrument to the human framing toolbox. In a sense, even reframing can be reframed. But it is no panacea. The choice exists only if such a broad frame is already being employed, and if that frame is flexible enough to elicit the more radical counterfactuals that the situation demands. As conceptually enticing as "reframing reframing" may be, it applies only to certain types of cases.

Regardless of whether we frame or reframe, there are ways to learn to get better at it. That is a good thing, since we will need to. The most profound problems in society require new thinking to address. We need to play with multiple possibilities and invite the ideas of others if we are to see the fullest variety of alternatives and make the best decisions. This means improving the activity of framing essential to our lives, our national well-being, and even our civilizational security and sustainability. We must get better at it. And there is one man in Silicon Valley who has dedicated his life to this mission.

7

learning

a wide variety of frames is crucial
for progress

Steve Jobs had a problem and Joel Podolny was the solution. Born in the 1960s and raised in Cincinnati, Podolny had had a career that was nothing short of extraordinary: three degrees from Harvard, a faculty position at Stanford, head of research at Harvard Business School, and then appointed dean of the Yale School of Management—all before turning forty. Jobs of course didn't care a whit about the credentials. It was what Podolny did at Yale that impressed Apple's boss.

Podolny was smart, charismatic, and driven. As soon as he got to Yale, in 2005, he uprooted the curriculum. For a century, business schools taught students to become able managers. For most of that time, this meant the ability to develop plans and ensure their unwavering execution. It also meant functionally separating activities: accounting in one corner, strategy in another. Thinking about business education in terms of the impact to be achieved wasn't part of the mix. Even the traditional pedagogical method in business school, which asks students to devise answers to real-world problems by applying a given mental model to reach a decision, has a short-coming: it presumes there is one preferred frame.

Podolny opposed such simplifications. He didn't think that learning prepackaged knowledge should be the goal of a modern business school. The objective had to be bigger. He wanted to change the MBA mind-set from uniformity to diversity. Not the fluffy diversity one finds in marketing brochures. Podolny was trained as a sociologist and understood the value of heterogeneity. Frames are tools for people to make better decisions. By promoting a wider range of them in the curriculum, Yale would be preparing its students to be better managers—and perhaps better individuals too.

Out were traditional courses like marketing and finance. In were interdisciplinary ones with names like "State & Society" and "Employee." They were better suited to the modern, complex world of business.

"The disciplinary silos are about teaching people to play functional roles," complained Podolny at the time. He pushed to make every element of learning interdisciplinary so a range of frames would flourish, reflecting the needs of real business. Teaching also changed to include cognitive diversity. Classes were taught not by one but several instructors—"team teaching," he called it—to expose students to a spectrum of views. Even physical classrooms were redesigned to be circular to foster interaction. And there would be less obvious hierarchy, like the knights at King Arthur's Round Table.

The reforms attracted attention. As a scholar of status in organizations, now Podolny was tipped as a future university president himself. But in 2008, after just three years at Yale, Podolny abruptly resigned to reframe his own career.

Steve Jobs had quietly courted Joel Podolny. Faced with the return of his cancer and the need to set Apple up to prosper without him, he convinced Podolny to join the company. Jobs wanted his legacy to be a team of executives who could "think different," in the words of the company's iconic advertising campaign. He hired Podolny to be the head of Apple University, where he needed to instill the importance of mental flexibility and of holding convictions but being ready to relinquish them for new perspectives.

Podolny instilled the same vision of frame diversity that he had championed at Yale. Doing so in a large organization required careful balancing. Employees needed to adhere to the firm's core beliefs and excel in their specific roles, while pursuing the cognitive diversity that Jobs wanted to encourage. There would be disagreement and friction, which is a headache to manage. But the benefits of diversity outweigh these difficulties.

Three years after Podolny started, Jobs passed away and his deputy, Tim Cook, took over as chief executive. Cook has long been an advocate of diversity in all its forms. His personal story may play a role, as he is one of the few bosses of a major company to come out as gay. Under his leadership, Apple would honor Jobs's belief that diversity makes for better framers and more successful companies.

A Mind-Set, Not a Method

Think of mental diversity as you might carpentry tools. We can't turn a screw by hammering it down, however hard we try. We need a screwdriver for it. If we only ever had a hammer, the very concept of a screwdriver might be alien to us. Yet once we encounter a screwdriver and understand the concept behind it, then we no longer attempt to hammer down screws. With a diversity of frames, we don't simply know *more*: we know *different*, we know *better*.

The world is a complex place, and no single frame can offer the right solution to every problem. Drawing on different perspectives to shape our judgments improves the odds of reaching better conclusions. Having fewer frames at our disposal when we need to pick one does the opposite: it reduces the range of potential choices and results in suboptimal decisions. But it isn't just that we need more frames, we need to choose them well.

The act of choosing a frame is akin to what psychologists call "insight problems." These are problems that can only be solved by switching to a less obvious frame or representation. In a famous experiment in the 1980s, Craig Kaplan, a psychologist, and Herbert Simon, a polymath scholar, AI pioneer, and Nobel laureate in economics, tested how people solved an insight problem known as the mutilated checkerboard.

They presented individuals with an ordinary eight-by-eight checkerboard of alternating white and black squares—but it had been slightly modified so that two squares were missing: a white square from the top-left corner and another white square from the bottom-right corner. Participants were asked whether it was possible to place dominoes on the board (with each domino covering two adjacent squares) so that no square was left uncovered and no domino hung over the side.

Kaplan and Simon discovered that almost everyone starts with the conventional problem-solving frame of trial and error. They want to "brute-force" the answer, trying many different combinations for fitting thirty-one rectangular dominoes onto sixty-two squares. They stay within the frame and work out counterfactuals. After all, the approach is action-oriented and familiar. But it isn't practical. Though the problem space is finite, trial and error entails hundreds of thousands of combinations, and few people persevere. One participant spent eighteen hours filling sixty-one pages of a notebook trying different arrangements—and still failed. The approach doesn't work; the nature of the problem is too complex.

It was only when people put aside their initial frame and looked for an alternative mental model that they realized something was amiss.

With a different perspective, the solution is actually quite simple. Any domino you place on a checkerboard has to cover one white square and one black square. So if there are not as many white squares as black ones, the dominoes cannot fit. When you think about it like that, it's obvious. But it requires a conceptual leap away from the trial-and-error, practice-and-persistence frame.

Problems like this one are all around us. In these moments, we can't sequentially reason our way through them. The very tools that improve our ability to apply a frame—that is, frequent practice of counterfactual thinking—provide little help for choosing a frame. That presents a huge challenge. If we can't do better at *choosing* a frame despite our advances in *applying* them, our framing will remain stunted. We will be stuck with an incomplete tool, the head of a hammer without a handle. We need a different strategy.

The starting point is remembering how the tasks of choosing and applying differ. Applying a frame is a process by which, with the help of causality, counterfactuals, and constraints—the three *C*'s—we drastically reduce the search space and identify a limited number of highly useful choices. The goal is speed of process and fit of options. It's fundamentally about efficiency that leads to action. It invites directed experimentation since the three *C*'s reduce cognitive complexity and lead to a streamlined version of trial and error. That is why applying a frame is an activity that we can get better at over time, and generally do.

In contrast, deliberately choosing a frame means leaving behind well-known territory and venturing into the unknown. It is inherently risky. There may be rewards, but failure always looms. There are no reliable guardrails nor signposts on the way toward success. The idea of "try, fail, try again" does not substantially improve the chances of a favorable outcome. Learning is no longer a sequential, structured process. Instead it is disruptive and binary. We need to be able to change perspectives; what is required is not so much a process but a mind-set. This means being primed to see the world from multiple vantage points, knowing about different perspectives and embracing the power that comes from that.

It may be tempting to think that mental diversity means exposing oneself to a great number of ideas, opinions, and views. But that misses the point. The advantage does not lie in volume but variation. Seven hundred similar ideas are not as valuable as seven that are very different from one another, in the same way that a toolbox containing seven different tools—hammer, screwdriver, wrench, and so on—is more useful than a toolbox containing seven hundred kinds of hammers.

For choosing a frame, we need to train a different cognitive muscle. It may sound simple, but it isn't. In principle, we say we welcome diversity. In practice, we tend to default to the known. Snap to grid. Yet over the long run, a diversity of frames is worth the effort required to identify them. Research shows that a willingness to leave our mental comfort zone for new intellectual quarters pays off.

Take the example of people who have lived the hustle and bustle of frame diversity literally since birth: people immersed in one culture but who also belong to another. In enterprising research, the economist Susan Pozo asked if American citizens who were born outside the country earned more than those born on American soil. They did: some 2.5 percent more for men and 5 percent more for women, rising even more in managerial and professional occupations that prize conceptual thinking.

Pozo called this premium the "returns to acquiring international human capital." The idea is that such people have their perspectives broadened by being exposed to different customs, languages, and ways of problem-solving—they grow up adroit at using both a hammer and a screwdriver, and know when to switch between them.

Expanding the Variety of Frames

The first and easiest strategy for adding mental models that are quite different from the ones we already know is to look at how others frame a problem. If we come in contact with new mental models we can add them to our armory.

This is a key feature of the learning process in business schools. Consider again the case study method that we described in chapter 4. On one level, the idea is to instill in students the ability to do counterfactual thinking. They are transported into a specific situation with numerous hard and soft constraints and need to imagine alternative options, evaluate them, and reach a decision. The method trains students to think within a frame.

However, on another level, each business case exposes students to a specific frame—and as they read and discuss case after case, they acquire a wide variety of mental models that they can keep in their repertoire. When confronted with a similar situation in their professional lives, they can trot out the frame they were exposed to as students and apply it to the matter at hand.

This objective was apparent from the very start, when Harvard handed its students the first business school case, "The General Shoe Company," in 1921. In it, workers are leaving their machines well before their shift ends to avoid the long wash-up queue. This hurts productivity. The one-page case concludes by asking: "What factors should be developed in the investigation on the part of management?" and "What are the general policies . . . [that] should be remedied?" Note that it is not simply looking for an answer for what to do: it first demands that students consider how they frame the problem.

Adding new frames to one's mental inventory in this way is

useful but it has limitations. As the number of cases that are considered in business school settings is relatively small, the method provides only a limited number of frames to students. This could be misinterpreted to suggest to students that these frames are sufficient to solve most real-world problems, thereby failing to prepare them for more radical reframing.

That concern is not new—it was understood by the Harvard Business School dean who launched the case study method, Wallace Donham. During the Great Depression, he worried that the case study method was too narrow, producing business leaders who failed "to see things in wide relations," as he put it in a *Harvard Business Review* article in 1933. Of course, this isn't a fatal flaw: it is better to be familiar with some of the most useful frames than none at all.

Another strategy for increasing mental diversity is to whet our appetite for new ideas. Call it "cognitive foraging": the pursuit of new ways of thinking and seeing the world without the specific aim to acquire frames. One swoops in hither and thither in pursuit of new ideas, experiences, and ways of seeing. Think of it as curiosity taken seriously. The aim is to be exposed to a plethora of perspectives, a variety of viewpoints, a cornucopia of concepts, all outside of one's domain. This helps us become more open to seeking and finding new mental models when we need to. It accustoms us to the task of being a hunter-gatherer of ideas; we exercise our inquisitiveness. By constantly looking, we're better at seeing.

People perform cognitive foraging when they seek out unfamiliar experiences—meeting new people, devouring a wide range of books, or going places they would not naturally gravitate to—for the purpose of evolving an open, inquiring mind. It often entails building connections with diverse groups of people beyond one's field not for any direct help, but for mental stimulation through novel inputs. People are often mystified when they see starched-shirt business leaders chatting away with people covered with tattoos and facial jewelry, wondering how such odd-seeming friendships might form. Behind it is that both become wiser from the association, albeit not in an obvious, immediate, and straightforward way.

The science of social networks backs this up. The sociologist Ronald Burt at the University of Chicago Booth School of Business has studied individuals in organizations to understand the role that information plays in performance. Some executives are more creative, make better decisions, and are promoted faster. Burt's research has shown that their success is associated with their social network and their willingness to be confronted with views from beyond their immediate circle of colleagues. He contrasts two archetypal people in organizations, whom he calls "James" and "Robert."

The Jameses of the world are inward-oriented. They emphasize sticking to rules and focus on efficiency. The Jameses' social network is filled with far more redundant information. Roberts, on the contrary, have connections to other domains, thrive on diverse information, and look for new perspectives. They bridge what Burt calls "structural holes" that separate organizations and domains from one another. Because they are cognitive foragers who are exposed to diverse ways of thinking, Roberts are able to see things in new ways. They build and maintain ties not because they have a concrete problem to solve, but because they see exposure to alternative views and perspectives as a value in itself.

But when a need arises, the Roberts are ready to look for mental models far beyond their own limited repertoire. Cognitive foraging prepares us for the moment when we need to surpass what we already know or can easily acquire. It's far less concrete than deliberately setting out to build a diverse repertoire of frames, but it is far more versatile. The only things that it does not prepare us for are the exceptional cases when we need to let go of all we know and devise a completely novel frame. To prepare for such extreme cases, we need yet another way.

The clean-slate strategy is the most radical approach. It is deliberately training our mind to be ready to put aside the familiar and to prepare ourselves for something fundamentally new: an acceptance of an emptiness that we will be able to fill, because within the void is the opportunity to see things in an entirely new way.

Of course, in practice we can never start from a completely clean slate. Our experiences and knowledge always influence how we conceptualize things and react to challenges, including novel ones. But much like the way our brain has the ability to forget (even if we can't control it directly), for this approach we must train to consciously cast aside the temptation to slot a situation into the categories of what we know. The clean-slate strategy is an effort to "unlearn" well-worn cognitive concepts and to deviate from the customary paths. It's the decision to not go to the tools we know, but to intentionally put our toolbox aside and conceive of the best possible way to solve our challenge. The clean-slate approach prepares us for that decision.

It's much like a child lifting both legs off the ground when learning to ride a bicycle, or jumping from a diving platform many feet above a pool for the first time. It's the step that, when we take it, separates us from those who have only read or seen or heard about what would happen, without actually experiencing it. It is a particular kind of courage, a cognitive readiness to take that mental step.

The story of the computer-science pioneer Alan Kay and "object-oriented" programming gives a sense of this. In the early 1970s, Kay was working at the legendary Xerox PARC, a research lab in Silicon Valley that gave birth to the personal computing revolution. Mainstream computer programming then was "procedural": programmers would carefully map out what their programs should do, and then diligently translate that into a step-by-step sequence of commands for the computer to follow. Human users provided input, but the program had its goal coded into it. It was a mental model for the era of mainframe computing.

Kay loathed this. He felt users were central to computing, and that computers should empower people to extend their mental abilities. Programmers could never foresee what users might do, much as toolmakers cannot foretell how and to what ends their tools will be employed. But this would require a vastly different way of programming.

Fortunately, half a decade earlier, on November 11, 1966, Kay had experienced a revelation. Looking over other people's computer code that tried to go beyond the existing programming paradigm, he realized that computers could be instructed to create a swarm of little virtual computers; each of which would handle an "object," and could interact among themselves by sending messages back and forth. "It was the promise of an entirely new way to structure computations that took my fancy," he explained years later.

At Xerox PARC, Kay implemented the audacious idea in Smalltalk, a programming language. It was a watershed moment, laying the conceptual foundation for software development in the digital age. A version of Smalltalk was shown to Steve Jobs when he famously visited in 1979, which inspired early Apple computers. Today, object-oriented programming remains the way most software is developed.

Kay is best known for his aphorism, "The best way to predict the future is to invent it." Less well known is what he calls "the tyranny of the present." In his view, institutions and schools do a poor job of encouraging novel thinking. In many ways, his life's project has been to help people think anew, by having the right mental model, or context. "Most creativity is a transition from one context into another," he said. "There are more contexts than the one that we're in—the one that we think is reality." There may be no better way to appreciate the power of framing and the clean-slate strategy.

Countless stories feature heroes—real and imagined—who push themselves into the unknown, from Odysseus setting sail upon the wine-dark sea to the early twentieth-century aviator Amelia Earhart crisscrossing the oceans. James Morris was a reporter on the first expedition to scale Everest in 1953 before becoming Jan Morris, one of the early recipients of sex reassignment surgery, in 1972, and a famed author. Their accomplishments were not only tangible, but mental too. They entailed letting go of the known.

Good framers need to mentally do the same, so that they are ready to open their minds to new perspectives and new frames. This is not easy, nor is it particularly comfortable. We are adrift—be it in still waters or tempest-tossed seas. But in this state of mental vacuity, new frames can form.

The three approaches—broadening the range of frames in our own repertoire, engaging in cognitive foraging, and practicing the clean-slate strategy—are useful tools for different situations. A way to see the differences is like this: if adding diverse frames to our repertoire is similar to acquiring relevant books, cognitive foraging is reading voraciously across a spectrum of subjects and the clean-slate strategy is being passionate for knowledge altogether.

As we engage multiple frames to explore different perspectives, it becomes apparent that different frames are often in tension with one another. One frame may highlight certain elements of a situation that another frame may neglect. Such tensions among frames are indicators of the complex and multifaceted nature of reality.

They are not uncommon. In physics, light is considered both a wave and a particle: the two frames conflict with each other, but one can't understand light with just one of them. In mathematics, frames overlap everywhere. Euclidian geometry is based on points and angles, but Descartes reframed it using numbers and algebra. We need both—Euclidian geometry for our intuitions and Cartesian "analytical" geometry to prove them with calculations. The

United Nations is based on human solidarity and globalism, and yet restricts full membership to nation-states.

The critical insight is: *it is not possible to reconcile these tensions— nor is that the point.* Only when we appreciate these tensions can we see beyond the individual frame and gain a fuller, more comprehensive picture. Actively navigating the tensions among frames translates into better choices of frames and strengthens our emotional stability.

Crucial to our understanding of the tension among frames is the idea of cognitive complexity. This is a term used in psychology to describe the degree to which one's thought patterns are intricate and nuanced versus basic and simple. Studies have shown that outstanding leaders have greater cognitive complexity; it's a trait that they appreciate, highlight, and embrace. Moreover, they coach colleagues to develop it. It isn't just exceptional leaders: children who are raised bilingual also think with more cognitive complexity.

Those who understand the value of being exposed to new mental models, even if they produce tensions, will actively insist on it. Lewis Branscomb, IBM's chief scientist in the 1970s who led Harvard's technology-policy program for years, was feared by new colleagues for critiquing presentations. "Don't tell me what I already know—tell me what I don't yet know," he'd bark. We should all be so wise as to adopt the Branscomb principle.

The Organizational Imperative

Individuals are not the only ones who benefit from a diversity of frames. Organizations as a whole profit when their members are better at picking frames; the organization is then able to find better solutions to the challenges it faces. The "diversity dividend" for framing doesn't just accrue to those framers, but is shared organization-wide. It helps the entire group succeed.

How can organizations protect mental diversity among their members and even increase it? It seems impossible, since one cannot peek into another human's mind for sure. Yet even if that trait cannot be directly observed, organizations can identify suitable proxies. And the most obvious proxy for mental diversity is social diversity.

It is clear that individuals with similar upbringings, educational backgrounds, and professional experiences are prone to think alike. In contrast, individuals from vastly different ethnicities, sociodemographic groups, and educations have divergent life experiences, which in turn likely translate into dissimilar mental models of the world. Bringing together a diverse group of people can maximize an organization's cognitive resources.

Yet fostering and working in diverse settings isn't something many of us are good at, even though reams of social-science studies have emphasized the benefits for decades. Strong forces hold us back. Research in social networks has shown that they have a significant tendency toward homophily, the idea that birds of a feather flock together. Not only do we tend to gravitate to people who look like us, but we are more comfortable with those who think like us as well. Going out of one's way to be exposed to perspectives that are different from our own takes determination.

Human framing is to blame, at least in part, for this seeming lack of effort. When applying frames, we quickly reduce the number of options to identify the most promising choices. That often leads to an emphasis on speed. Hence, we may not entertain all useful counterfactuals (as the victims of groupthink in chapter 4 found out). This may lead us to prefer the familiar to the novel and unknown.

When organizations need to reframe, establishing an environment that encourages a diversity of mental models is vital. It provides the space to think differently, to imagine anew. To appreciate the sort of mind-set that's useful (and the difficulties in achieving it), consider Norway's experience with board diversity.

In 2003 the country passed a law requiring that 40 percent of a company's board of directors had to be women by 2006—a big increase from an average of 9 percent at the time. However, a few years later, firms that had significantly increased their share of female directors experienced a deep drop in market value, and a decline in return on equity as large as 20 percent. Adding women to boards seemed to harm performance. Why didn't diversity help? Why did firms who brought in the most women do so poorly?

One reason may be that firms that had to make the biggest increase in female directors had been laggards not only in gender diversity but in commercial areas too. So it was just reality catching up with them. In industries like oil, gas, mining, and fishing—the main industries in the country—gender diversity may contribute less to financial success than it does in sectors like consumer goods and services. It certainly didn't help that to quickly comply with the law, some companies appointed executives' female family members to their boards.

Yet a deeper reason is that organizations need more than outward diversity like gender (though that's undoubtedly a good thing in its own right) to frame problems differently. They need mental diversity. And it was here where Norway may have failed. The country's pool of top female executives is limited, and they tended to come from the same communities, schools, and companies as their male counterparts. What was inside their heads was largely the same, even if what was inside their knickers wasn't. The situation is a powerful reminder that even when we strive for diversity we might end up with uniformity.

Research in the journal *Science* shows that teams with more gender diversity outperform homogenous ones at a variety of tasks. Yet it's not gender per se that is the decisive factor. The women who were contributing to team performance scored better on a social-sensitivity test, which measures the ability to evaluate social interactions in group dynamics. Their gender was not the decisive element, it was their ability to think differently, in this case, with more social sensitivity.

When an organization faces a reframing challenge, it is advantageous to assemble teams that are diverse in their backgrounds, outlooks, and perspectives. This improves the chances that the teams come up with a wide variety of mental models. The evidence has been piling up for years, so that by 2015 researchers were able to definitively state that diversity of team members produces better outcomes on tasks.

But there is a hitch. The research also shows that even diverse teams, when given a cognitive challenge to solve such as reframing, quickly coalesce around a consensus position without actually tapping too deeply into the different perspectives represented in the group. This is odd: it is almost as if the team deliberately forgoes harnessing the power of diversity that it possesses. However, the problem goes away when team members are asked to mull the issue individually before working as a group.

The reason why is compelling. By first thinking alone about the challenge, individual team members tap their diverse sets of frames, which they later use to debate as a group. In contrast, when they discuss the challenge as a team from the outset, each member gets influenced by others right away, leading swiftly to a consensus. Hence, a superior approach for organizations that face a reframing challenge is to have diverse team members initially consider the matter by themselves and only later come together as a group.

Apple achieves the same ends through different means, according to Podolny. Its managers are experts in a specific domain rather than only "general managers," as in most big companies, with just a generalist's knowledge. They hold strong but diverse opinions based on distinct frames. When they come together to discuss an issue, they don't quickly converge on a consensus and slap each other on the back, strolling to the executive dining room. That way group meetings produce the team benefit we mentioned. Crucial are three qualities Apple looks for in managers: area knowledge, command of details, and "a willingness to collaboratively debate other functions during collective decision-making," says Podolny.

The composition of groups and how they work together create an environment for productive framing. Other techniques include giving team members roughly equal time to make their case and adhering to majority rule. This may sound intuitive but it's not practiced widely in business—though in studies it worked best because it brought together the group's collective intelligence.

In recent years, organizations and companies have begun to experiment with going beyond their institutional boundaries to attract diverse insights. It's understandable. "No matter who you are, most of the smartest people work for someone else," chirped the consummate Silicon Valley geek Bill Joy in the 1990s. Even if an organization is able to attract diverse members to its teams, the most appropriate mental models may be held by individuals elsewhere, especially for tough reframing challenges. The internet lowers the transaction costs of involving outsiders, underpinning the open-innovation, crowdsourcing platforms like InnoCentive and Kaggle. They don't simply bring together different people but their diverse frames.

At times the approach works extremely well. The Japanese company Cuusoo created a site for fans to share Lego ideas. People from around the world proved so creative—far more than Lego's own master builders—that in 2008 the Danish company joined forces with the community of fans to sell their sets. One is the DeLorean time machine car from the 1985 cult movie *Back to the Future*, replete with fold-up wheels (and yes, a flux capacitor). The Cuusoo designs, now branded as "Lego Ideas," are made from the bricks and bits plundered from regular Lego sets. But they are put together in ways that force one to reimagine what is possible.

In Praise of Fools

Diversity isn't costless. In organizations, it may lead to fierce arguments about the right frame to apply to a problem. That takes extra energy, and if the tensions become too great, the organization's performance may suffer. But in many cases, the outcomes improve. And because in picking frames the outcome is crucial, the friction should be welcomed because the diversity leads to better results. Variation confers advantages when one is trying to identify the best solution to a problem.

The idea is nicely illustrated by Scott Page, a mathematician and expert on decision science at the University of Michigan. He offers the metaphor of trying to climb to the top of the tallest peak in a mountain range. It's easy to see which way is up from where you are, but the risk is that you climb to a high point but not the highest. You're stuck in a "local optimum" (the best for a particular area), not the "global optimum" (the best overall). You can't see the totality of the area; you can't survey the entire "problem space."

In this situation, most people either stay at the local optimum and declare victory, or—at best—descend to the valley and climb a few neighboring hills in the hope that it gets them higher or lets them see farther. In a resource-constrained world in which there is never enough time, money, or will, "satisficing"—accepting the highest of the first few hills you climb—is the norm. However, a better solution is to bring in other people who possess different frames, as they may start their climb in an entirely different part of the mountain range and they climb differently. Having several different starting points and approaches increases the likelihood that someone will reach the global optimum.

This is hard to achieve in practice. It is difficult to institutionalize the value of diversity if the organization is resistant to it. It takes a special sort of organization to let people with different frames exist, to hear them when they speak (since what they say is usually something the organization doesn't want to hear). In the business world, such intellectual outsiders and Cassandras need to be nurtured. But they rarely are.

In the ancient Greek myth of Cassandra, the beautiful daughter of King Priam was admired by the great god Apollo. To win her affection, he bestowed upon her a gift, the power of prophecy. But when she denied his advances, he cursed her (for a divine gift cannot be revoked). Though she could still see into the future, Apollo made it so that her visions were never to be believed. And so the curse of Cassandra is that she can foretell what will pass but must carry that knowledge alone. She screams into the wind, in a tongue no one understands. The fall of Troy! But people consider her mad and pay no heed.

It sounds like an ordinary day at a Fortune 500 company. Today it's not Greeks bearing gifts who we need to beware of but conformist thinking that leads to suboptimal decisions. Bureaucracies regularly fail to listen to the "corporate Cassandras" around them: the employees who foresee disasters and suggest correctives but are ignored. Andy Grove, the legendary cofounder of Intel, saw them as so essential to business success that he devoted an entire chapter in his memoir, called "Helpful Cassandras," to vaunt those who bring "a new way of looking at things."

The myth of Cassandra doesn't end well. Troy is indeed sacked. But Ed Catmull, the cofounder and president of the animated-movie studio Pixar, interprets the myth differently. "Why, I always wonder, do we think of Cassandra as the one who's cursed?" he asks. "The real curse, it seems to me, afflicts everyone else—all of those who are unable to perceive the truth she speaks."

As a business leader, Catmull takes the subject to heart. "I spend a lot of time thinking about the limits of perception. In the management context, particularly, it behooves us to ask ourselves constantly: How much are we able to see? And how much is obscured from view? Is there a Cassandra out there we are failing to listen to? In other words, despite our best intentions, are we cursed too?"

The hex isn't that the individual sees something that others do not. It is that others lack the cognitive dexterity to entertain many different models. It's not that some can't communicate; it's that those around them don't listen. Public-health experts warned for years about the threat of a global pandemic from coronaviruses that jump from animal to human, but few took note since the frame seemed so dramatic and alien. Both Eunice Foote in 1856 and Inez Fung in 1988 warned of carbon in the atmosphere leading to global warming, but the public wasn't willing to accept it until later.

To overcome the curse, institutions need to carve out a dedicated space to bring different frames to situations, and thereby expose people in organizations to diverse mental models. In politics, the notion of "Her Majesty's loyal opposition," a term coined in Britain in the 1800s, describes how political parties might clash in terms of practical policies but still share a common, higher goal of serving the country. Likewise, the concept of a "red team"—an internal group that takes an adversarial position against the organization to test its defenses—is a staple of military planning, corporate strategy, and computer security. The group tasks an outsider with probing its own weaknesses. By allowing a clash of frames (or in other cases, counterfactuals), the organization encourages the attack in order to view what it's doing from another perspective.

The medieval court jester served a similar function. With bells jingling from his three-pointed cap and marotte in hand, the jester had the air of a silly prankster amid the serious men at court, who brought the country to war, collected its taxes, and enforced its laws. But nothing could be further from reality. Though some of these courtly fools were minstrels or comics, only the jester could speak truth to the king (albeit in comic form, lest the majesty lose face . . .).

In 1386 the Austrian duke Leopold the Pious was planning with his generals to invade Switzerland. His jester took stock of the situation and opined: "You fools, you're all debating how to get into the country, but none of you have thought how you're going to get out again!"

In France, the jester Triboulet served kings Louis XII and Francis I. After he informed King Francis that a courtier threatened to kill him, Francis purportedly said, "If he does, I will hang him a quarter of an hour afterward." To which Triboulet is said to have replied: "Ah, sire, could you not contrive to hang him a quarter of an hour *before*?"

Certain "fools" continue to serve a useful function. Recent research for NASA on long-duration human space travel, for instance, has called for there to be one crew member on the team with the personality of the jester, prankster, or fool, as a way to defuse tense situations and introduce novel thinking when it's needed.

Getting the Setting Right

Individuals improve their ability to choose a frame by expanding their repertoire, cognitive foraging, and developing a clean-slate mentality to leap into a cognitive unknown. Organizations too have a critical role to play in fostering a myriad of frames. They can establish and maintain a diverse environment and make sure that teams employ the right ground rules to tap into the framing potential.

But for organizations it's often hard to do, and even the most well-meaning institutions stumble. That was the experience of the *New York Times*, which has long prided itself as a bastion of diversity and independent thinking. On July 14, 2020, one of its columnists, Bari Weiss, a journalistic gadfly who leans left on some issues and right on others, resigned in a huff.

She had been recruited to the *Times* from the conservative *Wall Street Journal* three years earlier in an attempt to broaden the spectrum of views in the *Times*'s op-ed section. Following the surprise election of Donald Trump—surprising for East Coast media elites most of all—the paper's leadership felt that it was out of step with the views of the country it covered. Bringing in right-of-center opinion writers was a way to present a diverse range of views to readers. It was inspired by the noblest of intentions from the opinion-page editor, James Bennet, and the paper's family owner.

But the sand in the oyster didn't produce a pearl. Many journalists on the news side of the paper, which is distinct from the opinion and editorial section, were uncomfortable with right-leaning commentaries. Over time, the internal grumbles made their way to Twitter, where reporters publicly condemned articles and authors. As an intelligent, sharp-tongued celebrity-journalist in her thirties who relishes challenging liberal dogma, Weiss fell into the crosshairs.

She criticized the Women's March following Trump's inauguration. She expressed alarm that #MeToo might go too far. She profiled the "intellectual dark web" of non-mainstream thinkers and denounced the censorship, microaggressions, and safe spaces that typify the culture wars. Her work generated animosity on both sides of the aisle. Jewish, she was labeled a Nazi by trolls.

In June 2020, after the op-ed section published a piece calling on Trump to use the military to quell incidents of looting and rioting that were happening alongside some of the Black Lives Matter protests, a staff insurrection forced out Bennet, the op-ed editor who had recruited Weiss. The heat on her increased, and she left five weeks later. "My own forays into Wrongthink have made me the subject of constant bullying by colleagues who disagree with my views," she wrote in her resignation letter.

"Standing up for principle at the paper does not win plaudits. It puts a target on your back." As she explained, "A new consensus has emerged in the press, but perhaps especially at this paper: that truth isn't a process of collective discovery, but an orthodoxy already known to an enlightened few whose job is to inform everyone else."

On one level, the dispute seems like a fight over free speech in an era of virtue signaling, identity politics, and cancel culture run amok. But there is something deeper. Cognitive diversity depends on the raw material of frames. And organizations play an essential role in fostering this. But it is hard. Even the Gray Lady tried and failed. Yet as tricky as it is for organizations to pull off, it's even more difficult at the level of society, where it matters most. It is there that we now turn.

8

pluralism

a coexistence of frames is essential to humanity's survival

The Gestapo officer liked her. For days, he interrogated the petite young woman sitting across from him. Her alleged crime was chronicling how organizations, institutions, and individuals were replacing their diverse understandings of the world with the monotone drumbeat of anti-Semitic, Nazi propaganda. Agents searched her apartment and found mysterious codes—philosophical quotations written in ancient Greek.

The officer did not know what to make of any of it. He had been a criminal investigator and had only just been promoted to the section looking after political crimes. "What am I supposed to do with you?" he'd ask aloud, over the course of the questioning.

She felt he had an "honest face." When she asked for cigarettes, he brought her several packets. When she complained about the quality of the coffee, he got her something better. In return she flattered him as she contrived and concocted elaborate lies. He promised to get her released, and as with the cigarettes and coffee, he came through. After being held for eight days in a jail cell in Berlin, Johanna Stern—later known as Hannah Arendt—was free.

The year was 1933. Hitler was consolidating his power. Arendt, age twenty-six, knew the next time she wouldn't be so lucky. So she fled Germany, eventually arriving in Paris. The Nazis had begun to "preventively" detain those with different opinions and beliefs, or just beat them up. Vibrant and colorful Berlin, with its opera and symphonies, art galleries and publishing houses, political salons and risqué cabarets, was slowly turning a dull, homogenous gray.

It was not only Berlin. For the previous decade, life in the major cities around the world bustled with energy and imagination. It was a time when new ideas and fresh thinking flourished. The excitement was sketched by Italian futurists, German expressionists, French dadaists. It was heard in Bolshevik speeches in Petrograd; radical politicians threatening successive French governments; Italian anarchists in Massachusetts and Chinese anarchists in San Francisco.

The 1920s and early '30s swelled with a cornucopia of frames— different ways to view the world. In Paris *les années folles* (the crazy years) saw Igor Stravinsky redefine music, Pablo Picasso reinvent painting, James Joyce reinterpret literature, Le Corbusier reimagine architecture—none of them French. In America's roaring twenties, women "flappers" danced, drank, and smoked, deliberately pushing against boundaries and redefining what was considered acceptable behavior.

"Everywhere was the atmosphere of a long debauch," wrote one literary critic. "The orchestras played too fast." It was a bubbling cauldron of political, social, economic, and artistic ideas. Capitalism and communism and fascism intermingled. Pacifism and militarism jostled for superiority. Cubism and surrealism; ultraism and minimalism; anti-Semitism and Nazism. It was all there colliding, bonding, repelling, and transforming.

But slowly the broad spectrum of ideas began to narrow. It happened gradually, barely perceptibly at times, like rust. Part of it was planned, the consequence of growing armies of extremists. Part of it was accidental, or at least unintended, as people looked on and hoped for the best. Where once a diversity of frames flowered, these were now starved or strangled. Scientists were pushed onto factory assembly lines. "Degenerate" art was removed from museum walls. Teachers, journalists, and businessmen were summoned to serve and adulate the dominant mental model rather than thrive in a pluralism of frames.

A darkness set in. Young men flooded the streets in paramilitary packs, committing everyday acts of barbarism. Hitler, Mussolini, and Stalin imprisoned dissidents and shot political rivals and their families. The cognitive invasion became a physical one. A fourteen-year-old girl in Poland ended a diary entry in 1943: "Oh, I forgot the most important thing. I saw how a soldier tore a baby, who was only a few months old, out of its mother's hands and bashed his head against an electric pylon. The baby's brain splashed on the wood. The mother went crazy"—an afterthought to the day.

The engine of industrialization was deformed to mechanize the killing of millions, from boxcar to gas chamber to crematorium. The war began with cavalry soldiers and horse-drawn artillery, and ended with fire bombings and atomic weapons. By the time the worst was over, humanity had inflicted upon itself an agony that defies imagination.

A Single Frame of Truth

Oppression takes many forms. Behind the outward violence, distorted institutions, hatred, and injustices are restrictions that are less visible. They crimp people's freedom to frame, to size up the world in a given way and reimagine what might be different. It is not apparent in itself but only noticeable by its effects. Cognitive oppression leaves a void; it is distinguished by what is absent, not what exists. When societies restrict the variety of mental models, when they deny the legitimacy or existence of alternative frames, it is not just individuals who suffer: all of humanity endures an invisible loss.

It happened with the rise of fascism and communism in the 1930s and '40s in Europe. It was a feature of China's Cultural Revolution in the 1960s and '70s. Its outward manifestations were seen in the killing fields of Cambodia and the genocide in Rwanda. And it does not always end with outward violence. The distortion of people's perception of reality is less horrific but no less wrong. This characterized America's "red scare"—the McCarthy hearings in the 1950s, when professors, writers, and Hollywood producers were hauled before Congress to testify whether they held communist sympathies. It happens today when university students—and Eastern European politicians—prevent people from expressing views, or hearing them, or associating together.

We use mental models to contemplate and interact with the reality around us, so choosing and applying a frame is our most powerful tool. A diverse mind makes us better individual framers, and a diverse team leads to better solutions. A similar advantage from embracing multiple frames holds true for society and humanity generally. Just as individuals benefit from diversity, so too does society benefit from pluralism. The point is less moral than pragmatic: an openness and tolerance to a multitude of diverse frames improves the chances that society will progress.

The idea of frame pluralism is apparent in the economic sphere. The essence of the market economy is that participants may interact as they judge best to self-coordinate their activities. Everyone has their varied frames to make decisions—to compete, cooperate, and transact. (When the moral philosopher Adam Smith called for an "open and free market," he was referring to freedom from obstacles that prevented this, like frivolous taxes, self-serving tariffs, and rentiers' unjust fees, but it applied to freedom from restraints on mental models too.) Likewise, pluralism is evident in the political sphere. A democracy, where people can decide their leaders and laws, allows for open competition for governance—and the freedom to frame.

In the social sphere, pluralism is the opposite of conformity. It accepts differences rather than tries to meld them into something singular and uniform. When all the colors of the rainbow are consolidated into a single beam it produces plain, white light. Pluralism celebrates keeping the hues: it strives for the colorful, not the colorless. A society that is open to and tolerant of a myriad of frames works better for all of its members.

Pluralism is not an end but a means to an end. The end is a society that supports the people who comprise it, that protects their rights and freedom, both physical and cognitive. The freedom to frame exalts human dignity but its power is in its effects: it enables better decisions where much is at stake, not just for one individual but for the community. At the societal level, the aim of pluralism is not to select one frame from an assortment and converge on it. Instead, the goal is to allow a multiplicity of clashing frames to flourish and be applied all at the same time. That creates the environment in which individuals and organizations can successfully frame.

Maintaining pluralism at all times also prepares society to respond to sudden and disruptive challenges. It offers resilience when sticking to an existing frame would be perilous, and the need to reframe is urgent. Pluralism provides the rich variety of frames that society needs to evolve, just as biological evolution relies on diversity in order to adapt. In evolutionary terms, if society fails at critical junctures to tap a vast tapestry of frames, it will fail the test of natural selection. That is why pluralism of frames in societies is such a vital strategy: it helps us rise to the challenge of the unknown unknowns.

Giving up pluralism endangers a society's survival. But embracing pluralism inevitably means some frames will emerge that see the variety of mental models as a blight. That is what happened in the 1930s, as Nazis, fascists, and communists succeeded in suffocating the diversity of thought. It is a concern that the philosopher Karl Popper called the "paradox of tolerance": that to tolerate intolerance eventually leads to no tolerance at all (fittingly, see note).

Throughout this book we have taken pains to suggest there is no such thing as a bad frame, only those that don't fit the circumstances well. And they should certainly be allowed to coexist. But we also carefully emphasized that there is a qualification to this generous rule. And this is it: *The only bad frame is one that denies other frames.*

We do not make the case for it primarily on moral or ethical grounds—or derived from religious precepts or a warm feeling in the solar plexus—but on practical ones. A pluralism of frames enables better framing. It is humanity's mental "insurance policy" for times of change. In contrast, when one limits a society's frame space, it leaves people's unique cognitive capabilities underutilized. It dumbs us down.

There is no easy way to identify bad frames, or a simple recipe for what to do with them. Only absolutists believe they have all the answers. Tackling bad frames requires a constant and pragmatic navigation between the need to remain open and accepting at all moments and the vigilance to prevent the rise of intolerant frames. But being aware of this challenge is already an important step.

Equally important is to understand that bad frames are often the exception, and that we should default to tolerance: when in doubt be more permissive than restrictive, because as framers we are biased to see other frames with an extra-critical eye. Furthermore, the task of evaluating these exceptional, bad frames is such a crucial one for society that it is something we cannot delegate or outsource. We need to tackle it as a common responsibility.

Unitary Versus Variety

The danger caused by single frames of truth is real, because humanity is so susceptible to them. As we have explained, humans love to apply a frame they have successfully used before; to reach for a hammer for anything that looks slightly like a nail. Being swift to apply a standard frame can be useful—but also has its downsides.

It locks us into a conventional response, which fails if what is required is switching to a different perspective. Worse, the more successful we have been in applying a frame, the more we stick with it. We may even be tempted to believe that the frame is so good that it's without alternatives. It's like the woeful stock trader who adopts a strategy and makes a killing, yet when the markets turn, sticks with the strategy and wonders what went wrong.

Single frames of truth are a threat to people individually, but they also afflict entire societies. Just consider: decades of economic and societal success have tempted many societies to believe in the validity of their dominant frame. In autocratic states, claims of success are used to trumpet the mental models that were employed. As much as it oils the propaganda machine, it also reinforces a regime's belief in its own righteousness. It is a dangerous dynamic that inches societies toward an intellectual void, as it empties the mind and the public sphere of any remaining diversity of frames.

However, the autocratic state's antipode, liberal democracy, is hardly immune. In democracies, the descent may be slower, the steps away from cognitive diversity smaller. But the fall still can happen, even if it is subtler and the initial slide often barely visible. If one is not vigilant, then over time a society's multitude of frames may be curtailed, if not explicitly and legally, then from social pressure.

Hannah Arendt, who escaped the Gestapo and fled Nazi Germany, risked death on several occasions before finding her way to the United States, where she became one of the leading public intellectuals of her time. She wrote eloquently on political philosophy—thick tomes bearing sparse, bold titles like *The Origins of Totalitarianism* and *On Revolution*. After attending the war crimes trial in 1960 of Adolf Eichmann, the Nazi bureaucrat who helped organize the Holocaust, she penned her most notable work, *Eichmann in Jerusalem,* and coined the term "the banality of evil."

Arendt is known for her ideas on politics, but her most intriguing work is on what she termed "the human condition." She described the essence of humanness as people's ability to think, decide, and act. She was a proponent of a pluralism of frames, or "standpoints," as she called them.

"The more people's standpoints I have present in my mind while I am pondering a given issue," she wrote, "the more valid my final conclusions."

She rebelled against homogenizing individual thinking into a collective. Rousseau aspired to a "general will." Not Arendt. She insisted on "a plurality of standpoints." Or as she succinctly put it: "Men, not Man, live on the earth and inhabit the world."

Arendt abhorred the monoculture of mental models in autocratic societies. She criticized the French and Russian revolutions for foisting a singular vision of reality on people, rather than enabling them to be free to express a variety of models.

But, importantly, she was also wary of the smug universalism of the West—the idea that the seemingly permissive liberal society's perspective can be imposed on all of the world as a single frame of truth. Instead, she wanted a myriad of mental models to coexist. It is a red thread through her life and her work, of which she herself was an embodiment: a Jewish woman and student of the greatest (and one of the most controversial) German philosophers of her time, Martin Heidegger, and then as an American woman studying what motivated "men in dark times." In whatever name a state constrains people's cognitive ability, it will impoverish society and make it vulnerable. Arendt wanted people to recognize the importance of frame pluralism, but few understood it.

The end of the Cold War and the fall of communism in the early 1990s only deepened the conviction among many in the West that not only Western values but also Western frames, their very mental models of the world, were superior to others. The American political scientist Francis Fukuyama famously gave voice to this belief in 1992, that human civilization had reached the "end of history" because the idea of liberal, market democracy—the dominant frame left standing after the Soviet Union collapsed—seemed to mark an end point in political thinking. The "liberal market democracy" frame, exemplified by the United States, faced no credible or coherent alternative for how to govern. So began a "unipolar moment" in world affairs.

As the sole superpower, America exported its values and mental models globally—a march of ideas and ideals that was triumphalist and universalist. A year after the Berlin Wall fell, there were posters in the subway of the former East Berlin, advertising a cigarette brand called West, that read, "Test the West!" The giddy optimism defined the decade. Russia was open to investment and holding elections. China's ascension into the World Trade Organization in 2001 was supported by the United States: few could fathom that the country wasn't on the path of economic openness and greater human freedom.

After September 11, America invaded Iraq and Afghanistan—and set about organizing elections. When the Arab Spring began in 2010, American pundits saw it as confirmation that the spirit of 1776 finally stretched between Tehran and Tunis. They looked at events through the frame they knew best, though this view said more about the individuals who employed it than about the situation itself; more about who was looking than what was there to see. One can sympathize with the mistake: "If the frame works well, why change it?" is a natural bias.

But the problem isn't merely that people use frames that no longer work. The danger is that as alternative frames are excluded, challenges to conventional wisdom will subside. The risk is that the environment will no longer support a range of frames that can coexist and vie for acceptance.

Variety improves the likelihood that we find new solutions to our challenges and thereby overcome them. A narrow set of frames or a single, dominant one makes it more likely that we fall into a mental trap and fail to address our challenges—and like the inhabitants of ancient kingdoms and remote islands, see our civilization destroyed by our inability to respond. But there are ways to avert this.

Avoiding Mental Monocultures

At the dawn of the information age, America's East Coast dominated. Telecom giant AT&T was headquartered in New Jersey. Electronics powerhouse GE was based in Connecticut. Computer behemoth IBM hailed from New York state, as did Kodak for photography and Xerox for copiers. A slew of computer companies lined

Boston's Route 128. In 1959, tech jobs in the Route 128 corridor were almost triple that of Silicon Valley. Yet by 1990 Silicon Valley's technology employment was far larger and the region was creating three times as many new jobs. How did Silicon Valley succeed?

The answer is that the East Coast tech titans were run like government bureaucracies: monolithic and highly centralized. This was the era of the company man in the gray flannel suit. The Route 128 firms (with now-forgotten names like Digital Equipment Corp., Apollo Computer, and Wang Labs) were formal, hierarchical organizations where decision-making was concentrated at the top and information was cordoned off rather than shared outside the firm. The labor market wasn't open to people changing jobs—a lack of employment migration meant that workers were rewarded for hewing to what the business thought was the one right way, and lacked exposure to outside ideas. Stability was prized, not novel thinking, notes the business scholar AnnaLee Saxenian, in her landmark work, *Regional Advantage.*

In contrast, Silicon Valley was home to a flourishing network of small, nimble firms that competed against one another and actively searched for new ideas. There were no domineering players, start-ups were decentralized, and risk-taking was respected. Competition amounted to lots of small experiments that made everyone smarter. Workers from different firms met outside the office to share ideas, and the labor market encouraged job hopping, letting companies draw on a fuller set of frames from employees. The result was that fragmented Silicon Valley was more innovative and efficient than conformist East Coast firms.

According to the economic historian Joel Mokyr and the anthropologist Jared Diamond, a similar situation unfolded in the economic competition between China and Europe over the past roughly two thousand years. For most of history Asia was more advanced scientifically and economically and Europe was a primitive backwater. To appreciate the role that a pluralism of frames played in the destiny of societies, it is useful to look back in time—to the year 221 BC.

After a period of warring among states, China was unified under the Qin dynasty. As a single power, it could make many things more efficient. Decision-making happened at the center and was disseminated throughout the land. For well over a thousand years, China led the world in science and innovation. Its inventions included cast iron, gunpowder, shipbuilding, the compass, intricate clock building, paper, and printing. At the start of the 1400s, well before Columbus traveled with three small ships across the Atlantic, China sent fleets of large ships across the Indian Ocean to reach East Africa.

But after internal power struggles in the mid-1400s, an insular faction took over. The Chinese fleets stopped, the shipbuilding was discontinued, and the shipyards were dismantled. Oceangoing vessels were banned. Trade was prohibited. In 1661 the emperor moved people in southern China seventeen miles inland and waved away European traders and diplomatic missions. After just a few decisions in the highly centralized country, China's great epoch of exploration, invention, and globalization halted.

Compare that with Europe. In the fourteenth century, the region was divided into a thousand statelets, all competing with one another. Wars over religion basically ended by the mid-1500s with the doctrine *Cuius regio, eius religio* ("whose realm, his religion"), paving the way for religious pluralism. Instead, the fiefdoms, principalities, and kingdoms fought over power and wealth. It caused significant friction and led to countless bloody battles. But the disunity of Europe was also fertile ground for experimentation, a laboratory of novel frames in the domains of politics, economics, and science.

Where China's policies were unitary, Europe's were scattered. Where China had a dominant language, Europe had many, often with their own alphabetical characters. Where China had central control, European lands were just far enough apart to allow independent thinking while close enough and porous enough to exchange ideas and share what worked. Italian city-states and German *Länder* flourished. Attempts to unify Europe, from Charlemagne to Napoleon, failed. At its height, the Roman Empire comprised less than half the area of Europe. Decentralization meant diversity, and that produced different frames for sizing up problems and trying out solutions.

China was a homogenous state, centrally run. Europe was fragmented and teemed with a wide range of frames. Societal conditions inhibited frame pluralism in one place, and incentivized frame pluralism in another. China invented gunpowder but lacking constant rivalries, used it for fireworks. Europeans, economically competitive and always fearful of their neighbors, saw other uses for it—including, alas, to make munitions. Today the economic situation looks different. China is a hotbed of commercial rivalry and the West seems to have lost its business dynamism and thirst for innovation. Dominance does that to individuals, companies, and countries. Conditions matter.

Ironically, Silicon Valley has become the new monoculture. The engineers, developers, and designers tend to look alike, think alike, and are often motivated by the same values. Large, monolithic companies, run by all-powerful leaders, stand like totems towering over Lilliputian start-ups. Whether a Caltech research scientist or a hacker high-school dropout, the people seem to lack cognitive diversity; the social equivalent of Norwegian board directors. Patrick Collison, the founder of the fintech firm Stripe, and Tyler Cowen, an economist, have called for a new discipline of "progress studies," to understand in greater detail why some innovative ecosystems do better than others—and how to sustain success. Perhaps the geeks resemble clones of one another because they have all gone through

Joel Podolny's classes at Apple University only to strive to "think different" in the same way.

Monocultures never work. A homogeneity of mental models fails for economic clusters as for entire societies. The principle of frame pluralism (that is, we must accept all frames save for ones that deny others) offers a solution that is simple and powerful.

Frame pluralism does not imply that all frames are equal in utility or value. Some frames are clearly much worse in most situations than others, and we should be incredibly careful before considering any of them. Of course, frames can be critical of other frames, implying another's inferiority to circumstances, or its own superiority under certain conditions. That's precisely the kind of robust give-and-take on framing well that we all benefit from.

Hence, the frame of the Earth being flat is flawed but may still be useful for measuring short distances easily, because the planet's curvature is insignificant on local scales. We are entitled to explain why it does not correspond with reality, but we must not refuse the frame to exist altogether. Nor should we try to stamp out a mental model that global warming is *not* being caused by humans. It is incorrect in the face of science, and leads to erroneous decisions—but that is a reason to resist the mistaken frame, not deny its existence.

Frame pluralism's very goal is for frames to compete, complement, contradict, and coexist with one another. But no frame would be acceptable that aims to eliminate or negate altogether the existence of alternative frames. That is what makes social pressure to censor others' views, today's cancel culture, so pernicious. It is not simply a restriction of free speech. It is a refusal to accept another's thinking—their comprehension of reality.

Frame pluralism produces better outcomes, but there may nevertheless be good ethical and moral grounds for banning additional frames from our shared repositories. However, if such bans take place, we need to be aware of and accept them for what they are—a reduction of our frame space.

Nor is frame pluralism costless: it causes societal friction. If everybody sees the world the same way, there is little to debate and quarrel about. But there also may be no one to stop a society from jumping off a cliff—that is, from making bad decisions because it failed to mentally size up the situation well. Societies that encourage different perspectives make a deliberate investment; they accept a clash of frames and find ways to turn the friction into a feature.

So how can communities live and breathe frame pluralism successfully? The most fundamental way is to establish the right setting, one that fosters different and competing frames. In the previous chapter, we explained how cognitive diversity in individuals is linked to a more generally diverse environment. A wide variety of friends and colleagues is the fertile ground that lets our own range of mental models develop. The same holds true on a societal level.

Pluralist societies aren't necessarily congruent with liberal democracies. We can, for instance, imagine a democracy whose members hold very similar views. (Think of Victorian England of the 1800s, or Japan's consensus model of decision-making in the twentieth century.) In the same vein, we can imagine societies that are accepting of many different frames, but are not necessarily democratic. (The Roman Empire was culturally diverse but certainly not democratically governed.) The majority may not rule, but the plurality of frames may lead to innovations and better societal decisions, especially in times of disruptive change.

An environment that protects cognitive freedom and promotes a multiplicity of frames is not the natural state of affairs. In fact, our tribalism pushes us toward cognitive homogeneity, like an invisible, intellectual gravitational force. (Everyone in a meeting with their boss knows how that feels.) A climate that fosters frame pluralism has to be established and maintained. We can't declare victory and be done. Sustaining the conditions for pluralism is a significant societal task. But it is also empowering: even a smidgeon of effort can go a long way—provided one resists complacency and passivity, which only help those who would erode cognitive diversity.

Let a Thousand Frames Flourish

Society can foster frame pluralism so the widest range of views can flourish. Four strategies enable this: embracing variation and harnessing education on the personal level, and encouraging migration and accepting friction on the societal level. Consider each facet in turn.

First is variation. It is to actively strive for differences in viewpoints rather than passively hope they crop up. Regard the range of views as a feature to celebrate, not an uncomfortable fact of life to be avoided. The simple line "I see this differently" highlights the tension, yet at the same time respects the other's views as well as one's own. It validates the idea that people holding diverse frames can still enjoy fruitful interactions. It means accepting that our world is not cognitively homogenous, but that a range of mental models is a mark of civilization's progress.

This was done in a shrewd but subtle way by campaigners for same-sex marriage in the United States. In 1995 only a quarter of Americans supported gay marriage. By 2020 the number was almost 70 percent. What happened? Sociodemographic changes can explain part of it: couples had fewer children, making marriage less about reproduction than about stable relationships. But there was something deeper at work.

From the 1980s onward, marriage was a mainstay of the gay rights movement, which emphasized just that: legal rights. But it got them nowhere. "God made Adam and Eve, not Adam and *Steve*," thundered conservatives. As Kevin Nix, who led the communications strategy of the activist organization Freedom to Marry, explains: "That legal frame, including the word *rights*, didn't work. It was sterile, materialistic, and unpersuasive."

In the early 2000s Nix and others pored over public opinion data, polls, and focus groups to learn what the public's reservations were. "We needed to figure out how to meet those folks—and onetime opponents—where they were in their own mental template and help get them on board," he said. "We settled on a values frame that hit on why most people get married: love, commitment, and family."

In other words, the group changed how they characterized gay marriage, not as a liberty or a right, but as an expression of and commitment to love. It was a decisive shift. They had gay people from all walks of life make the case. They found third-party "validators" like straight parents to stand up for their child's right to marry. They ran ads, placed the narrative into the political media and celebrity press, and plugged it into television story lines.

The goal wasn't to discredit or invalidate how others saw the world, presuming there was a "right" frame—rather, it was to show that there were numerous legitimate frames. And they positioned gay marriage in the frame of love and commitment that many straight people already had.

And it worked. In 2011 the crossover moment came when more Americans supported than opposed gay marriage. Strikingly, only 14 percent of the population described gay marriage in terms of liberty, but 32 percent in terms of love and human affection. On June 26, 2015, the Supreme Court ruled that the Constitution guarantees the right of same-sex couples to wed. A significant social victory was achieved not by forcing people to accept a particular frame. The notion that a multitude of mental models can coexist, the cornerstone of a pluralistic society, was at the heart of the success.

The second way to boost frame pluralism is within education and childhood socialization. Teaching and pedagogy today are increasingly open and encouraging of different viewpoints than they were a century ago. It is a universal change that is far more pronounced than the differences that remain in education, such as the rural versus urban divide in performance. The openness to new ideas is a hallmark of modern learning. As a result, young adults are more articulate, more confident, and less intimidated. But more important, society benefits because individuals who have been educated in this way sustain frame pluralism.

To be sure, more can and should be done, especially in places that lag behind. Creating a classroom experience that embraces different perspectives is challenging for teachers, who may have grown up in less permissible climes. Having one's views questioned requires knowing more, in particular knowing the viewpoints' strengths and weaknesses. It also requires skills of managing discussions and a willingness to potentially accept the superiority of another's view. That's a tall order for a profession already struggling to manage the growth of knowledge, more administrative tasks, and fewer resources. It's tempting to feel certain of one's views when the entire class is nodding and taking notes.

Challenging ideas and accepting the legitimacy of the clash is at the heart of the open society. Recruiters have long argued that liberal-arts graduates with a solid academic background enjoy an advantage in the job market. This suggests that a central task of higher education isn't necessarily skills training but facilitation of cognitive diversity: not what to think but how to think. This helps individuals become better framers. But from a broader standpoint, it deputizes the next generation to guarantee frame pluralism in our society.

How we teach people to accept that there can be multiple lenses through which to see the world will be crucial: seeing and cele-brating the differences rather than ignoring or hiding them. By rendering them overt, it dignifies the differences; it honors and legitimates them. We can talk about what we can see. A fascinating area of sociological research where this comes into play is the stark difference between how some white and black American parents talk to their children about race.

Well-meaning white parents tend not to point out race or bring up racial issues, in the belief that such "color-blind" behavior will lead to nonracist children. The message, channeling Martin Luther King Jr., is that a person's character counts, not the color of their skin. But black parents regularly discuss race and racial matters with their children. To be color-blind is to willfully ignore the obvious—and fail to see how it affects everyday life, from walking down a store aisle to being pulled over for a traffic stop. Black kids are taught to see the "colorful," to be aware of race.

Sociologists believe that "color-blindness," as a frame, is actually a significant source of racial discrimination. By suggesting that race all of a sudden should not matter, white people with the best intentions are inadvertently denying the experience of people of color who live with daily discrimination. The frame of absolute color-blindness erases variation and disregards diversity, turning a rainbow into in-distinguishable shades of gray. It neglects the reality that people live and vaunts homogeneity, the very opposite of frame pluralism.

The alternative frame, "colorfulness" (in the words of sociologists of race), not only acknowledges variation but in so doing highlights the pain, hardships, and tensions that the differences signify, eventu-ally translating them into the diversity that human framing thrives on. The goal of education and socialization is to see the actual differ-ences in our society as both a responsibility and an opportunity.

A third set of measures to foster frame pluralism is in the domain of migration and mobility. The more that people carry their culture and ways of thinking from one place to another—where they can mix and metamorphize—the more the environment is enriched and different frames can flourish. Throughout history, hubs of fresh, dynamic thinking have regularly cropped up, from Athens and Rome to innovative clusters like seventeenth-century Cremona for violins. Paris's Latin Quarter got its name because it was a crossroads for scholars from all over Europe who spoke Latin to communicate.

What makes mobility and migration so important is the openness that it presupposes. In the early 2000s Richard Florida, an urban theorist, considered the factors that undergird the economic success or failure of regions and urban areas. He trumpeted his findings in a book, *The Rise of the Creative Class*, where he examined a vast set of metrics to tease out what was behind the success. Three elements stood out: technology, talent, and tolerance.

The last one, tolerance, is the linchpin. The places that were most open performed best. "They have a bigger mental map, if you will. They are the kinds of places that enable people to take risks, that don't have this homogenous outlook," Florida said. The creative class moves to areas that are more tolerant and open. It is an early indicator of diversity and pluralism—and of the economic dividend that frame pluralism creates.

However, openness requires long-term commitments. As relatively tolerant cities like Dubai and Singapore (tolerant, that is, compared to their geographic neighbors) have found out, the best of the creative class is hypermobile. They will decamp quickly when tolerance is not sustained. Rather than going after these hypermobile creative elites, it may be more sensible to signal sufficient openness to those willing to come and stay for good.

At a larger scale, an entire society's frame pluralism can also be deliberately influenced by migration. With birth rates low in many advanced economies, immigration is one way to replenish the population. But societies differ in their expectations of immigrants. In continental Europe, for instance, significant public spending programs have been in place for decades to help new immigrants assimilate quickly. The goal is for them to blend in—the right strategy when the economy needs additional hands and society has no interest in increased tensions.

When Europe received millions of immigrants, mostly from the Middle East and Africa starting around 2015, pundits predicted that the influx would change the relative homogeneity of many European nations and lead to societal tensions. They were right: it did. Diversity is not costless.

However, from a human framing point of view, the influx may turn out to be a blessing in disguise. There is now more cultural diversity in Europe than there has been in decades. More cultural diversity translates into more frame pluralism. It insulates European nations from the threat of cognitive monocultures by facilitating many new perspectives. It is not so vital during times of stability, when the sailing is smooth and no reframing is necessary. But it is crucially important when circumstances change and switching to alternative frames is imperative, say, if society faces existential environmental challenges, a catastrophic pandemic, or canyons of economic inequalities.

The United States, in contrast, is balancing the myth of the "melting pot" with the "stew," where the individual pieces remain distinct. One can live comfortably in Koreatown in Los Angeles without speaking a word of English, or in Chinatown in San Francisco, among Latinos in South Texas, Cubans in Florida, or Brazilians in Boston. It slows the pace of assimilation, but gives the United States a sustained diversity dividend. The outsider sees things that insiders do not and can use their novel frames to their advantage.

Think about it: Google cofounder Sergey Brin was born in Russia, as was conservative darling and author Ayn Rand. Microsoft CEO Satya Nadella is Indian, and so is Google's CEO, Sundar Pichai. Google's CFO, Ruth Porat, is British; Elon Musk, of Tesla and SpaceX fame, is South African; aerospace entrepreneur turned astronaut Anousheh Ansari is Iranian. Media czar Rupert Murdoch is from Australia. Intel cofounder Andy Grove was born in Hungary, and NVIDIA cofounder Jen-Hsun Huang in Taiwan. Outspoken venture capitalist Peter Thiel was born in Germany, as was actor Bruce Willis. Steve Jobs's father immigrated from Syria. Only Barack Obama is a naturally born American.

They all broke a mold and became models for others to follow. And by doing so enhanced America's frame pluralism and ensured the country's ability to tap into a rich and varied repertoire of mental models. This is especially useful as the country faces tensions over the wide spectrum of identities that characterize American political and social life.

Pluralism has a price. Fittingly, friction is the final domain to foster frame pluralism. The discord produced by the collision of different frames can be transformed from a drawback to an advantage.

Maintaining a pluralism of frames in a society will cause unease and conflict among its members. It explicitly relies on people seeing and interacting with people with whom they do not agree. This will prompt discussions and debate, but may very well aggravate tensions. After all, that is the normal course of life when people with different perspectives confront each other. If there is no clear hierarchy or priority of frames in a society (be it emperor, pope, or king), choosing the ones that society should adopt is left to the people (be it as consumers, citizens, etc.). If one values tranquility, predictability, and efficiency, then the prospect of robust societal disagreement may sound frightening.

Yet it also signifies the energy and motivation to shape a society's trajectory. The opportunity lies in channeling this friction in a suitable path—not by putting a lid on it, or papering over it, but by embracing debate and accepting the existence of different and conflicting views. This has been an ideal for centuries—the bedrock of liberalism (in the classical, not the American, meaning), which is the liberty to reimagine and voice disagreement. But after the horrors of the Second World War, ensuring that society not only allowed but actively promoted and protected differences became a priority.

The friction produced when one frame rubs up against another one happens in the "public sphere," in the words of the German philosopher Jürgen Habermas. It is the space where individuals meet and debate societal issues. Don't think rarefied Oxford debates but those in pubs and coffee shops, associations and clubs. Friction can be productive when it occurs in these places.

The issue is that societal debates have shifted from regular people to professional politicians, media pundits, and other public voices—that is, direct democracy has been replaced by representative democracy. This deprives people of active, personal participation. Political debate becomes theatrical battles fought by proxies representing people's views rather than by the people themselves. In this respect, Americans outsourced their critical faculties and political voices to Fox's Tucker Carlson on the right and MSNBC's Rachel Maddow on the left to slug it out for them. But America isn't alone. This is a tension in societies everywhere, from the *Yomiuri* versus *Asahi* newspapers in Japan to the squabbles between the French intellectuals Bernard-Henri Lévy and Michel Houellebecq.

We need to revive the public sphere, where frames are rendered apparent and can clash, collide, and combine. Central to that, argued Habermas, are activists and groups that get people involved in public matters and energize individuals to engage in civic debates. The activity lets society harness the power of diversity to discuss and decide in which direction to go. Deliberative democracy—combining elements of both consensus decision-making and majority rule— makes discussion central to the political process. Proponents have advocated for adoption of a "deliberation day," which would bring people in many communities together on a public holiday, perhaps even compensating them in return for their willingness to discuss public issues. The goal is to entice more citizens to engage in the kind of talkative tussle that is the foundation of democratic governance.

In a more modest version a diverse set of individuals is brought together to deliberate on an important policy issue. The participants are polled before the discussion begins and at the end. Briefing materials and experts are provided to answer questions and offer input. Views are permitted to clash. While there is no expectation of a consensus, there is an expectation of earnest engagement and consideration of one another's views. Deliberative polls have been held in dozens of nations, and one was even made into a TV program in Britain in 1994 called *Power and the People*.

Another way to deepen political participation and turn friction into a benefit is a concept called "empowered" democracy. It is advanced by Roberto Unger, a vibrant and original thinker on alternative social orders at Harvard Law School. He calls for "raising the temperature of politics" by actively bringing together different mental models. For example, he advocates greater political decentralization "to create 'counter-models' of the national future."

"As a society advances decisively along a certain path it should be able to hedge its bets and to allow particular localities or sectors to secede from general solutions and to undertake experiments that point in a different national direction," he explains.

Unger vaults frame friction everywhere. On education he believes it should be "dialectical: that every subject be taught from at least two contrasting points of view"—a value he shares with Podolny at Apple University. The idea is to ensure that society "not be pinned down to a single version of itself—that we be able to experiment with alternative ways of organizing."

The friction that results from pluralism need not be regarded as a threat but can be productively channeled for societal advantage—provided there is a sense of a common future. At a time when it is easy to feel despair, our point is an optimistic one: we are not buffeted by forces beyond our control. On the contrary, as framers we are armed with strategies to build the society we want.

Charging Bull, Fearless Girl

Hannah Arendt died in Manhattan in 1975 shortly after her sixty-ninth birthday. Until the end, she worried that the "plurality of standpoints," so vital to protect, was dissipating. She disliked the fact that there was an absence of societal mechanisms to learn and benefit from others' framing. But the foundation had been laid. Judith Shklar built atop it.

Like Arendt, Shklar was a Jewish war refugee (though some twenty years younger). She too was a political philosopher in a male environment. Four years before Arendt died, Shklar became the first woman to receive tenure in Harvard's Department of Government, albeit fifteen years after she joined the faculty. Shklar and Arendt shared a distaste for individual rights—not because individual rights are wrong, but because they are insufficient. A pluralism of views can't be guaranteed through individual rights alone.

Instead, as Shklar pointed out (and as we have explained in this chapter), it requires the creation and maintenance of the right societal conditions for a pluralism of frames. That is what she meant when she wrote, in a landmark essay in 1989, that "every adult should be able to make as many effective decisions without fear or favor about as many aspects of her or his life." Arendt emphasized "thinking" and "actions"; Shklar stressed "decisions without fear."

Arendt and Shklar differed in some of their views. The younger philosopher particularly disliked Arendt's theoretical ideas about freedom without offering practical ways that the freedom could be realized. But they were united in highlighting pluralism rather than majority rule, and emphasizing conditions rather than rights. For Shklar, societal progress is directly correlated with the absence of fear, correlated with possessing not just an abstract right, but the concrete ability for humans to rise, and to stand up against power fearlessly. Only then is a pluralism of frames realized.

A tangible symbol of Shklar's pluralism of frames might be the confrontation of two statues near Wall Street in New York. Since 1989, *Charging Bull*, a hulking 7,100-pound bronze statue, measuring eleven feet tall and sixteen feet long, has stood beside a small park in the financial district. With nostrils flaring, tail whipping, and head lowered to gore, it's a potent symbol of aggressive capitalism. Yet on March 7, 2017, another bronze statue was placed in front of the bull. This one was just four feet high and weighed a mere 250 pounds.

Staring down the bull was *Fearless Girl*, by the sculptor Kristen Visbal. With her head held high, chin jutting out, ponytail billowing, and hands defiantly on her hips in a "power pose," the petite figure was a symbolic counterpoint to the raging beast in front of her. The juxtaposition of statues represented the plurality of frames. It did not reflect power versus impotence but coexistence. There was no obvious hierarchy, no status differentiation. Both were legitimate. Yet there is no doubt who was stronger.

As statues around the world, from General Robert E. Lee in America to King Leopold II in Belgium, were defaced and toppled in the summer of 2020, the face-off between *Charging Bull* and *Fearless Girl* offers a lesson that Arendt and Shklar would appreciate. One need not feel powerless before a great force but can stand alongside it, provided the conditions instill a sense of fearlessness. Pluralism, the objective, can only exist if there is confidence, not fear. But who possesses such confidence?

9

vigilance

we must remain on guard not to cede our power

In the spring of 2020, as America's Covid-19 lockdown began in earnest, a series of short TikTok videos went viral on social media. The chaotic word salad sounded familiar, as did the raspy voice: "We hit the body with a tremendous—whether it's ultraviolet, or just very powerful light." But the words emanated from the youthful, dynamic Sarah Cooper, lip-synching the proposed Covid-19 remedy of Donald Trump. "Supposing you brought the light inside the body, which you can do either through the skin or in some other way . . . Sounds interesting, right? And then I see the disinfectant, which knocks it out in a minute."

The effect was stunning. Other comedians have tried to impersonate Trump by imitating him physically, down to his girth, red cap, and comb-over. Cooper's art was shrewder: she played his actual voice and stuck to her real self in all other ways. Cooper is everything that Trump is not: a young svelte black woman mimicking an old chunky white man. She made us stop short and rethink our assumptions.

Changing the constraints in this way, in order to imagine an alternative reality, makes all the difference. The effect is revealing; what is spoken becomes shocking. The method, she explains, was deliberate. "What I did was basically, *What if I, Sarah Cooper, said these words?* Like I really believe that this is a valid idea," she says. "I had taken away the suit and the podium and the people behind him smiling and nodding and calling him sir, and all that was left were his empty words."

Cooper reframed comic impersonation, by completely abandoning the constraints of looking like the person being mocked. This is comedy that exposes rather than imitates. Like the fearless girl staring down the charging bull, an unknown comedian took on America's president. She attained the highest mark of professional success: Trump blocked her on Twitter.

Then there is Nie Yunchen.

In 2012, after leaving school at nineteen in Jiangmen, a city in southern China, Nie looked for a business idea to change the world. He noticed that tea, a mainstay of Chinese history and culture, wasn't popular among his peers. It was either too expensive and marketed to the elderly, or a cheap, bland concoction made of instant tea and powdered milk. Companies spent handsomely marketing a product that no one especially liked.

Nie realized that the tea business, like any enterprise, could be refashioned, and he played with the constraints to conjure up a new counterfactual of what a tea business could be. With a few thousand dollars, he opened up a shop in Jiangmen called Heytea that catered to hip Chinese. The teas were affordable but were brewed from premium tea leaves, used real milk, and came in innovative flavors. Nie covered the cost of the fancy ingredients by resisting traditional marketing campaigns and spread the word via social media.

Heytea was a hit. More shops opened. They were bright and

sparse, their design signaling quality and freshness. People would queue for hours to try the flavored teas. By 2020 there were more than four hundred Heytea shops in China, the company was branching out internationally, and the business had earned Nie more than half a billion dollars before he was thirty.

Where Starbucks founder Howard Shultz made coffee a gourmet item and his stores a "third place" between home and work, Nie did something different. He tapped into cultural pride and the demand for quality among style-conscious youth to create a brand in tune with the times. Nie stayed within the frame of the classical Chinese teahouse but refashioned it for a new generation. In so doing, he reacquainted young Chinese with an old custom.

A third successful framer is Nthabiseng Mosia, a South African–Ghanaian entrepreneur bringing electricity to Africa.

Growing up in a township outside Johannesburg, Mosia learned the importance of dependable electricity early on. "The national grid would occasionally go down in my home, leaving my family and I scrounging around in the dark," she said. "Suddenly you're like, 'Oh wait! I can't do all the things that I need and want to do!' It was around the time of my high school exams, so I was studying by candlelight on some nights."

After grad school in America, she moved to Sierra Leone in West Africa. Around 85 percent of people in the region lack electricity. Because they live in mostly rural areas, it's not feasible to connect them to the grid. So they're stuck using dangerous and toxic kerosene lanterns for light, and having to travel to charge their mobile phones. Mosia realized that instead of trying to expand the national power grid, people could get power directly with inexpensive solar panels.

So Mosia and two cofounders created Easy Solar in 2016. It provides sets of solar panels and batteries to power lighting and home appliances. Yet even though the system is affordable, most people can't buy it outright. But they are familiar with the "pay as you go" plans of mobile phone operators. So Mosia and her colleagues asked, what if customers don't have to pay in full for the kits right away but can pay for them over time? Easy Solar adapted its business model by offering a clever financing plan: customers use their kit till the cost is paid, and then they own it.

By 2020 Easy Solar was providing power to 300,000 households serving nearly half a million people, letting small businesses stay open later, improving the security of homes and farms at night, and giving students an easier time studying—as Mosia had wished for. The innovation wasn't technical. It repurposed a business model from the mobile phone industry to make power generation not only decentralized and dependable but affordable too.

The American comedian Sarah Cooper, the Chinese business-man Nie Yunchen, and the African impact-entrepreneur Nthabiseng Mosia are all framers. They played with mental models to devise new alternatives, which exposed different choices, led to better decisions, and created successful outcomes. And they were unafraid to consider what the world could be rather than being content with what it already was.

While none of them changed the course of rivers, discovered a new law of physics, or left a dent in the universe that had humanity gaping in awe, they made choices that matter. An essential message of this book is that framing can happen at all levels, commoner or king, and still shape our world. It happens more frequently than we think. We lose out if we focus only on the exceptional acts of paradigm-shattering reframers. Instead, we need to celebrate humanity's widespread capacity to frame.

Framing requires skill. It benefits from training and experience. But framing also requires cognitive diversity and a mind-set that is open to the new. Successful framers aren't only old and wise, or audacious and young. The capacity to frame well is an ability that transcends obvious categories like age, gender, education, income, and occupation. Good framers are rare, but they can be found everywhere.

Thinking New, Thinking Different

Human progress is typically measured through the lens of human cooperation. By working together, people advance their societies. We build cities, travel oceans, explore the heavens. Roman roads and the Chinese wall; courts of law and blockchain updates. Whether in the form of infrastructure, institutions, or inventions, society's achievements are attributed to the organization and coordination of people. For good reason too. Most of what people do and know cannot be captured in a single mind. It takes a village, today a global village, to achieve humanity's potential.

We may believe the answer to our problems is to double down on human coordination in the future. All we need is to link together more and better. For the historian Yuval Noah Harari, human coordination marks not just the apex of our past but the elixir of our future. Speaking with Facebook's boss Mark Zuckerberg in 2019, he argued, "We need global cooperation like never before because we are facing unprecedented global problems."

Yet this is only half the story. Inside every achievement is an idea; embedded in each monument is a mental model. Our economic, scientific, and social successes stem from our ability to comprehend and conceptualize, to see what is and what can be, and to connect our ideas with our actions. It is the actual basis of human betterment, underpinning the Wright brothers' liftoff and Neil Armstrong's giant leap.

Why, then, have we focused so much on coordination and so little on the cognitive process underlying it?

To an extent, the fixation on coordination is understandable: it is visible and obvious. It is something we can easily shape and directly influence. In contrast, our cognitive processes are locked in our heads. For most of human history, we were unable to peek into the minds of people. The philosopher and the shaman could eloquently ponder the results of their introspection and speculate about the cognitive processes of others. But for the rest of us, it was a great unknown. Human framing remained a black box—a process, the consequences of which we experienced, but without real knowledge of its inner workings. We had neither the methods nor the concepts to plumb those cognitive depths. We barely had a language to describe it.

That changed only about a century ago. Cognitive science, neuroscience, and decision science are subjects that began to blossom in the early 1900s, with powerful new methods and concepts to understand the mind. Much of the research we've highlighted stems from the past three decades, and important discoveries made more recently still. Though we have always been human framers, only now can we appreciate what this means.

This is hugely consequential, as humanity's gaze is shifting from human interaction that undergirds coordination to human framing that prompts better decisions. It is a change in focus from the interpersonal to the personal, from the organizational to the individual. Cooperation still matters, but framing matters more. It is emerging as the central lever for how humanity can improve its lot.

This gives reason to cheer. By appreciating the power of framing and learning how to get better at it, we can enhance our decision-making—thereby improving our lives, our communities, our societies, and civilization. By understanding the ingredients of successful framing, we also have identified essential tools to evolve our framing skills. Most important, framing offers human beings the scarcest of treasures: hope.

And yet . . .

Diverse models are not always embraced. Yes, people have never been able to tap as numerous and varied frames as today. Yes, the flow of information, vital for cooperation, produces huge benefits. Yes, cognitive diversity makes us better framers. However, we at times squander this inheritance. We feel uncomfortable with the unfamiliar. Confronted with a cornucopia of alien frames, we retreat to the ones we know best.

Globally, but especially in America, "ideological silos" have become common across the spectrum. In the United States, those with strongly held views increasingly say that they want to live in places where the people around them share their opinions. In 1980 areas with a dominant ideological frame made up 4 percent of the country. By 2016 this had grown to 30 percent, and by 2020 it had increased to 35 percent, according to the Pew Research Center.

With ideas, as with diets, there is a chasm between what we crave and what sustains us. It may soothe our souls to be surrounded by those who agree with us, but to be good at framing we need to expose ourselves to diverse perspectives that challenge our own. Cognitive homogeneity is the death of a wide spectrum of counterfactuals. Uniformity is the end of successful framing.

The stakes have never been higher. The difficulties before us are profound: from climate to conflict; racial inequality to economic inequity; pandemics to populism and algorithmic authoritarianism. For some, the past half century has been a time of certainty, stability, and relative comfort. Yet in the arc of human history, that period is over.

Our generation's curse is to confront a transition to more troubling times. On the near horizon is a dark period when the pathologies that our progress has produced must be addressed, else they risk eradicating us. As we face the gravity of the challenges—as societies and as a species—we can no longer be simply guided by our past but must fix our vision on our potentialities. For that, both emotional impulses and AI-inspired answers fail us. Our ability to cooperate, so essential in the past, is now only part of the answer.

We may not know the solutions to the problems before us, but we know how to go about finding them. The response of humanity cannot be to acquiesce, or wish for gifts from the gods, or abandon action due to a failure to reach a decision. Before it will take cooperation, it will need new conceptions. The answer is to embrace what humans do well, to cherish our unique cognitive capabilities, and to refocus our minds on our ability to frame.

Framing the Universe and Ourselves

"We do not see things as they are. We see things as we are," goes a saying attributed to the Talmud, the Jewish book of law. We have made the case that our frames are the foundation of our thought, they direct how we size up reality and how we choose to act. We understand the world through mental models and use them to imagine alternative realities. This offers us an intellectual richness and variety no other species possesses. Our framing makes us unique.

Framing combines two distinct processes. The first, applying a frame, entails thinking with causality, counterfactuals, and constraints. It is ideal for efficiently identifying valuable options and preparing for swift action. Applying a frame is how we spend most of our time, and with good reason: it is the most effective way to help us make decisions in situations that are at least somewhat familiar. And we are good at it; it's a skill that we begin honing in early childhood. The effective application of frames is the secret ingredient in the stream of continuous, incremental improvements across human history.

The second process involves switching to a different frame. It is far riskier but may offer bigger rewards by letting us see reality differently. A new perspective begets alternative options for our decisions and may open up new ways of responding to a challenge. We don't need to reframe when a situation is stable and circumstances are constant. But when the context changes, reframing is often a good strategy.

Whether we choose a different frame from our repertoire, repurpose a frame from another context, or invent a new frame altogether, the act of reframing has us jettison a mental model that no longer works, so we can better conceptualize the problem we face. It's like seeing the world through somebody else's eyes: it opens our mind and helps us to cast aside the limitations of our conventional thinking.

Reframers, especially those who devise an entirely new frame, are often hailed for their accomplishments. Throughout history, societies have celebrated their successes in part because they change the world, and in part because they are relatively rare. There is no obvious linear path to follow to develop this skill. Reframing depends on an unpredictable aha moment to strike. Practice doesn't help. Yet there are strategies we can harness to get better at reframing.

By having a language to think about framing and a method to work with frames, people can become better at it. In so doing, it transforms a process of cognition into a tool for action.

Still, despite the obvious advantages, the emotionalists and the hyper-rationalists reject the power of framing. Emotionalists charge that the mainstream over-intellectualizes everything. In contrast, they feel simpler is better: it's authentic, faster, gets results. Those driven by emotion argue it's more suitable to follow impulse—and make decisions without the fuss of weighing every iota of an issue.

It's not a left-right thing: the appeal of emotionalism transcends ideological categorization. Emotionalists are found among liberals who oppose vaccines and conservatives who reject global warming. Both sides revel in extremes—but understood more deeply, both appeal to emotions. Stripped of the content, the sentiment is an expression of essentially the same frame.

And it is global. In Peru in 2020 a president is ousted after five days as the country is gripped by a popular uprising, while Bolivia's former president (accused of vote rigging) triumphantly returns from exile, advocating a populist revolution against moderates. In the Philippines, President Rodrigo Duterte called on citizens to simply kill suspected drug dealers and saw his popularity soar. In Germany, some emotionalists call themselves *Querdenker* or "lateral thinkers" and protest Covid-19 lockdown measures and mask mandates. With a touch of nostalgia (and a dose of anti-Semitism) they wave flags of the German Empire from before the First World War. The emotional seems on the ascendency and the Enlightenment in descent.

However, the solutions that the emotionalists advocate are odd cognitive concoctions. They are ostensibly put forward as alternatives to "dangerous" deliberate framing—but in so doing, the emotionalists can't help but frame themselves. How they interpret the world is a mental model. Despite the rhetoric, emotionalists aren't anti-framers: they're just bad at framing. That doesn't make their causes irrelevant or suggest they don't honestly believe what they say. It simply means that they are not using the full cognitive powers that their minds offer.

The situation is different for the group skeptical of the human endeavor of framing, the hyper-rationalists. They see humanity as a lost cause, forever trapped in the flaws of its thinking. For them, the answer lies not in emotion but in silicon; not impulse but in evidence. Their hope is that by relying on technology, society can outsource the decisions it must make. They aspire to replace imperfect human framing with the rational power of data and algorithms. But that is not just shortsighted; it misconceives the role of humans and AI.

Recall how Regina Barzilay, who used AI to discover an antibiotic, explained that the real breakthrough was not the machine's number crunching but humans adjusting mental models. In fact, human framing has been an essential feature in every case of AI's supposed superiority, from playing Go, chess, and *Dota 2* to Daniel Dennett's fictional robot, Waymo's Carcraft, and Cheng-Zhi Anna Huang's harmonious Coconet. The vital attribute is framing, the necessary element to produce novel but generalizable insight.

This leads to a striking conclusion: rather than undermine mental models, AI reinforces their significance. Since the systems cannot frame or reframe by themselves, they depend on human beings. Robots will certainly take over many jobs, and algorithms will make decisions affecting all of us. But instead of sidelining people, AI actually reaffirms humanity's place at the center—so long as individuals embrace and hone their framing. We will be needed to manage the machines.

François Chollet, a rising star in AI, expresses it neatly: "This ability to handle hypotheticals, to expand our mental model space far beyond what we can experience directly—to perform *abstraction* and *reasoning*—is arguably the defining characteristic of human cognition." Chollet refers to it as "extreme generalization," that is, "an ability to adapt to novel, never-before-experienced situations using little data or even no new data at all."

This is both a redemption and a warning for humanity. Through our ability to frame, we matter; but if we give up on being good framers, we stand to lose our privileged position.

As AI continues to evolve, identifying patterns in data at a speed, scale, and accuracy far greater than that of humans, we will apply it to an increasing array of situations. It's hard to imagine how we are going to feed the planet, care for its sick, and power our glistening Teslas without AI embedded in all that we do. So framing will be more important, not less.

As we make a plea for framing, as an antidote to the emotionalists and the rationalists, we need to acknowledge the danger of using badly formed mental models, or using them in the wrong way. If we aren't careful, it prompts bad decisions and actions—but at its worst, it begets horrors.

A Rigidity of Frames

On November 13, 2015, at around ten o'clock in the evening, shots rang out at the Bataclan, a live-music venue in Paris. Some of the roughly fifteen hundred young people in the audience initially thought the noise and small spurts of flame were part of the heavy-metal act. But after a few seconds it was clear that they weren't. Three terrorists had stormed the building with M70 assault rifles and opened fire. Bodies were ripped open by the spray and began piling up on the floor. Those scrambling to escape were mowed down. Screams filled the darkness as the assailants reloaded and resumed the fusillade.

It was a night of terror across Paris. At roughly the same time, three terrorists detonated suicide vests outside the city's big stadium, where the national soccer team was playing Germany. Another group drove through parts of the city shooting into restaurants. Back at the Bataclan, the terrorists took twenty hostages. When a police raid began, they blew themselves up. One could only be identified by his fingertip. In the end, 130 people were killed and hundreds wounded.

The French began a manhunt to find those responsible. Many of the terrorists were known to the police, and some had been under surveillance. So establishing connections, suspects, and accomplices wasn't too hard. The police quickly settled on Abdelhamid Abaaoud, twenty-eight, as the leader. Born in Belgium of Moroccan descent, he had fought in Syria and was accused of previous terror attacks in Europe. Five days after the terrible night, around one hundred police descended on an apartment in the northern suburbs of Paris. After an hour-long shootout and explosions, Abaaoud was dead.

There is a commonly held view that terrorists act irrationally and illogically. It is easy to come to this conclusion, since it is hard for most people to comprehend their motivation to kill as indiscriminately and as dispassionately as they did on that dark night at the Bataclan. But according to recent studies, many terrorists aren't irrationally following their instincts but are just the opposite: coolly rational in their grotesque violence.

Terrorists typically are deliberate, even meticulous, framers. They apply a carefully crafted mental model to the world. In the words of Gérald Bronner, a sociologist at Université de Paris who has studied "extreme thinking," terrorists possess an "almost inhuman consistency" and "mechanical rationality, accepting no compromise."

Abaaoud falls into this category. Everything that happened to him, he explains as a gift from Allah. When he tried to enter the country while wanted by Belgian authorities, an immigration officer stopped him and compared him to a photo, but let him pass. The officer was "blinded by Allah," Abaaoud told *Dabiq*, an Islamic-militant magazine, before the Paris attack. When Belgian commandos raided an apartment he was occupying, two associates were killed but he slipped away.

"All this was arranged by Allah," he explained. The mental model of how reality unfolded was applied squarely, even if its substance was amiss, from causality to counterfactuals to constraints.

When terrorists frame, they cripple a key element, flexibility. Our mental models need to be adjusted, amended, and challenged to unleash the cognitive power within them. In contrast, terrorists, though believing to act rationally, see no room to deviate in their minds. They are incapable of adjusting their frames and instead take them as the sole way to view the world.

In fact, research has suggested that terrorists despise others precisely because ordinary people are ready to make these adjustments. They judge this cognitive flexibility as a form of corruption, while they see the rigidity of their framing as a form of purity and order. Where for most people their framing is a source of their personal agency, for terrorists, it eliminates their free will. They happily abandon it in pursuit of their ideals. Reality for them becomes "simpler and clearer," explains Bronner.

Even when we deduce actions from counterfactual thinking under constraints, even when we feel we frame well, we can be terribly, shockingly wrong. We may believe we think perfectly rationally, but the options we elicit are gray reflections of the true rainbow of alternatives. Instead of helping us be agents in a malleable world, overly rigid frames turn us into blind executioners of bastardized reasoning.

This is just one of many ways that our rational framing can confine us. But what greatly adds to the danger that results from such framing is that we believe we acted perfectly logically, that we consciously framed just as we should. The deeply flawed nature of our decisions is hidden behind a veneer of seeming reason, making it harder for us to escape and for others to comprehend. Framing done poorly is more dangerous and consequential than disregarding framing altogether, because it presumes to be right—and is therefore doubly mistaken.

Human framing requires our vigilance. Only done well will it yield its power. But how do we ensure that?

Agility of Mind

The free flow of information has been the filament of cooperation and the fertilizer of collaboration. It's what makes markets function efficiently and enables science to iterate and improve. Stunting the flow of ideas stifles human progress. When this has happened in the past, it has inflicted colossal suffering—from burning books to burning people. To encourage, maintain, and protect the flow of knowledge, societies have enacted rules, created institutions, and established processes.

We see it in disclosure requirements for public companies and for environmental polluters. We recognize it in the transparency of parliaments and courts. It permeates the rules of business transactions and the principles of scientific accountability. Tenure emerged so scholars could study and speak without unjust restraint. It's guaranteed in modern constitutions as the freedom of expression.

However, today, as the essential element of progress is not so much cooperation but cognition, our focus needs to shift too, from outward information flows to inward decision-making. The onus is on imagining alternative realities, not just working together in common cause. This raises the question, what is the new principle for the twenty-first century that deserves protecting—our generation's equivalent to the free flow of information?

What needs to be nurtured is the intellectual nimbleness to conceive of the unarticulated idea, the unspoken ideal, the latent notion, and the new reality locked in potentiality. For framing to be successful, what is required is *agility of mind*.

This is not simply being open to new ideas, nor is it mental flexibility or cognitive diversity. Rather, we mean something more profound. It is a plasticity and elasticity of how we conceive—and reconceive—the world. It is the idea that the pathways of our thoughts are fundamentally adaptable, not fixed. It is the conviction that our thinking is not limited to following the cognitive steps we have taken before; that our mind can venture into new directions, and even after having taken the same mental steps a thousand times, we can make a new mental leap if we wish. We can "hold two opposing ideas in mind at the same time," in F. Scott Fitzgerald's famous formulation.

The principle rests on our mind's deep-seated ability to think beyond the obvious and the familiar. We have the capability to dream with a purpose, to push our imagination a particular way, to give it direction without unduly shackling it down to the known and the common. It is a mental alchemy that transforms the old into the new; the past into the future; the base into the precious.

Agility of mind is not a given; it is something we have to work for. To obtain and sustain it, we need to train it. We do this by continually nurturing our curiosity for new perspectives, including the courage to disagree and be disagreed with.

Consider it similar to a gymnast or dancer who can twist, bend, or undulate his body to produce a new form. Or a sprinter whose every motion propels her faster. Most people have the same physical capacity—torso, arms, legs, and so on—but not the same ability or honed physique. We can run when we need to, but it takes training and discipline to sprint like an athlete. Few of us can contort our bodies like a professional dancer. But we could with dedicated practice.

So too agility of mind: we all have the capacity but not the ability, unless we prepare. It takes serious effort. It's not a utopian aspiration but a state we can attain. We possess the right strategy framing, the mental models that have gone from being an ordinary aspect of cognition to a powerful tool we can use to improve our lives. But we need to work to develop our agility of mind: to stretch our conceptions and conceptualizations and incorporate the frames of others, or ones not yet conceived, to appreciate different perspectives and values, and devise new alternatives when confronted with new problems.

Framers see the world not as it is, but as it can be. They do this by understanding, considering, rejecting, or accepting frames and communicating them to others. The principle of agility of mind asks us to never stop honing our skills of framing: seeing causation, generating a variety of counterfactuals and altering their features— in short, dreaming with constraints. Just as the free flow of information is the basis of interpersonal coordination, agility of mind is the foundation of human framing.

Information flows were enabled by processes and institutions, much as societies can facilitate agility of mind by creating the right environment for it to flourish. We can adjust our educational system so that children not only acquire the skills to frame, but develop a thirst for it. We can revisit policies from immigration to labor laws to economic development to bolster our exposure to new ideas. We can even consider fashioning innovative participatory processes to foster agile minds; the "deliberative democracy" programs could play a part. And there is much more, from economic incentives for older people to intensify their mental agility to initiatives that purposefully expose individuals to very different perspectives. Perhaps we even need a new foundation or government agency dedicated to agility of mind. . . . But of course, that somewhat misses the point.

Though these programs and policies are helpful, we must not

forget that unlike human coordination, human framing takes place within. Societal institutions and processes can't do the cognitive heavy lifting for us. Agility of mind is a project for all of us, individually. Framers frame frames, organizations don't.

The frontiers of our imagination are the boundaries of our world. Humanity is not locked into one reality but can enjoy any it decides to create. The power is within us, by how we conceive of and conceptualize our world and lives—all that we are, and all that we hope to be. We thrive through cooperation but we can only survive as framers.

a guide to working with frames

I. Harness mental models

Framing happens all the time but can deliberately be used to improve decisions.

- Identify and inspect the assumptions in your mental models.
- Ask "why" and "how" questions: Why did you reach this conclusion? How must the world work if you anticipate this happening?
- Imagine how a wise friend, a historical hero, or a rival might frame a certain challenge.
- Ask yourself what would need to change for you to want to frame a situation differently.
- When your views clash with another's, try to characterize the underlying way they see the world.

II. Dream with constraints

Applying a frame is about swiftly and efficiently identifying appropriate options.

- Focus on those elements that are most easily changeable.
- Start by making minimal changes to your constraints, and gradually contemplate more elaborate modifications.
- Be careful to remain consistent by weighing whether the change contradicts any underlying assumptions or beliefs.
- Embed constraints in a physical model if it is too difficult to keep all of them in mind at once.

III. Reframe wisely

Switching to an alternative frame lets you see the world differently, but it is risky.

- See if you already have a frame in your repertoire that will work.
- Try repurposing a frame that you can apply from a different domain.
- Invent a new frame as a last resort, since it's the hardest option.
- Keep in mind the trade-offs between tight frames (fast but limited) and broad ones (comprehensive but time-consuming).
- Don't reframe repeatedly, since it leads to disorientation.

IV. Conditions matter

We can improve our framing through cognitive diversity.

- Develop a curiosity for the unfamiliar to continually challenge your worldview.
- Be willing to accept tensions among frames: they are less an indication of faulty reasoning than of the complexity of reality.

- Speak the truth, even when it is not comforting for individuals or organizations. The courage is respected by those who matter.
- Seek dissent rather than confirmation.
- When deciding in teams, have each person frame the problem independently before sharing views and deciding as a group.

V. Think beyond yourself

The role of society is to ensure frame pluralism to produce optimal responses in times of change.

- Strive to see the colorful; don't be color-blind. Speak openly but respectfully about differences.
- Regard societal friction as an advantage, not a drawback.
- Use education to instill respect for others' frames.
- Promote a commingling of cultures as a way to foster imagination, innovation, and dynamism in a society.
- Reject anything that presents itself as a single frame to encompass all of reality.

notes

Quote from Amanda Gorman poem: Recited at the inauguration of President Joe Biden. Amanda Gorman, "The Hill We Climb: The Amanda Gorman Poem That Stole the Inauguration Show," *Guardian*, January 20, 2021, https://www.theguardian.com/us-news/2021/jan/20/amanda-gorman-poem-biden-inauguration-transcript.

1. decisions

On antibiotics in history and resistance: World Health Organization, "New Report Calls for Urgent Action to Avert Antimicrobial Resistance Crisis," joint news release, April 29, 2019, https://www.who.int/news/item/29-04-2019-new-report-calls-for-urgent-action-to-avert-antimicrobial-resistance-crisis. Estimated deaths due to antibiotic resistance: on track to hit ten million by 2050, according to WHO statistics.

On a death every three seconds: Joe Myers, "This Is How Many People Antibiotic Resistance Could Kill Every Year by 2050 If Nothing Is Done," World Economic Forum, September 23, 2016, https://www.weforum.org/agenda/2016/09/this-is-how-many-people-will-die-from-antimicrobial-resistance-every-year-by-2050-if-nothing-is-done/.

Coolidge's son's infection: Chelsea Follett, "U.S. President's Son Dies of an Infected Blister?," HumanProgress, March 1, 2016, https://www.humanprogress.org/u-s-presidents-son-dies-of-an-infected-blister/.

AI to identify antibiotics: Jonathan M. Stokes et al., "A Deep Learning Approach to Antibiotic Discovery," *Cell* 180, no. 4 (February 20, 2020): 688–702.

Barzilay quotes: Regina Barzilay, in an interview with Kenneth Cukier, February and November 2020.

On Colin Kaepernick: Eric Reid, "Why Colin Kaepernick and I Decided to Take a Knee," *New York Times*, September 25, 2017, https://www.nytimes.com/2017/09/25/opinion/colin-kaepernick-football-protests.html.

Fasciculus Medicinae: For body parts associated with zodiac signs, see: "Historical Medical Library," College of Physicians of Philadelphia, accessed November 1, 2020, https://www.cppdigitallibrary.org.

On Lysenkoism: Sam Kean, "The Soviet Era's Deadliest Scientist Is Regaining Popularity in Russia," *Atlantic*, December 19, 2017, https://www.theatlantic.com/science/archive/2017/12/trofim-lysenko-soviet-union-russia/548786/; Edouard I. Kolchinsky et al., "Russia's New Lysenkoism," *Current Biology* 27, no. 19 (October 9, 2017): R1042–47.

On telephone and phonograph framing: Rebecca J. Rosen, "The Magical, Revolutionary Telephone," *Atlantic*, March 7, 2012, https://www.theatlantic.com/technology/archive/2012/03/the-magical-revolutionary-telephone/254149/; "History of the Cylinder Phonograph," Library of Congress, accessed November 10, 2020, https://www.loc.gov/collections/edison-company-motion-pictures-and-sound-recordings/articles-and-essays/history-of-edison-sound-recordings/history-of-the-cylinder-phonograph/.

On Edison and education: Todd Oppenheimer, *The Flickering Mind: Saving Education from the False Promise of Technology* (New York: Random House, 2004).

On Kahneman and Tversky's "framing effect": Amos Tversky and Daniel Kahneman, "The Framing of Decisions and the Psychology of Choice," *Science* 211, no. 4481 (January 30, 1981): 453–58.

On Kuhn's "paradigm shift": Thomas S. Kuhn, *The Structure of Scientific Revolutions* (Chicago: University of Chicago Press, 1962).

On the origin of art perspective: Giorgio Vasari, "The Life of Filippo Brunelleschi, Sculptor and Architect," in *The Lives of the Artists*, trans. Julia C. Bondanella and Peter Bondanella (Oxford: Oxford University Press, 2008), 110–46.

On hyper-rationalists: We refer to a general sentiment and not to a specific group, i.e., the American tech-and-society thinkers called the Rationalists. Klint Finley, "Geeks for Monarchy: The Rise of the Neoreactionaries," *TechCrunch*, November 23, 2013, https://techcrunch.com/2013/11/22/geeks-for-monarchy/?guccounter=1. Also, Cade Metz, "Silicon Valley's Safe Space," *New York Times*, February 13, 2021, https://www.nytimes.com/2021/02/13/technology/slate-star-codex-rationalists.html.

On the singularity: Ray Kurzweil, *The Singularity Is Near: When Humans Transcend Biology* (New York: Viking, 2005).

On AI's potential and limitations: The great AI developer, entrepreneur, and cognitive scientist Gary Marcus is also a great AI critic, pointing out all the ways that current AI technologies are riddled with problems. See Gary Marcus and Ernest Davis, *Rebooting AI: Building Artificial Intelligence We Can Trust* (New York: Pantheon, 2019).

Rousseau quote: Jean-Jacques Rousseau, "Correspondence Générale XVII, 2–3," in *The Question of Jean-Jacques Rousseau*, Ernst Cassirer (Bloomington: Indiana University Press, 1963), quoted in Claes G. Ryn, *Democracy and the Ethical Life: A Philosophy of Politics and Community*, 2nd ed. (Washington, DC: Catholic University of America Press, 1990), 34.

On Welch's gut: Jack Welch, *Jack: Straight from the Gut* (New York: Grand Central, 2003).

On the benefits of using data and statistics: Paul E. Meehl, *Clinical Versus Statistical Prediction: A Theoretical Analysis and a Review of the Evidence* (Minneapolis: University of Minnesota Press, 1954).

On AlphaZero: This section benefited greatly from interviews in March 2019 by Kenneth Cukier with Demis Hassabis of DeepMind, as well as the chess grand master Matthew Sadler and master Natasha Regan, for which the authors extend their thanks.

AlphaZero's specifics on model training: David Silver et al., "A General Reinforcement Learning Algorithm That Masters Chess, Shogi and Go," DeepMind, December 6, 2018, https://deepmind.com/blog/article/alphazero-shedding -new-light-grand-games-chess-shogi-and-go; David Silver et al., "Mastering Chess and Shogi by Self-Play with a General Reinforcement Learning Algorithm," DeepMind, December 5, 2017, https://arxiv.org/pdf/1712.01815.pdf. Note: a successor project to AlphaZero, called MuZero, can learn the rules of a board game by itself. See Julian Schrittwieser et al., "Mastering Atari, Go, Chess and Shogi by Planning with a Learned Model," *Nature* 588, no. 7839 (December 23, 2020): 604–609, https://www.nature.com/articles/s41586-020 -03051-4.

AlphaZero and chess strategy: Matthew Sadler and Natasha Regan, *Game Changer: AlphaZero's Groundbreaking Chess Strategies and the Promise of AI* (Alkmaar, the Netherlands: New in Chess, 2019).

Our World in Data: Information about the project and its financial supporters is at "Our Supporters," Our World in Data, accessed November 2, 2020, https:// ourworldindata.org/funding.

On Harari: Yuval N. Harari, *Homo Deus: A Brief History of Tomorrow* (London: Harvill Secker, 2016).

On Fukuyama: Francis Fukuyama, *The End of History and the Last Man* (New York: Free Press, 1992).

2. framing

Story of Alyssa Milano and the origin of MeToo: The information was compiled from an interview with Alyssa Milano by Kenneth Cukier in August 2020, as well as from the articles that follow: Useful references include: Jessica Bennett, "Alyssa Milano, Celebrity Activist for the Celebrity Presidential Age," *New York Times*, October 25, 2019, https://www.nytimes.com/2019/10 /25/us/politics/alyssa-milano-activism.html; Anna Codrea-Rado, "#MeToo Floods Social Media with Stories of Harassment and Assault," *New York Times*, October 16, 2017, https://www.nytimes.com/2017/10/16/technology/metoo -twitter-facebook.html; Jim Rutenberg et al., "Harvey Weinstein's Fall Opens the Floodgates in Hollywood," *New York Times*, October 16, 2017, https:// www.nytimes.com/2017/10/16/business/media/harvey-weinsteins-fall -opens-the-floodgates-in-hollywood.html.

Milano's thinking: The words in quotation marks come from our interview with Milano, as well as from an interview in which she was asked what she was thinking at the time. See: Nadja Sayej, "Alyssa Milano on the #MeToo Movement: 'We're Not Going to Stand for It Any More,'" *Guardian*, December 1,

2017, https://www.theguardian.com/culture/2017/dec/01/alyssa-milano
-mee-too-sexual-harassment-abuse.

Milano's assault: Two years after her tweet, Milano went public with her own assault. See: Joanne Rosa, "Alyssa Milano on Sharing Alleged Sexual Assault Story 25 Years Later," *ABC News*, October 16, 2019, https://abcnews.go.com /Entertainment/alyssa-milano-sharing-alleged-sexual-assault-story-25/story? id=66317784.

On the MeToo movement: The term "MeToo" was coined in 2006 by an activist, Tarana Burke, on MySpace, an early social network. Creating a mass movement online to call out sexual assault had been less effective before 2017.

On defining frames: There is no firm definition, since the idea spans many disciplines. As José Luis Bermúdez of Texas A&M University put it: "The concept of a frame is itself something that can be framed in many different ways." See José Luis Bermúdez, *Frame It Again: New Tools for Rational Decision-Making* (Cambridge: Cambridge University Press, 2020), 11. A seminal, earlier analysis is Erving Goffman, *Frame Analysis: An Essay on the Organization of Experience* (Cambridge, MA: Harvard University Press, 1974).

On OKRs: Eric Schmidt and Jonathan Rosenberg, *How Google Works* (New York: Grand Central, 2014).

On Cassirer and Wittgenstein: See the accessible Wolfram Eilenberger, *Time of the Magicians: Wittgenstein, Benjamin, Cassirer, Heidegger, and the Decade That Reinvented Philosophy* (New York: Penguin, 2020).

On mental models: The idea of a mental model is sometimes attributed to the Cambridge philosopher Kenneth Craik. In a short book, in 1943, he wrote: "If the organism carries a 'small-scale model' of external reality and of its own possible actions within its head, it is able to try out various alternatives, conclude which is the best of them, react to future situations before they arise . . . [and] to the emergencies which face it." See Kenneth Craik, *The Nature of Explanation* (Cambridge: Cambridge University Press, 1952), 61. The scholar Philip Johnson-Laird describes it as "a mental representation that serves as a model of an entity in much the same way as, say, a clock functions as a model of the earth's rotation." See Philip Johnson-Laird, *Mental Models: Towards a Cognitive Science of Language, Inference, and Consciousness* (Cambridge, MA: Harvard University Press, 1983), 2. Also, Philip Johnson-Laird, *How We Reason* (Oxford: Oxford University Press, 2006). Neuroscientists argue that the main purpose of the brain is to create a model of the world. For a recent analysis, see David Eagleman, *Livewired: The Inside Story of the Ever-Changing Brain* (London: Pantheon Books, 2020). A fuller treatment is Chris D. Frith, *Making Up the Mind: How the Brain Creates Our Mental World* (Oxford: Blackwell Publishing, 2007).

On purposeful dreaming: Katherine L. Alfred et al., "Mental Models Use Common Neural Spatial Structure for Spatial and Abstract Content," *Communications Biology* 3, no. 17 (January 2020).

On maps and frames: Bas van Fraassen, a philosopher of science, argues that maps and scientific representations are in many respects the same. In his view, we could also consider scientific models as scientific maps. See Bas van Fraassen, *The Scientific Representation* (Oxford: Oxford University Press, 2008).

On the map's Mercator projection: John Noble Wilford, "Arthur H. Robinson, 89, Geographer Who Reinterpreted World Map, Dies," *New York Times*, November 15, 2004, https://www.nytimes.com/2004/11/15/obituaries/arthur-h -robinson-89-geographer-who-reinterpreted-world-map-dies.html; John Noble Wilford, "The Impossible Quest for the Perfect Map," *New York Times*, October 25, 1988, https://www.nytimes.com/1988/10/25/science/the-impossible -quest-for-the-perfect-map.html.

Constitutional framers: Michael J. Klarman, *The Framers' Coup: The Making of the United States Constitution* (New York: Oxford University Press, 2016); on Europe and *demos* versus *demoi*, Kalypso Nicolaïdis, "We, the Peoples of Europe . . . ," *Foreign Affairs*, November/December 2004, https://www.foreignaffairs.com /articles/europe/2004-11-01/we-peoples-europe.

World Health Organization Versus Médecins Sans Frontières response to Ebola: Francis de Véricourt, "Ebola: The Onset of a Deadly Outbreak," ESMT-317-0177-1 (Berlin: European School of Management and Technology, 2017). MSF raised the alarm on March 31, 2014, see: "Mobilisation Against an Unprecedented Ebola Epidemic," MSF, press release, March 31, 2014, https:// www.msf.org/guinea-mobilisation-against-unprecedented-ebola-epidemic. WHO responded to MSF during a press conference held in Geneva the day after, see: "Geneva/Guinea Ebola," Unifeed, 2:39, posted by CH UNTV, April 1, 2014, https://www.unmultimedia.org/tv/unifeed/asset/U140/U140401a/.

Trump's Ebola tweet: Ed Yong, "The Rank Hypocrisy of Trump's Ebola Tweets," *Atlantic*, August 3, 2019, https://www.theatlantic.com/health/archive/2019 /08/the-rank-hypocrisy-of-trumps-ebola-tweets/595420/.

About coronaviruses: "Coronaviruses: SARS, MERS, and 2019-nCoV," Johns Hopkins Center for Health Security, updated April 14, 2020, https://www.center forhealthsecurity.org/resources/fact-sheets/pdfs/coronaviruses.pdf.

Italy's Covid experience: The news was reported in UK media, denied by the Italian government, but affirmed by Italian doctors. See: Lucia Craxì, et al., "Rationing in a Pandemic: Lessons from Italy," *Asian Bioeth Rev* (June 16, 2020): 1–6, https://www.ncbi.nlm.nih.gov/pmc/articles/PMC7298692.

New Zealand's brilliant Covid response: Interview by Kenneth Cukier with Michael Baker, health adviser to the government, June 2020.

Britain's pathetic Covid response: "Britain Has the Wrong Government for the Covid Crisis," *Economist*, June 18, 2020, https://www.economist.com/leaders /2020/06/18/britain-has-the-wrong-government-for-the-covid-crisis.

Britain's Covid performance in June: "Coronavirus: UK Daily Deaths Drop to Pre-lockdown Level," *BBC News*, June 8, 2020, https://www.bbc.co.uk/news /uk-52968160.

UK data on deaths and cases: "COVID-19 Pandemic Data in the United Kingdom," Wikipedia, accessed October 30, 2020, https://en.wikipedia.org/wiki /Template:COVID-19_pandemic_data/United_Kingdom_medical_cases _chart.

Neil Armstrong's "small step": Robbie Gonzalez, "Read the *New York Times'* 1969 Account of the Apollo 11 Moon Landing," *Gizmodo*, August 25, 2012, https://io9.gizmodo.com/277292567?jwsource=cl.

On the *New York Times*'s retraction of its 1920 article: Bjorn Carey, "*New York Times* to NASA: You're Right, Rockets DO Work in Space," *Popular Science*,

July 20, 2009, https://www.popsci.com/military-aviation-amp-space/article/2009-07/new-york-times-nasa-youre-right-rockets-do-work-space/.

On the Higgs boson: Sabine Hossenfelder, "The Uncertain Future of Particle Physics," *New York Times*, January 23, 2019, https://www.nytimes.com/2019/01/23/opinion/particle-physics-large-hadron-collider.html. On black holes, see: Jonathan Amos, "Dancing Gargantuan Black Holes Perform on Cue," *BBC News*, April 29, 2020, https://www.bbc.com/news/science-environment-52464250.

On Blue Ocean Strategy: W. Chan Kim and Renée Mauborgne, *Blue Ocean Strategy: How to Create Uncontested Market Space and Make the Competition Irrelevant*, expanded ed. (Boston: Harvard Business Review Press, 2015).

On the Wright brothers: See: Johnson-Laird, *How We Reason*; David Mc-Cullough, *The Wright Brothers* (New York: Simon & Schuster, 2015). Richard P. Hallion, *Taking Flight: Inventing the Aerial Age, from Antiquity Through the First World War* (Oxford: Oxford University Press, 2003).

Orville's description of the propeller: Orville Wright, "How We Made the First Flight," *Flying and the Aero Club of America Bulletin* 2 (December 1913): 10, https://www.faa.gov/education/educators/curriculum/k12/media/k-12_how_we_made_the_first_flight_orville_wright.pdf.

On framing and economic development: World Bank Group, *World Development Report 2015: Mind, Society, and Behavior* (Washington, DC: World Bank, 2015).

On Black-Scholes: Donald MacKenzie, *An Engine, Not a Camera: How Financial Models Shape Markets* (Cambridge, MA: MIT Press, 2006).

On the persistence of bad frames: Karla Hoff and Joseph E. Stiglitz, "Equilibrium Fictions: A Cognitive Approach to Societal Rigidity," *American Economic Review* 100, no. 2 (May 2010): 141–46, https://www.aeaweb.org/articles?id=10.1257/aer.100.2.141.

Eugene Kleiner quote: Rhonda Abrams, "Remembering Eugene Kleiner," *Inc.*, December 1, 2003, https://www.inc.com/articles/2003/12/eugenekleiner.html.

On silent reading: Paul Saenger, *Space Between Words: The Origins of Silent Reading* (Palo Alto: Stanford University Press, 1997).

On the frame problem: John McCarthy and Patrick Hayes, "Some Philosophical Problems from the Standpoint of Artificial Intelligence," vol. 4 of *Machine Intelligence*, eds. Bernard Meltzer and Donald Michie (Edinburgh: Edinburgh University Press, 1969), 463–502.

On Dennett's robot: Daniel Dennett, "Cognitive Wheels: The Frame Problem of AI," in *Minds, Machines and Evolution*, ed. Christopher Hookway (Cambridge: Cambridge University Press, 1984), 129–51, dl.tufts.edu/concern/pdfs/7d279568g.

On the nine-dot test: John Adair, *Training for Decisions* (London: Macdonald, 1971). Puzzle book: Sam Loyd, *Sam Loyd's Cyclopedia of 5000 Puzzles* (New York: Lamb, 1914). In psychological experiments on creativity: Norman Maier, "Reasoning in Humans: I. On Direction," *Journal of Comparative Psychology* 10, no. 2 (1930): 115–43; Norman Maier, "Reasoning in Humans: II. The Solution of a Problem and Its Appearance in Consciousness," *Journal of Comparative Psychology* 12, no. 2 (1931): 181–94.

3. causality

Bernanke's recollection at the window: Ben Bernanke, *The Courage to Act: A Memoir of a Crisis and Its Aftermath* (New York: Norton, 2015), 83.

On economic history: Joel Mokyr, "The Intellectual Origins of Modern Economic Growth," *Journal of Economic History* 65, no. 2 (June 2005): 285–351, https://www.jstor.org/stable/3875064; Daniel R. Fusfeld, *The Age of the Economist*, 9th ed. (Boston: Addison-Wesley, 2002); Callum Williams, "Who Were the Physiocrats?," *Economist*, October 11, 2013, https://www.economist.com/free-exchange/2013/10/11/who-were-the-physiocrats; Kate Raworth, "Old Economics Is Based on False 'Laws of Physics'—New Economics Can Save Us," *Guardian*, April 6, 2017, https://www.theguardian.com/global-development-professionals-network/2017/apr/06/kate-raworth-doughnut-economics-new-economics.

Bernanke's view of the Fed's flawed policy after 1929 crash: Ben Bernanke, "Federal Reserve and the 2008 Financial Crisis," speech given at George Washington University, March 27, 2012, C-SPAN video, 1:15:12, https://www.c-span.org/video/?305130-1/federal-reserve-2008-financial-crisis Ben Bernanke interviewed by Scott Pelley, *60 Minutes*, "The Chairman," March 15, 2009, YouTube video, 13:23, https://www.youtube.com/watch?v=odPfHY4ekHA.

The nickname "Helicopter Ben": Ben Bernanke, "Deflation: Making Sure 'It' Doesn't Happen Here," speech to the National Economists Club, Washington, DC, November 21, 2002, transcript, https://www.federalreserve.gov/BOARDDOCS/SPEECHES/2002/20021121/default.htm.

Sequence of financial-institution collapses: For an authoritative account, see: Andrew Ross Sorkin, *Too Big to Fail: The Inside Story of How Wall Street and Washington Fought to Save the Financial System—and Themselves* (New York: Viking, 2009).

On McDonald's franchise uncertain of making payroll: Andrew Ross Sorkin interviewed by Robert Smith, "Inside the Minds of Wall Street Execs," *NPR Weekend Edition*, September 18, 2010, transcript and audio, https://www.npr.org/templates/story/story.php?storyId=129953853.

On cash machines drying up: *Panic: The Untold Story of the 2008 Financial Crisis*, directed by John Maggio, aired December 11, 2018, on HBO, https://www.hbo.com/vice/special-reports/panic-the-untold-story-of-the-2008-financial-crisis.

The Fed's balance sheet, 2008 to 2015: Elizabeth Schulze, "The Fed Launched QE Nine Years Ago—These Four Charts Show Its Impact," *CNBC*, November 24, 2017, https://www.cnbc.com/2017/11/24/the-fed-launched-qe-nine-years-ago—these-four-charts-show-its-impact.html. See also: Michael Ng and David Wessel, "The Fed's Bigger Balance Sheet in an Era of 'Ample Reserves,'" Brookings, May 17, 2019, https://www.brookings.edu/blog/up-front/2019/05/17/the-feds-bigger-balance-sheet-in-an-era-of-ample-reserves/.

On humans thinking causally: We are not referring to the chain of causality but some causal connection. For more on this, see Joseph Henrich, *The Secret of Our Success: How Culture Is Driving Human Evolution, Domesticating Our Species, and Making Us Smarter* (Princeton, NJ: Princeton University Press, 2015).

On monkeys scared of snakes: Eric E. Nelson, Steven E. Shelton, and Ned H. Kalin, "Individual Differences in the Responses of Naïve Rhesus Monkeys to

Snakes," *Emotion* 3, no. 1 (March 2003): 3–11; Masahiro Shibasaki and No-
buyuki Kawai, "Rapid Detection of Snakes by Japanese Monkeys (*Macaca fus-
cata*): An Evolutionarily Predisposed Visual System," *Journal of Comparative
Psychology* 123, no. 2 (May 2009): 131–35.

On preschool children detecting snakes: Vanessa LoBue and Judy S. De-
Loache, "Detecting the Snake in the Grass: Attention to Fear-Relevant Stimuli
by Adults and Young Children," *Psychological Science* 19, no. 3 (March 2008):
284–89.

Babies and falling objects: Renée Baillargeon, "Infants' Physical Knowledge: Of
Acquired Expectations and Core Principles," in *Language, Brain, and Cognitive
Development: Essays in Honor of Jacques Mehler*, ed. Emmanuel Dupoux (Cam-
bridge, MA: MIT Press, 2001), 341–61.

On clever crows: Leyre Castro and Ed Wasserman, "Crows Understand Analogies," *Scientific American*, February 10, 2015, https://www.scientificamerican
.com/article/crows-understand-analogies.

On the limitation of crow cleverness: Alex H. Taylor et al., "Do New Caledo-
nian Crows Solve Physical Problems Through Causal Reasoning?," *Proceedings
of the Royal Society B* 276, no. 1655 (January 22, 2009): 247–54.

Crows versus other birds on dinner plates: The quip is inspired by Alison
Gopnik's delightful TED Talk. See: Alison Gopnik, "What Do Babies Think?,"
filmed July 2011, TED video, https://www.ted.com/talks/alison_gopnik
_what_do_babies_think.

Pinker's "cognitive niche": The term is not Pinker's per se, though he's most
closely associated with it. As he points out, the idea and phrase come from
the anthropologists John Tooby and Irven DeVore. See: "Listen to Psycholin-
guist Steven Pinker Speak About 'Cognitive Niche' in Early Modern Human
Evolution," transcript, *Britannica*, May 29, 2015, https://www.britannica
.com/video/193409/Psycholinguist-Steven-Pinker-humans-evolution
-niche.

Metaphorical abstraction: The specific example and quote come from: Steven
Pinker, "The Cognitive Niche: Coevolution of Intelligence, Sociality, and Language," *Proceedings of the National Academy of Sciences* 107, supplement 2 (May
2010): 8993–99, https://www.pnas.org/content/pnas/early/2010/05/04
/0914630107.full.pdf. It is worth noting that a pioneer of AI, Douglas Hofstadter, has spent his later years studying a similar phenomenon, analogies,
which he regards as a backbone of how humans comprehend reality. See:
Douglas Hofstadter and Emmanuel Sander, *Surfaces and Essences: Analogy as
the Fuel and Fire of Thinking* (New York: Basic Books, 2014).

Human cooperation and cognition: Michael Tomasello, *A Natural History of
Human Thinking* (Cambridge, MA: Harvard University Press, 2014); Michael
Tomasello, *Becoming Human: A Theory of Ontogeny* (Cambridge, MA: Harvard
University Press, 2019).

Tomasello's tube experiment: Felix Warneken, Frances Chen, and Michael Tomasello, "Cooperative Activities in Young Children and Chimpanzees,"
Child Development 77, no. 3 (May/June 2006): 640–63.

On a mix of cognitive and cultural niches: Rachel L. Kendal, "Explaining
Human Technology," *Nature Human Behaviour* 3, no. 5 (April 2019): 422–23,
https://www.nature.com/articles/s41562-019-0578-6.

notes

The wheel experiment: Maxime Derex et al., "Causal Understanding Is Not Necessary for the Improvement of Culturally Evolving Technology," *Nature Human Behaviour* 3, no. 5 (April 2019): 446–52, https://www.nature.com/articles/s41562-019-0567-9. Also see: "Can Technology Improve Even Though People Don't Understand What They Are Doing?," press release, Arizona State University, April 1, 2019, https://www.eurekalert.org/pub_releases/2019-04/asu-cti032819.php.

On the speed of technical change and the cognitive niche: Kendal, "Explaining Human Technology."

On biasing the way humans explore alternatives: Maxime Derex and Robert Boyd, "The Foundations of the Human Cultural Niche," *Nature Communications* 6, no. 1 (September 24, 2015): 8398.

On our ancestors' domestication: John R. McNeill and William H. McNeill, *The Human Web: A Bird's-Eye View of World History* (New York: Norton, 2003).

The story of Semmelweis: Sherwin Nuland, *The Doctors' Plague: Germs, Childbed Fever, and the Strange Story of Ignác Semmelweis* (New York: Norton, 2004). Also see: Rebecca Davis, "The Doctor Who Championed Hand-Washing and Briefly Saved Lives," *NPR Morning Edition*, January 12, 2015, transcript and audio, https://www.npr.org/sections/health-shots/2015/01/12/375663920/the-doctor-who-championed-hand-washing-and-saved-women-s-lives?t=1577014322310.

On Louis Pasteur: Louise E. Robbins, *Louis Pasteur and the Hidden World of Microbes* (New York: Oxford University Press, 2001).

On Joseph Lister: Lindsey Fitzharris, *The Butchering Art: Joseph Lister's Quest to Transform the Grisly World of Victorian Medicine* (New York: Farrar, Straus and Giroux, 2017).

Brain hemispheres and the Coke experiment: Michael S. Gazzaniga, *The Ethical Brain* (New York: Dana Press, 2005).

On explanation and causality: Joseph J. Williams and Tania Lombrozo, "The Role of Explanation in Discovery and Generalization: Evidence from Category Learning," *Cognitive Science* 34, no. 5 (July 2010): 776–806.

On Lombrozo's work: Our thanks to Lombrozo for her help in how we described her work. Also see Reginald Lahens, "Tania Lombrozo Shares the Benefits of Brief Explanations," *Brown and White*, September 30, 2018, https://thebrownandwhite.com/2018/09/30/tania-lombrozo-breaks-down-the-benefits-of-brief-explanations-the-brown-and-white. Lombrozo is not the first or only scholar to study the effects of explanation on learning. See Michelene T. H. Chi et al., "Eliciting Self-Explanations Improves Understanding," *Cognitive Science* 18, no. 3 (1994): 439–477.

On rewards experiment: Koichi Ono, "Superstitious Behavior in Humans," *Journal of the Experimental Analysis of Behavior* 47, no. 3 (May 1987): 261–71.

On social structures: Anthony Giddens, *The Constitution of Society: Outline of the Theory of Structuration* (Berkeley: University of California Press, 1984).

Train history and fears: Christian Wolmar, "How Railways Changed Britain," Christian Wolmar, October 29, 2007, https://www.christianwolmar.co.uk/2007/10/how-railways-changed-britain.

Always revising what we know: Samuel Arbesman, *The Half-Life of Facts: Why Everything We Know Has an Expiration Date* (New York: Current, 2012).

Pearl on causation: Judea Pearl and Dana Mackenzie, *The Book of Why: The New Science of Cause and Effect* (New York: Basic Books, 2018), 5. Our thanks to Pearl for sharing his ideas over the course of several years with Kenneth Cukier.

***Dota 2* prize money:** Arda Ocal, "Dota 2's the International Surpasses $40 Million in Prize Money," ESPN, October 9, 2020, https://www.espn.com/esports/story/_/id/30079945/dota-2-international-surpasses-40-million-prize-money.

AI wins *Dota 2*: Nick Statt, "OpenAI's Dota 2 AI Steamrolls World Champion e-Sports Team with Back-to-Back Victories," *The Verge*, April 13, 2019, https://www.theverge.com/2019/4/13/18309459/openai-five-dota-2-finals-ai-bot-competition-og-e-sports-the-international-champion.

OpenAI *Dota 2* research paper: Christopher Berner et al., "Dota 2 with Large Scale Deep Reinforcement Learning," OpenAI, 2019, https://arxiv.org/abs/1912.06680. For more on the work, see also: Ng Wai Foong, "Beginner's Guide to OpenAI Five at Dota2," Medium, May 7, 2019, https://medium.com/@ngwaifoong92/beginners-guide-to-openai-five-at-dota2-3b49ee5169b8; Evan Pu, "Understanding OpenAI Five," Medium, August 12, 2018, https://medium.com/@evanthebouncy/understanding-openai-five-16f8d177a957.

OpenAI's "team spirit" hyper-parameter: Christy Dennison et al., "OpenAI Five," OpenAI, June 25, 2018, https://openai.com/blog/openai-five.

On connecting nothing: T. S. Eliot, *The Waste Land* (New York: Boni and Live-right, 1922).

4. counterfactuals

Foote's paper: Eunice Foote, "Circumstances Affecting the Heat of the Sun's Rays," *American Journal of Science and Arts* 22, no. 66 (November 1856): 382–83, https://archive.org/stream/mobot31753002152491#page/382/mode/2up.

Details on the setting of Foote's paper: Henry's remarks from: Raymond P. Sorenson, "Eunice Foote's Pioneering Research On CO_2 And Climate Warming," Search and Discovery article #70092, January 31, 2011, http://www.searchanddiscovery.com/pdfz/documents/2011/70092sorenson/ndx_sorenson.pdf.html. See also: Tara Santora, "The Female Scientist Who Discovered the Basics of Climate Science—and Was Forgotten," *Audubon*, July 17, 2019, https://www.audubon.org/news/the-female-scientist-who-discovered-basics-climate-science-and-was-forgotten; Leila McNeill, "This Suffrage-Supporting Scientist Defined the Greenhouse Effect but Didn't Get the Credit, Because Sexism," *Smithsonian Magazine*, December 5, 2016, https://www.smithsonianmag.com/science-nature/lady-scientist-helped-revolutionize-climate-science-I-get-credit-180961291. Also: John Schwartz, "Overlooked No More: Eunice Foote, Climate Scientist Lost to History," *New York Times*, April 21, 2020, https://www.nytimes.com/2020/04/21/obituaries/eunice-foote-overlooked.html.

On climate models: Inez Fung, interviewed by Kenneth Cukier, April 2020.

On James Hansen's statement: James Hansen, "Hearing Before the Committee on Energy and Natural Resources," US Senate, June 23, 1988, https://babel.hathitrust.org/cgi/pt?id=uc1.b5127807&view=1up&seq=48; Philipp Shabecoff, "Global Warming Has Begun, Expert Tells Senate," *New York Times*, June 24, 1988, https://www.nytimes.com/1988/06/24/us/global-warming-has

-begun-expert-tells-senate.html. Hansen, ever diplomatic, does not use the term "human activity" in his testimony but a euphemism: "larger than natural climate variability."

On Inez Fung: Renee Skelton, *Forecast Earth: The Story of Climate Scientist Inez Fung* (Washington, DC: Joseph Henry Press, 2006). Also: National Academies of Science, "InterViews: Inez Fung," 2011, http://nasonline.org/news-and -multimedia/podcasts/interviews/inez-fung.html.

John, the king, and arsenic: Roger Carl Schank and Robert P. Abelson, *Scripts, Plans, Goals, and Understanding: An Inquiry into Human Knowledge Structures* (Hillsdale, NJ: Erlbaum, 1977).

Mandžukić's sad goal: "Mandzukic Makes World Cup History with Early Own Goal," *FourFourTwo*, July 15, 2018, https://www.fourfourtwo.com/news/man dzukic-makes-world-cup-history-early-own-goal.

Eye-tracking experiment for counterfactual thinking: Tobias Gerstenberg et al., "Eye-Tracking Causality," *Psychological Science* 28, no. 12 (December 2017): 1731–44.

On Galileo: José Manuel Montejo Bernardo, "Galileo's Most Famous Experiment Probably Never Took Place" (original: "El Experimento Más Famoso de Galileo Probablemente Nunca Tuvo Lugar"), *Conversation*, May 16, 2019, https://the conversation.com/el-experimento-mas-famoso-de-galileo-probablemente -nunca-tuvo-lugar-111650. See also: Paolo Palmieri, "'Spuntar lo Scoglio Più Duro': Did Galileo Ever Think the Most Beautiful Thought Experiment in the History of Science?," *Studies in History and Philosophy of Science Part A* 36, no. 2 (June 2005): 223–40.

On Parkinson's disease and counterfactual thinking: Patrick McNamara et al., "Counterfactual Cognitive Deficit in Persons with Parkinson's Disease," *Journal of Neurology and Psychiatry* 74, no. 8 (August 2003): 1065–70.

On monkeys and bananas: Yuval N. Harari, *Sapiens: A Brief History of Humankind* (New York: HarperCollins, 2015).

Rousseau, James, Freud, and *The Onion* on children: Paul Bloom, "The Moral Life of Babies," *New York Times Magazine*, May 5, 2010, https://www.nytimes .com/2010/05/09/magazine/09babies-t.html; "New Study Reveals Most Children Unrepentant Sociopaths," *The Onion*, December 7, 2009, https://www .theonion.com/new-study-reveals-most-children-unrepentant-sociopaths -1819571187. On Freud: Alison Gopnik and Caren M. Walker, "Considering Counterfactuals: The Relationship Between Causal Learning and Pretend Play," *American Journal of Play* 6, no. 1 (Fall 2013): 15–28.

Details about Gopnik: Alison Gopnik, "A Midcentury Modern Education," in *Curious Minds: How a Child Becomes a Scientist*, ed. John Brockman (New York: Vintage, 2005), 43–51. Also see: Audio interview and article by Michael Gordon, "The Intellectual Wonderland of Dr. Alison Gopnik," *Journey2Psychology*, March 25, 2019, https://journey2psychology.com/2019/03/25/the -intellectual-wonderland-of-dr-alison-gopnik; Alison Gopnik, "How an 18th-Century Philosopher Helped Solve My Midlife Crisis," *Atlantic*, October 2015, https://www.theatlantic.com/magazine/archive/2015/10/how-david-hume -helped-me-solve-my-midlife-crisis/403195/.

Gopnik hails children as "Scientists" and "Philosophical": Alison Gopnik, *The Philosophical Baby: What Children's Minds Tell Us About Truth,*

Love and the Meaning of Life (New York: Farrar, Straus and Giroux, 2009); Alison Gopnik, Andrew N. Meltzoff, Patricia K. Kuhl, *The Scientist in the Crib: Minds, Brains, and How Children Learn* (New York: William Morrow, 1999).

The "zando test": Daphna Buchsbaum et al., "The Power of Possibility: Causal Learning, Counterfactual Reasoning, and Pretend Play," research paper, *Philosophical Transactions of the Royal Society B* 365, no. 1599 (August 5, 2012): 2202–12. Also, Alison Gopnik, "Let the Children Play, It's Good for Them!," *Smithsonian Magazine*, July 2012, https://www.smithsonianmag.com/science-nature/let-the-children-play-its-good-for-them-130697324. The account also appears in Alison Gopnik, *The Gardener and the Carpenter: What the New Science of Child Development Tells Us About the Relationship Between Parents and Children* (New York: Farrar, Straus and Giroux, 2016).

Script to child research subjects: The sentences, spoken by the experimenter, are gently edited for readability. See: Buchsbaum et al., "The Power of Possibility."

Gopnik on pretend play and better counterfactuals: Gopnik, "Let the Children Play."

Children as R&D division of humanity: Gopnik, "What Do Babies Think?" TED video.

Three excerpts from literature: Patrick Süskind, *Perfume: The Story of a Murderer*, trans. John E. Woods (New York: Knopf, 1986); Erich Maria Remarque, *All Quiet on the Western Front*, trans. A. W. Wheen (Boston: Little, Brown, 1929); Chimamanda Ngozi Adichie, *Americanah* (New York: Knopf, 2013).

On computers as theater: Brenda Laurel, *Computers as Theatre* (Reading, MA: Addison-Wesley, 1993).

History of the Harvard case study method: Todd Bridgman, Stephen Cummings, and Colm McLaughlin, "Restating the Case: How Revisiting the Development of the Case Method Can Help Us Think Differently About the Future of the Business School," *Academy of Management Learning & Education* 15, no. 4 (December 2016): 724–741. See also: Bruce A. Kimball, *The Inception of Modern Professional Education: C. C. Langdell, 1826–1906* (Chapel Hill: University of North Carolina Press, 2009). Our sincere thanks to Alberto Moel, a former Harvard Business School lecturer, and Robert Merton of MIT, for their invaluable insights on the pros and cons of the case method in interviews with Kenneth Cukier in 2019.

First Harvard Business School case: Clinton Bittle, "The General Shoe Company," Harvard Business School, 1921. Harvard Business School archives.

On athletes' "film study": Marc Lillibridge, "A Former Player's Perspective on Film Study and Preparing for an NFL Game," *Bleacher Report*, November 29, 2012, https://bleacherreport.com/articles/1427449-a-former-players-perspective-on-film-study-and-preparing-for-a-nfl-game.

On counterbalance to "causal determinism": Philip E. Tetlock and Erika Henik, "Theory- Versus Imagination-Driven Thinking about Historical Counterfactuals: Are We Prisoners of Our Preconceptions?," in *Psychology of Counterfactual Thinking*, eds. David Mandel, Denis J. Hilton, and Patrizia Catellani (London: Routledge, 2005); Ruth Byrne, *The Rational Imagination: How People Create Alternatives to Reality* (Cambridge, MA: MIT Press, 2005).

notes

Kennedy and the Cuban missile crisis: Graham T. Allison, *Essence of Decision: Explaining the Cuban Missile Crisis* (Boston: Little, Brown, 1971). Also: Ernest May, "John F. Kennedy and the Cuban Missile Crisis," BBC, November 18, 2013, http://www.bbc.co.uk/history/worldwars/coldwar/kennedy_cuban _missile_01.shtml. The term *groupthink* comes from George Orwell's novel *Nineteen Eighty-Four.* Some social scientists have challenged the idea that "groupthink" was a main factor in the Bay of Pigs disaster.

On counterfactuals, options, and choices: Byrne, *Rational Imagination.*

Kahneman on mental simulation: Daniel Kahneman, "Varieties of Counterfactual Thinking," in *What Might Have Been: The Social Psychology of Counterfactual Thinking*, eds. Neal J. Roese and James M. Olson (Mahwah, NJ: Lawrence Erlbaum, 1995).

MacGyver's hacks: "15 Insane MacGyver Hacks That Would Totally Work in Real Life," CBS, accessed November 2, 2020, https://www.cbs.com/shows/recom mended/photos/1003085/15-insane-macgyver-hacks-that-would-totally -work-in-real-life/. See also: Sam Greenspan, "11 Most Absurd Inventions Created by MacGyver," *11 Points*, March 18, 2018, https://11points.com /11-absurd-inventions-created-macgyver/.

Our sense of predictability and control: Keith D. Markman et al., "The Impact of Perceived Control on the Imagination of Better and Worse Possible Worlds," *Personality and Social Psychology Bulletin* 21, no. 6 (June 1995): 588–95.

Introductory example of self-driving cars: Videos from research in an Arxiv paper at: Mayank Bansal, Alex Krizhevsky, and Abhijit Ogale, "Chauffeur-Net: Learning to Drive by Imitating the Best and Synthesizing the Worst," Waymo, accessed November 2, 2020, https://sites.google.com/view/waymo -learn-to-drive. The scenario was "recovering from a trajectory perturbation (M2 = M1 + environment losses)." The paper itself is at "ChauffeurNet," Waymo, Arxiv, December 7, 2018, https://arxiv.org/abs/1812.03079.

On Carcraft: An article with superb reporting is: Alexis C. Madrigal, "Inside Waymo's Secret World for Training Self-Driving Cars," *Atlantic*, August 23, 2017, https://www.theatlantic.com/technology/archive/2017/08/inside-waymos -secret-testing-and-simulation-facilities/537648.

Data on the amount of simulation driving: "The Virtual World Helps Waymo Learn Advanced Real-World Driving Skills," Let's Talk Self-Driving, accessed November 2, 2020, https://letstalkselfdriving.com/safety/simulation.html.

On self-driving technology: Bansal, Krizhevsky, and Ogale, "ChauffeurNet."

Waymo's performance relative to rivals': California Department of Motor Vehicles, "2020 Disengagement Reports," https://www.dmv.ca.gov/portal /vehicle-industry-services/autonomous-vehicles/disengagement-reports.

On counterfactuals and AI: In the AI community, there has been an increase in interest in counterfactual logic to improve explainability of AI systems; see, e.g., Sandra Wachter et al., "Counterfactual Explanations Without Opening the Black Box: Automated Decisions and the GDPR," *Harvard Journal of Law & Technology* 31, no. 2 (2018), https://jolt.law.harvard.edu/assets/articlePDFs /v31/Counterfactual-Explanations-without-Opening-the-Black-Box-Sandra -Wachter-et-al.pdf.

5. constraints

On the Entebbe raid: Interview with Noam Tamir by Kenneth Cukier in March 2020. The authoritative work is: Saul David, *Operation Thunderbolt: Flight 139 and the Raid on Entebbe Airport, the Most Audacious Hostage Rescue Mission in History* (New York: Little, Brown, 2015). An excellent resource is: Ronen Bergman and Lior Ben-Ami, "Operation Entebbe as Told by the Commandos: Planning the Mission," *Ynet*, June 27, 2016, https://www.ynetnews.com/articles /0,7340,L-4815198,00.html.

On separating passengers: The Air France pilots and crew refused to be released and chose to remain as hostages with the Jewish passengers, an act of inspiring nobility. There are many excellent accounts. For one, see: Sam Roberts, "Michel Bacos, Hero Pilot of Jet Hijacked to Entebbe, Dies at 94," *New York Times*, March 28, 2019, https://www.nytimes.com/2019/03/28/obituaries /michel-bacos-dead.html.

Shomron's quote "It's a dud": From: David, *Operation Thunderbolt*.

For details of this account: There are many good articles, including: Jenni Frazer, "40 Years after Israel's Most Daring Mission," *Jewish News*, June 28, 2016, https://jewishnews.timesofisrael.com/40-years-after-israels-most -daring-mission/; David E. Kaplan, "A Historic Hostage-Taking Revisited," *Jerusalem Post*, August 3, 2006, https://www.jpost.com/Features/A-historic -hostage-taking-revisited; Lauren Gelfond Feldinger, "Back to Entebbe," *Jerusalem Post*, June 29, 2006, https://www.jpost.com/Magazine/Features/Back -to-Entebbe; Saul David, "Israel's Raid on Entebbe Was Almost a Disaster," *Telegraph*, June 27, 2015, https://www.telegraph.co.uk/news/worldnews/mid dleeast/israel/11701064/Israels-raid-on-Entebbe-was-almost-a-disaster .html.

On Dr. Seuss's *Green Eggs and Ham*: Louis Menand, "Cat People: What Dr. Seuss Really Taught Us," *New Yorker*, December 16, 2002, https://www.new yorker.com/magazine/2002/12/23/cat-people.

On Martha Graham: Jenny Dalzell, "Martha Graham: American Modern Dance Pioneer," *Dance Teacher*, January 2, 2013, https://www.dance-teacher.com /history-lesson-plan martha-graham-2392370093.html; "Martha Graham: The Graham Technique," Human Kinetics (Canada), accessed November 10, 2020, https://canada.humankinetics.com/blogs/excerpt/martha-graham the-graham-technique; "About," MarthaGraham.org, accessed November 10, 2020, https://marthagraham.org/history.

Frank Gehry on gravity: "Frank Gehry Teaches Design and Architecture," MasterClass, video course, accessed November 4, 2020, https://www.masterclass .com/classes/frank-gehry-teaches-design-and-architecture.

Gehry on building without constraints: "What It Takes—Frank Gehry," American Academy of Achievement, April 6, 2018, https://learningenglish .voanews.com/a/what-it-takes-frank-gehry/4302218.html.

On a French novel without the letter *e*: In 1969 the French writer Georges Perec wrote a three-hundred-page novel *La Disparition* (*A Void*) entirely devoid of *e*, following the restrictions dictated by the Oulipo artistic movement to which he belonged. See: Georges Perec, *A Void*, trans. Gilbert Adair

(London: Harvill, 1995). Also see: Harry Mathews and Alastair Brotchie, *Oulipo Compendium* (London: Atlas Press, 2005).

On early space shuttle thinking: T. A. Heppenheimer, "SP-4221 The Space Shuttle Decision," NASA, accessed November 10, 2020, https://history.nasa.gov/SP-4221/contents.htm.

On the hang glider and NASA: "Space History Photo: The Birth of Hang Gliding," NASA Archives, Space, May 21, 2012, https://www.space.com/15609-hang-gliding-birth-paresev-1.html.

On learning to apply constraints: Byrne, *Rational Imagination*, 122.

On mutability and social norms: Rachel McCloy and Ruth M. J. Byrne, "Counterfactual Thinking About Controllable Events," *Memory & Cognition* 28, no. 6 (November 2000): 1071–78; Clare R. Walsh and Ruth M. J. Byrne, "The Mental Representation of What Might Have Been," in *The Psychology of Counterfactual Thinking*, eds. David. R. Mandel, Denis. J. Hilton, and Patrizia Catellani (London: Routledge, 2005).

On jumping the taxi queue: To be sure, cutting in line at a taxi rank is perfectly normal behavior in certain cultures. But the larger point holds.

On minimal change: Christopher Prendergast, *Counterfactuals: Paths of the Might Have Been* (London: Bloomsbury Academic, 2019), 42–56.

On Austrian wine and antifreeze: "Österreichs Weinexporte im Höhenflug," Oesterreich Wein, March 12, 2018, https://www.oesterreichwein.at/presse-multimedia/pressetexte/news-1/article/oesterreichs-weinexporte-im-hoehenflug.

Erich Polz quote: He spoke on the twenty-fifth anniversary of the scandal. See: Kester Eddy, "Wine: Antifreeze Scandal 'Was the Best Thing That Happened,'" *Financial Times*, October 21, 2010, https://www.ft.com/content/38f2cb2c-dbd9-11df-af09-00144feabdc0.

On control and mutability: Byrne, *Rational Imagination*, 124–25.

On cognitive effort and minimal change experiments: Byrne, *Rational Imagination*, 47, 53. Also see: Ruth M. J. Byrne, "Counterfactual Thought," *Annual Review of Psychology* 67 (January 2016): 135–57, http://www.modeltheory.org/papers/2016counterfactuals.pdf.

The setting of the film *Minority Report*: Interview with Peter Schwartz by Kenneth Cukier in January and February 2019. See also: Christina Bonnington et al., "Inside *Minority Report*'s 'Idea Summit,' Visionaries Saw the Future," *Wired*, June 21, 2012, https://www.wired.com/2012/06/minority-report-idea-summit. For the original short story, see: Philip K. Dick, *Minority Report* (London: Gollancz, 2002). Remarks by participants based on Schwartz's recollections.

Carter and the nuclear reactor: Kenneth Cukier, "Jimmy Carter and Fukushima," *Economist*, April 2, 2011, https://www.economist.com/banyan/2011/04/02/jimmy-carter-and-fukushima. See also: Ian MacLeod, "Chalk River's Toxic Legacy," *Ottawa Citizen*, December 16, 2011, https://ottawacitizen.com/news/chalk-rivers-toxic-legacy; Arthur Milnes, "Jimmy Carter's Exposure to Nuclear Danger," *CNN*, April 5, 2011, https://edition.cnn.com/2011/OPINION/04/05/milnes.carter.nuclear/index.html.

On simulated surgery: Peter Weinstock gave a TED Talk on his approach and in a talk for OPENPediatrics. Peter Weinstock, "Lifelike Simulations That Make

Real-Life Surgery Safer," filmed January 2016, TED video, https://www.ted.com /talks/peter_weinstock_lifelike_simulations_that_make_real_life_surgery _safer/; *Building an Enterprise-Wide Simulation 2.0 Program: Part 1 "Rationale, Origins and Frameworks,"* OPENPediatrics, YouTube video, 35:48, November 26, 2018.

On AI music: Cheng-Zhi Anna Huang et al., "Coconet: The ML Model Behind Today's Bach Doodle," Magenta, Google, March 20, 2019, https://magenta .tensorflow.org/coconet.

On Flipkart: Sneha Jha, "Here's How Flipkart Is Innovating to Redefine Customer Experience," ETCIO.com, June 27, 2017, https://cio.economictimes.india times.com/news/strategy-and-management/heres-how-flipkart-is-innovating -to-redefine-customer-experience/59331335.

On will.i.am: Interviews with will.i.am by Kenneth Cukier in 2011, 2018, and 2020. The quote comes from: Reid Hoffman, "Make It Epic, w/ will.i.am," *Masters of Scale* 47, podcast audio, October 30, 2019, https://podcasts.apple .com/ca/podcast/masters-of-scale-with-reid-hoffman/id1227971746?i=10004 55551842.

6. reframing

Peter Habeler comments: Interview with Habeler by Viktor Mayer-Schönberger, May 2020.

On the Habeler and Messner ascent of Everest: Peter Habeler, *Der Einsame Sieg: Mount Everest '78* (München: Goldmann, 1978); Karin Steinbach and Peter Habeler, *Das Ziel ist der Gipfel* (Innsbruck: Tyrolia, 2007); Reinhold Messner, *Überleht—Meine 14 Achttausender* (München: Piper, 2013); Reinhold Messner, *Alle meine Gipfel* (Stuttgart: LangenMüller, 2019).

On Munger's many models: Tren Griffin, *Charlie Munger: The Complete Investor* (New York: Columbia University Press, 2017).

On IKEA: Bertil Torekull, *Leading by Design: The Ikea Story*, trans. Joan Tate (New York: HarperBusiness, 1999). Note that the company has begun to move away from the disposable nature of the products toward recycling.

Models of the economy: For a literal instantiation, the economist Bill Phillips of LSE in 1949 built a physical model of the economy using water (representing money) flowing through tanks, pumps, sluices, and valves to simulate income, taxation, savings, exports, etc. Ones are on display at the British Science Museum and the University of Cambridge.

On Andrew Lo and economics: Andrew W. Lo, *Adaptive Markets: Financial Evolution at the Speed of Thought* (Princeton, NJ: Princeton University Press, 2017).

Reframing the economy: For a fascinating reframing of economics through the lens of Claude Shannon's information theory, see: George Gilder, *Knowledge and Power: The Information Theory of Capitalism and How It Is Revolutionizing our World* (Washington, DC: Regnery, 2013). The idea of a "circular economy" is another example, viewing products in terms of a life cycle.

On being open-minded and curious: A good resource is David Epstein, *Range: Why Generalists Triumph in a Specialized World* (New York: Riverhead, 2019).

On Rousseau's social contract: Jean-Jacques Rousseau, *The Social Contract*, trans. Maurice Cranston (Harmondsworth, UK: Penguin, 1968).

notes

On the discovery of DNA's structure: James Watson, *The Double Helix: A Personal Account of the Discovery of the Structure of DNA* (New York: Athenaeum, 1968). See also: "The Answer," Linus Pauling and the Race for DNA, Oregon State University Libraries, accessed November 10, 2015, http://scarc.library .oregonstate.edu/coll/pauling/dna/narrative/page30.html.

Lise Meitner and Otto Hahn: Ruth Lewin Sime, *Lise Meitner: A Life in Physics* (Berkeley: University of California Press, 1996).

Hertz's quotes: Petri Launiainen, *A Brief History of Everything Wireless: How Invisible Waves Have Changed the World* (Cham, Switzerland: Springer, 2018).

On Amazon: Robert Spector, *Amazon.com—Get Big Fast: Inside the Revolutionary Business Model That Changed the World* (New York: HarperBusiness, 2000).

On changing the Camden police force: Scottie Andrew, "This City Disbanded Its Police Department 7 Years Ago. Here's What Happened Next," *CNN,* June 10, 2020, https://edition.cnn.com/2020/06/09/us/disband-police-camden -new-jersey-trnd/index.html; Steve Tawa, "NJ Agency OKs Layoff of Camden's Entire Police Force," CBS, January 3, 2013, https://philadelphia.cbslocal .com/2013/01/03/nj-agency-oks-layoff-of-camdens-entire-police-force; Josiah Bates, Karl Vick, and Rahim Fortune, "America's Policing System Is Broken. It's Time to Radically Rethink Public Safety," *Time,* accessed November 10, 2020, https://time.com/5876318/police-reform-america/.

Hedges's description of Camden: Chris Hedges and Joe Sacco, *Days of Destruction, Days of Revolt* (New York: Nation Books, 2012). See also: Hank Kalet, "Camden Didn't Defund Its Police Department—It Just Handed It Off," *Progressive,* June 30, 2020, https://progressive.org/dispatches/camden-didnt -defund-police-department-kalet-200630/.

Views of Camden official Louis Cappelli Jr.: Jersey Matters, "County Freeholder Louis Cappelli Reacts to Camden Earning Praise," YouTube, 8:07, June 15, 2020, https://www.youtube.com/watch?v=KeA79kq9pF8. The authors thank Cappelli for his help in our description of the changes.

Quotes from Camden's then police chief Scott Thomson: Mary Louise Kelly, "New Police Force from Scratch: N.J. City Proves It's Possible to Reform the Police," *All Things Considered,* NPR, June 8, 2020, transcript and audio, https:// www.npr.org/2020/06/08/872470135/new-police-force-from-scratch -n-j-city-proves-its-possible-to-reform-the-police.

Jennifer Doudna on her discovery: Sabin Russell, "Cracking the Code: Jennifer Doudna and Her Amazing Molecular Scissors," *California,* Winter 2014, https:// alumni.berkeley.edu/california-magazine/winter-2014-gender-assumptions /cracking-code-jennifer-doudna-and-her-amazing.

Andrew Wiles and Fermat's Last Theorem: "Fermat's Last Theorem," BBC video, 50 minutes, accessed November 4, 2020, https://www.bbc.co.uk/pro grammes/b0074rxx.

Einstein's quote: Albert Einstein and Max Born, *The Born-Einstein Letters,* trans. Irene Born (New York: Walker, 1971).

On unlearning: See, e.g.: Viktor Mayer-Schönberger, *Delete—The Virtue of Forgetting in the Digital Age* (Princeton, NJ: Princeton University Press, 2009).

On Tesla and German cars: See, e.g.: Martin Gropp, "Autohersteller verdoppeln Investitionen in Elektromobilität," *Frankfurter Allgemeine Zeitung,* June 2,

2019, https://www.faz.net/aktuell/wirtschaft/auto-verkehr/autohersteller-verdoppeln-investitionen-in-elektromobilitaet-16218061.html.

On Singapore: See, e.g.: W. G. Huff, "What Is the Singapore Model of Economic Development?," *Cambridge Journal of Economics* 19, no. 6 (December 1995): 735–59; Winston T. H. Koh, "Singapore's Transition to Innovation-Based Economic Growth: Infrastructure, Institutions, and Government's Role," *R&D Management* 36, no. 2 (March 2006): 143–60; the authors' own observations and interviews.

On Spotify: Sven Carlsson and Jonas Leijonhufvud, *The Spotify Play: How CEO and Founder Daniel Ek Beat Apple, Google, and Amazon in the Race for Audio Dominance* (New York: Diversion Books, 2021).

7. learning

Podolny on business education: David Leonhardt, "Revamping the MBA," *Yale Alumni Magazine*, May/June 2007, http://archives.yalealumnimagazine.com/issues/2007_05/som.html. See also: Joel M. Podolny, "The Buck Stops (and Starts) at Business School," *Harvard Business Review*, June 2009, https://hbr.org/2009/06/the-buck-stops-and-starts-at-business-school.

On Apple University: The authors thank Apple for its careful feedback on the content of this section. The information was also compiled from conversations with Podolny when he was at Yale, interviews, firsthand experience, and written accounts, including: Jessica Guynn, "Steve Jobs' Virtual DNA to Be Fostered in Apple University," *Los Angeles Times*, October 6, 2011, https://www.latimes.com/archives/la-xpm-2011-oct-06-la-fi-apple-university-20111006-story.html; Brian X. Chen, "Simplifying the Bull: How Picasso Helps to Teach Apple's Style," *New York Times*, August 10, 2014, https://www.nytimes.com/2014/08/11/technology/inside-apples-internal-training-program-.html; Adam Lashinsky, *Inside Apple: How America's Most Admired—and Secretive—Company Really Works* (New York: Business Plus, 2012).

On insight problems: Marvin Levine, *A Cognitive Theory of Learning: Research on Hypothesis Testing* (Hillsdale, NJ: Lawrence Erlbaum, 1975); Janet Metcalfe and David Wiebe, "Intuition in Insight and Noninsight Problem Solving," *Memory & Cognition* 15, no. 3 (May 1987): 238–46.

The mutilated checkerboard: Original paper presented to the US military: Craig A. Kaplan and Herbert A. Simon, *In Search of Insight*, Technical Report AIP 55 (Arlington, VA: Office of Naval Research, August 15, 1988). Academic citation: Craig A. Kaplan and Herbert A. Simon, "In Search of Insight," *Cognitive Psychology* 22, no. 3 (July 1990): 374–419.

On trials and errors: Levine, *Cognitive Theory of Learning*; Metcalfe and Wiebe, "Intuition."

Rewards to diverse-minded Americans abroad: Susan Pozo, "Does the US Labor Market Reward International Experience?," *American Economic Review* 104, no. 5 (2014): 250–54.

On the case study method: Bridgman, Cummings, and McLaughlin, "Restating the Case."

First Harvard Business School case: Bittle, "The General Shoe Company."

notes

Quote from Wallace Donham: Wallace Donham, "The Failure of Business Leadership and the Responsibilities of the Universities," *Harvard Business Review* 11 (1933): 418–35. He wrote: "We need in business and politics administrators who are able not only to handle their specialized problems well, but also to see things in wide relations and do their part in maintaining society's stability and equilibrium." (Quoted in Bridgman, Cummings, and McLaughlin, "Restating the Case.")

On Burt's Roberts and Jameses: Ronald S. Burt, *Brokerage and Closure: An Introduction to Social Capital* (Oxford: Oxford University Press, 2005).

On clean-slate strategy: The idea is similar to the concept of "jootsing"—i.e., jumping out of the system—introduced by Douglas Hofstadter in his classic *Gödel Escher Bach: An Eternal Golden Braid* (New York: Basic Books, 1979), and later developed in Daniel C. Dennett, *Intuition Pumps and Other Tools for Thinking* (New York: Norton, 2013).

On Alan Kay and object-oriented programming: Interview with Kay by Kenneth Cukier, January 2021. The authors thank Kay for generously sharing his time and insights for this book. See also Eric Elliott, "The Forgotten History of OOP," Medium, October 31, 2018, https://medium.com/javascript-scene /the-forgotten-history-of-oop-88d71b9b2d9f. Kay was the first to develop the OOP idea in its fullest extent, building on other work, notably the Sketch-Pad and Simula programming languages.

Kay's quotes: On "an entirely new way": from Alan Kay, "The Early History of Smalltalk," 1993, worrydream.com/EarlyHistoryOfSmalltalk. On "predict the future": Kay has been expressing the thought since the 1970s. On "tyranny of the present": from Robin Meyerhoff, "Computers and the Tyranny of the Present," *Forbes*, November 11, 2015, https://www.forbes.com/sites/sap /2015/11/11/computers-and-the-tyranny-of-the-present. On "transition from one context": from Stuart Feldman, "A Conversation with Alan Kay: Big Talk with the Creator of Smalltalk—and Much More," *Association for Computing Machinery* 2, no. 9 (December 27, 2004), https://queue.acm.org/detail .cfm?id=1039523.

On influences for Smalltalk: Kay stresses (as do we) that it is impossible to think of things with a truly clean slate. In interviews, he is quick to name technologies that he feels provided the mental building blocks for object-oriented programming. An excellent intellectual history of Smalltalk is Kay, "The Early History of Smalltalk," 1993. Also see: Alan Kay, "The Power of the Context," remarks upon being awarded the Charles Stark Draper Prize, National Academy of Engineering, February 24, 2004.

On James/Jan Morris: Jan Morris, *Conundrum* (London: Faber, 1974).

On geometry: Cartesian geometry (often referred to as analytic geometry in mathematics) can sometimes provide intuitions that Euclidian geometry does not easily allow, while some proofs can be easier and very elegant in Euclidian geometry.

On self-complexity: Patricia Linville, "Self-complexity and Affective Extremity: Don't Put All of Your Eggs in One Cognitive Basket," *Social Cognition* 3, no. 1 (1985): 94–120.

On bilingual kids: Jared Diamond, "The Benefits of Multilingualism," *Science* 330, no. 6002 (October 15, 2010): 332–33. See also: Ellen Bialystok, "The

Bilingual Adaptation: How Minds Accommodate Experience," *Psychological Bulletin* 143, no. 3 (March 2017): 233–62; Cristina Crivello et al., "The Effects of Bilingual Growth on Toddlers' Executive Function," *Journal of Experimental Child Psychology* 141 (January 2016): 121–32.

On Lewis Branscomb: Two of the authors have experienced his rigorous intellectual charm firsthand.

On diversity dividend: The decision-science expert Scott Page calls it a "diversity bonus." See Scott E. Page, *The Diversity Bonus: How Great Teams Pay Off in the Knowledge Economy*, ed. Earl Lewis (Princeton, NJ: Princeton University Press, 2017).

On homophily in social networks: Miller McPherson, Lynn Smith-Lovin, and James M. Cook, "Birds of a Feather: Homophily in Social Networks," *Annual Review of Sociology* 27 (August 2001): 415–44.

Norway's gender diversity on corporate boards: Kenneth R. Ahern and Amy K. Dittmar, "The Impact on Firm Valuation of Mandated Female Board Representation," *The Quarterly Journal of Economics* 127, no. 1 (February 2012): 137–97. See also: David A. Matsa and Amalia R. Miller, "A Female Style in Corporate Leadership? Evidence from Quotas," *American Economic Journal: Applied Economics* 5, no. 3 (July 2013): 136–69. An excellent account is in Page, *The Diversity Bonus*. Note, the purpose of the law was not to improve corporate performance but to reduce gender inequality. In this, the law ensured that female leaders received board experience to develop their talents and contacts, and inspire other women.

On firm performance and gender diversity: Some studies suggest women on boards lead to better financial performance, cf. Julia Dawson et al., "The CS Gender 3000: The Reward for Change," Credit Swiss Research Institute, September 2016. However, the studies have been criticized as methodologically simplistic, cf. "100 Women: Do Women on Boards Increase Company Profits?," *BBC News*, October 2017, https://www.bbc.com/news/41365364. More rigorous analyses have found a positive correlation (but not a causal link) between firm performances and female representation in top management in some instances. Cf. Corinne Post and Kris Byron, "Women on Boards and Firm Financial Performance: A Meta-Analysis," *Academy of Management Journal* 58, no. 2, November 7, 2014, https://journals.aom.org/doi/abs/10.5465/amj.2013.0319.

Diversity ending up with uniformity: An illustration is Greg Lukianoff and Jonathan Haidt's argument that American universities' approach to diversity has undermined the free exchange of ideas. Greg Lukianoff and Jonathan Haidt, "The Coddling of the American Mind," *Atlantic*, September 2015, https://www.theatlantic.com/magazine/archive/2015/09/the-coddling-of-the-american-mind/399356/. See also: Jonathan Haidt, "Viewpoint Diversity in the Academy," jonathanhaidt.com, accessed December, 31, 2020, https://jonathanhaidt.com/viewpoint-diversity/.

Teams with women outperform male-only groups: Anita W. Woolley et al., "Evidence for a Collective Factor in the Performance of Human Groups," *Science* 330, no. 6004 (October 29, 2010): 686–88.

On team diversity benefiting the organization: The reference work, stating, "In general, groups performing creative or innovative tasks often benefit from diversity," is Anita W. Woolley, Ishani Aggarwal, and Thomas W. Malone, "Collective Intelligence and Group Performance," *Current Directions in Psychological Science* 24, no. 6 (December 2015): 420–24. For a survey on the role of diversity in team performance spanning more than sixty years of research, see also: Hans van Dijk, Marloes L. van Engen, and Daan van Knippenberg, "Defying Conventional Wisdom: A Meta-Analytical Examination of the Differences Between Demographic and Job-Related Diversity Relationships with Performance," *Organizational Behavior and Human Decision Processes* 119, no. 1 (September 2012): 38–53. A robust finding of this literature is that diversity tends to benefit groups when they are performing creative tasks, but may impair them for more regular work, where efficiency is more important.

On thinking alone before deliberating in groups: André L. Delbecq and Andrew H. Van de Ven, "A Group Process Model for Problem Identification and Program Planning," *Journal of Applied Behavioral Science* 7, no. 4 (July 1, 1971); Andrew H. Van de Ven and André L. Delbecq, "The Effectiveness of Nominal, Delphi, and Interacting Group Decision Making Processes," *Academy of Management Journal* 17, no. 4 (December 1974): 605–21.

On Apple's teams: Joel M. Podolny and Morten T. Hansen, "How Apple Is Organized for Innovation," *Harvard Business Review*, November/December 2020, https://hbr.org/2020/11/how-apple-is-organized-for-innovation.

On adhering to majority rule: Reid Hastie and Tatsuya Kameda, "The Robust Beauty of Majority Rules in Group Decisions," *Psychological Review* 112, no. 2 (May 2005): 494–508. For more on decision-making in groups, see: R. Scott Tindale and Katharina Kluwe, "Decision Making in Groups and Organizations," in *The Wiley Blackwell Handbook of Judgment and Decision Making II*, eds. Gideon Keren and George Wu (Hoboken, NJ: Wiley Blackwell, 2015), 849–74.

Bill Joy quote: Rich Karlgaard, "How Fast Can You Learn?," *Forbes*, November 9, 2007, https://www.forbes.com/forbes/2007/1126/031.html.

Cuusoo and Lego: Hasan Jensen, "Celebrating 10 Years of Your Ideas!," Lego, accessed November 8, 2020, https://ideas.lego.com/blogs/a4ae09b6-0d4c-4307-9da8-3ee9f3d368d6/post/bebe460c-fd4c-413a-b0a7-ca757aad1ecc.

On diversity hindering group performance: Ishani Aggarwal and Anita W. Woolley show in a control experiment that teams with heterogenous cognitive styles have more difficulty reaching a strategic consensus, which increases errors, compared with homogenous teams. See: Ishani Aggarwal and Anita W. Woolley, "Do You See What I See? The Effect of Members' Cognitive Styles on Team Processes and Performance," *Organizational Behavior and Human Decision Processes* 122, no. 1 (September 2013): 92–99.

On global and local optima: Scott E. Page, *The Difference: How the Power of Diversity Creates Better Groups, Firms, Schools, and Societies* (Princeton, NJ: Princeton University Press, 2008). Page, in an interview with Kenneth Cukier in January 2021, noted: "It's not just in two dimensions [up or down]. Most ideas and products have dozens or hundreds of dimensions—not just you look left and right and don't see a higher point. Metaphorically, you could step in any one of dozens of directions." A deep look at how models shape society is Scott E. Page, *The Model Thinker: What You Need to Know to Make Data* (New York: Basic Books, 2018).

Andy Grove's "Helpful Cassandras": Andrew Grove, *Only the Paranoid Survive* (New York: Doubleday Business, 1996).

Ed Catmull and Cassandras: Ed Catmull and Amy Wallace, *Creativity, Inc.: Overcoming the Unseen Forces That Stand in the Way of True Inspiration* (New York: Random House, 2014).

History of the fool: Beatrice K. Otto, *Fools Are Everywhere: The Court Jester Around the World* (Chicago: University of Chicago Press, 2001). Note the jester is universal: The role appears in ancient Rome and India, courts of the Middle East and in China, as well as Europe.

Quip by Triboulet: Magda Romanska, "The History of the Court Jester," Boston Lyric Opera, March 24, 2014, http://blog.blo.org/the-history-of-court-jester-by-magda.

NASA and fools: Interview with Jeffrey Johnson of the University of Florida by Ian Sample, "Jokers Please: First Human Mars Mission May Need Onboard Comedians," *Guardian*, February 15, 2019, https://www.theguardian.com/science/2019/feb/15/jokers-please-first-human-mars-mission-may-need-onboard-comedians.

On Bari Weiss and the Gray Lady: Edmund Lee, "Bari Weiss Resigns from *New York Times* Opinion Post," *New York Times*, July 14, 2015, https://www.nytimes.com/2020/07/14/business/media/bari-weiss-resignation-new-york-times.html; Elahe Izadi and Jeremy Barr, "Bari Weiss Resigns from *New York Times*, Says 'Twitter Has Become Its Ultimate Editor,'" *Washington Post*, July 14, 2020, https://www.washingtonpost.com/media/2020/07/14/bari-weiss-resigns-new-york-times. Quotes from: Bari Weiss, "Resignation Letter," Bariweiss.com, July 14, 2020, https://www.bariweiss.com/resignation-letter. The authors thank the sources who helped in producing this account.

8. pluralism

Hannah Arendt and the Gestapo: The account is from Elisabeth Young-Bruehl, *Hannah Arendt: For Love of the World* (New Haven, CT: Yale University Press, 2004). The codes being Greek quotations from: Jeremy Adelman, "Pariah: Can Hannah Arendt Help Us Rethink Our Global Refugee Crisis?," *Wilson Quarterly*, Spring 2016, https://www.wilsonquarterly.com/quarterly/looking-back-moving-forward/pariah-can-hannah-arendt-help-us-rethink-our-global-refugee-crisis/. Our thanks to Arendt scholar Samantha Rose Hill for confirming the name style that Arendt used in 1933 (Stern was her last name through marriage).

Quote on America in the 1920s from a literary critic: Malcolm Cowley, *Exile's Return: A Literary Odyssey of the 1920s* (New York: Penguin, 1994), 279.

Diary entry of Nazi atrocity: The entry was on February 6, 1943. See: Rutka Laskier, *Rutka's Notebook: A Voice from the Holocaust*, eds. Daniella Zaidman-Mauer and Kelly Knauer (New York: Time/Yad Vashem, 2008), 29–30.

On market coordination: Charles E. Lindblom, *The Market System—What It Is, How It Works, and What to Make of It* (New Haven, CT: Yale University Press, 2001).

On Karl Popper's "paradox of tolerance": Karl Popper, "The Principle of Leadership," in *The Open Society and Its Enemies,* vol. 1 (Abington, UK: Routledge, 1945), note 4. The idea is raised only in a note, not the text. Building on

Plato's "paradox of freedom" (giving a tyrant the freedom to destroy freedom
means society ends up with no freedom), Popper writes: "Unlimited tolerance must lead to the disappearance of tolerance. If we extend unlimited tolerance even to those who are intolerant, if we are not prepared to defend a
tolerant society against the onslaught of the intolerant, then the tolerant will
be destroyed, and tolerance with them.—In this formulation, I do not imply,
for instance, that we should always suppress the utterance of intolerant phi-
losophies; as long as we can counter them by rational argument and keep
them in check by public opinion, suppression would certainly be most un-
wise. But we should claim the *right* to suppress them if necessary even by
force; for it may easily turn out that they are not prepared to meet us on the
level of rational argument, but begin by denouncing all argument; they may
forbid their followers to listen to rational argument, because it is deceptive,
and teach them to answer arguments by the use of their fists or pistols. We
should therefore claim, in the name of tolerance, the right not to tolerate the
intolerant." Note that even advocates of openness and diversity are not immune to the temptation to restrain expression. For instance, for many years
Popper taught "The Open Society and Its Enemies" at the London School of
Economics, where students jokingly nicknamed the course "The Open Society *by Its Enemy.*"

Arendt's books: Hannah Arendt, *The Origins of Totalitarianism* (New York:
Schocken Books, 1951); *The Human Condition* (Chicago: University of Chicago Press, 1958); *On Revolution* (New York: Penguin Books, 1963); *Eichmann
in Jerusalem: A Report on the Banality of Evil* (New York: Viking Press, 1963); *On
Violence* (Boston: Houghton Mifflin Harcourt, 1968); *Men in Dark Times* (Boston: Houghton Mifflin Harcourt, 1970); *Crisis of the Republic* (New York: Harcourt Brace Jovanovich, 1972); *Rahel Varnhagen: The Life of a Jewish Woman*
(New York: Harcourt Brace, 1974).

Arendt quotes: On "final conclusions": from Hannah Arendt, *Between Past and
Future: Eight Exercises in Political Thought* (New York: Penguin, 2006), 237.
"General will" is a term by Rousseau. "Men, not Man" appears in Arendt, *The
Human Condition*, 7. A "plurality of standpoints" is from Hannah Arendt, *The
Promise of Politics* (New York: Schocken, 2007), 175.

The "end of history": Fukuyama, *End of History.*

Silicon Valley versus Route 128: AnnaLee Saxenian, *Regional Advantage: Culture
and Competition in Silicon Valley and Route 128* (Cambridge, MA: Harvard University Press, 1994), 2–3. See also: "Silicon Valley Is Changing, and Its Lead over
Other Tech Hubs Narrowing," *Economist*, September 1, 2018, https://www
.economist.com/briefing/2018/09/01/silicon-valley-is-changing-and-its-lead
-over-other-tech-hubs-narrowing; "Why Startups Are Leaving Silicon Valley,"
Economist, August 30, 2018, https://www.economist.com/leaders/2018/08/30
/why-startups-are-leaving-silicon-valley.

Imperial China and Europe's fragmented states: Joel Mokyr, *A Culture of
Growth: The Origins of the Modern Economy* (Princeton, NJ: Princeton University Press, 2016). See also: Jared Diamond, *Guns, Germs, and Steel: The Fates of
Human Societies* (New York: Norton, 1997). A readable romp is: John Mickle-
thwait and Adrian Wooldridge, *The Fourth Revolution: The Global Race to Reinvent the State* (New York: Penguin, 2015).

On Collison's "progress studies": Interview with Patrick Collison by Kenneth Cukier, January 2020. Also see Patrick Collison and Tyler Cowen, "We Need a New Science of Progress," *Atlantic*, July 30, 2019, https://www.theatlantic .com/science/archive/2019/07/we-need-new-science-progress/594946. For a critical assessment, see: Cukier, "Innovation Around Innovation—Studying the Science of Progress," *The Economist, Babbage* podcast, September 4, 2019, https://www.economist.com/podcasts/2019/09/04/innovation-around -innovation-studying-the-science-of-progress.

Silicon Valley groupthink from Podolny's classes: It's a joke.

Reframing gay marriage: Kevin Nix, "It's All in the Frame: Winning Marriage Equality in America," Open Democracy, September 8, 2015, https://www .opendemocracy.net/en/openglobalrights-openpage/its-all-in-frame-win ning-marriage-equality-in-america.

On gay marriage as liberty versus love: "In Depth: Gay and Lesbian Rights," Gallup, poll of November 26–29, 2012, https://news.gallup.com/poll/1651 /gay-lesbian-rights.aspx.

Public opinion poll on gay marriage: Justin McCarthy, "U.S. Support for Same-Sex Marriage Matches Record High," Gallup, June 1, 2020, https:// news.gallup.com/poll/311672/support-sex-marriage-matches-record-high .aspx).

On the liberal arts: Epstein, *Range*.

On race and sociology: On parenting: Megan R. Underhill, "White Parents Teach Their Children to Be Colorblind. Here's Why That's Bad for Everyone," *Washington Post*, October 5, 2018, https://www.washingtonpost.com/nation /2018/10/05/white-parents-teach-their-children-be-colorblind-heres-why -thats-bad-everyone; on colorblind racism, see also: Meghan Burke, *Colorblind Racism* (Cambridge: Polity Press, 2019)

On the creative class and openness: Richard Florida, *The Rise of the Creative Class* (New York: Basic Books, 2002), chap. 14. Quote from his video course: Richard Florida, "Technology, Talent, and Tolerance in the Creative City," Coursera, accessed November 9, 2020, https://www.coursera.org/lecture /city-and-you-find-best-place/technology-talent-and-tolerance-in-the-creative -city-instructor-video-uVp5h.

On the public sphere: Jürgen Habermas, *The Structural Transformation of the Public Sphere: An Inquiry into a Category of Bourgeois Society*, trans. Thomas Burger (Cambridge, MA: MIT Press, 1989).

On deliberative democracy: James S. Fishkin, *Democracy When the People Are Thinking: Revitalizing Our Politics Through Public Deliberation* (Oxford: Oxford University Press, 2018).

On empowered democracy: Roberto Mangabeira Unger, *False Necessity: Anti-Necessitarian Social Theory in the Service of Radical Democracy* (Cambridge: Cambridge University Press, 1987).

Unger quotes: On federalism: Roberto Mangabeira Unger, "Big Thinkers: Roberto Mangabeira Unger on Empowered Democracy in the UK," Institute for Government, November 15, 2013, https://www.instituteforgovernment.org.uk /events/big-thinkers-roberto-mangabeira-unger-empowered-democracy-uk.

Unger on education: Roberto Mangabeira Unger, "No One Should Have to Do Work That Can Be Done by a Machine," talk at Harvard Thinks Big 4, You-

Tube video, 10:47, February 28, 2013, https://www.youtube.com/watch?v=N8n5ZL5PwiA.

On Judith Shklar: Judith Shklar, "The Liberalism of Fear," in *Liberalism and the Moral Life,* ed. Nancy Rosenblum (Cambridge, MA: Harvard University Press, 1989), 31–38.

On *Fearless Girl*: The statue was placed in front of the bull on March 7, 2017, yet was relocated to another area of the financial district in November 2018. A plaque with two footprints now marks the spot where she once stood her ground.

9. vigilance

On Covid-19 remedy skit: Sarah Cooper, "How to Medical," YouTube video, 0:49, https://www.youtube.com/watch?v=RxDKW75ueIU.

On Sarah Cooper: James Poniewozik, "Trump Said, 'I Have the Best Words.' Now They're Hers," *New York Times*, May 27, 2020, https://www.nytimes.com/2020/05/27/arts/television/trump-sarah-cooper.html. See also: ZZ Packer, "Sarah Cooper Doesn't Mimic Trump. She Exposes Him," *New York Times*, June 25, 2020, https://www.nytimes.com/2020/06/25/magazine/sarah-cooper-doesnt-mimic-trump-she-exposes-him.html. The authors thank Cooper for her help in producing this account.

Cooper quote: Shirley Li, "Sarah Cooper Has Mastered the Trump Joke," *Atlantic,* May 8, 2020, https://www.theatlantic.com/culture/archive/2020/05/comedian-behind-viral-trump-pandemic-tiktok-sarah-cooper/611329. See also: Sarah Cooper and Sarah Cristobal, "Comedian Sarah Cooper on How Her Viral Trump Parodies Came to Be," *InStyle*, July 10, 2020, https://www.instyle.com/news/sarah-cooper-essay-trump-impressions.

Heytea's success: Farhan Shah, "Heytea Founder Neo Nie on the Ingredients to the Brand's Success," *Peak*, July 23, 2020, https://www.thepeakmagazine.com.sg/interviews/heytea-founder-neo-nie-business-success/; Li Tao, "How Chinese Tea-Drink Brand Heytea Saves Millions in Marketing Costs Thanks to Its Millennial Customers," *South China Morning Post*, August 28, 2018, https://www.scmp.com/tech/start-ups/article/2161529/how-chinese-tea-drink-brand-heytea-saves-millions-marketing-costs. See also: "He Is a Post-90s CEO Worth 4 billion," *DayDay News*, September 23, 2020, https://daydaynews.cc/en/technology/812466.html.

Nthabiseng Mosia quotes on growing up: Interview with Mosia by Kenneth Cukier, January 2021. Also see "Nthabiseng Mosia, an Entrepreneur Finding Affordable Clean Energy Solutions for Africa by Harnessing the Power of Solar Technology," Lionesses of Africa, December 11, 2016, https://www.lionessesofafrica.com/blog/2016/12/11/startup-story-nthabiseng-mosia. See also: World Economic Forum, "Bring the Power of Solar to Sierra Leone," YouTube video, 3:17, December 16, 2019, https://www.youtube.com/watch?v=auzkln9MMjk&feature=emb_title.

On Mosia: Dhivana Rajgopaul, "This SA Entrepreneur Creates Solar Solutions for Communities in Sierra Leone," *Independent Online*, May 7, 2018, https://www.iol.co.za/business-report/entrepreneurs/this-sa-entrepreneur-creates-solar-solutions-for-communities-in-sierra-leone-14819523. See also: Pavitra Raja, "This Is How Social Innovators Are Leading the Race to Zero Emissions," World Economic Forum, November 9, 2020, https://www.weforum.org

/agenda/2020/11/this-is-how-social-innovators-are-leading-the-race-to-zero-emissions.

On Easy Solar: Easy Solar, "Easy Solar Raises $5M in Series A Equity and Debt Funding to Scale Operations in West Africa," press release, September 30, 2020, https://www.pv-magazine.com/press-releases/easy-solar-raises-5m-in-series-a-equity-and-debt-funding-to-scale-operations-in-west-africa.

Yuval Noah Harari on human cooperation: "A Conversation with Mark Zuckerberg and Yuval Noah Harari," Facebook, April 26, 2019, transcript, https://about.fb.com/wp-content/uploads/2019/04/transcript_-marks-personal-challenge-yuval-noah-harari.pdf.

Looking into the mind: It is only recently (i.e., the late nineteenth century) that scholars have looked deeper into decision-making abilities. The field of "judgment and decision-making" was founded in the 1950s.

On "ideological silos": "How Politics Has Pulled the Country in Different Directions," *Wall Street Journal*, November 10, 2020, https://www.wsj.com/graphics/polarized-presidential-elections/.

On global economic improvements: "Decline of Global Extreme Poverty Continues but Has Slowed: World Bank," World Bank, press release, September 19, 2018, https://www.worldbank.org/en/news/press-release/2018/09/19/decline-of-global-extreme-poverty-continues-but-has-slowed-world-bank.

Talmud quote: This is a popular rendition of the passage: "A man is shown only what is suggested by his own thoughts." From Rabbi Shemuel ben Nachmani, as quoted in the tractate Berakhot (55b.), *Tractate Berakhot: Edition, Translation, and Commentary*, ed. Heinrich W. Guggenheimer (Berlin: de Gruyter, 2000). The passage is in reference to the interpretation of dreams.

The emotionalists around the world: In Peru: Michael Stott, "Peru President's Ousting Underlines Resurgent Latin American Populism," *Financial Times*, November 11, 2020, https://www.ft.com/content/5c4c4411-e648-4681-bdde-186ff5b20d3e. In the Philippines: "More than 7,000 Killed in the Philippines in Six Months, as President Encourages Murder," Amnesty International, May 18, 2020, https://www.amnesty.org.uk/philippines-president-duterte-war-on-drugs-thousands-killed. In Germany: Alexander Frölich, "Rechtsextremisten steuern die Corona-Proteste zum Teil schon," *Der Tagesspiegel*, November 16, 2020, https://www.tagesspiegel.de/berlin/berliner-sicherheitsbehoerden-alarmiert-rechtsextremisten-steuern-die-corona-proteste-zum-teil-schon/26627460.html; Tilma Steffen and Ferdinand Otto, "Aktivisten kamen als Gäste der AfD in den Bundestag," *Die Zeit*, November 19, 2020, https://www.zeit.de/politik/deutschland/2020-11/bundestag-afd-stoerer-corona-protest-einschleusung.

On François Chollet: François Chollet, *Deep Learning with Python* (Shelter Island, NY: Manning, 2017). See https://blog.keras.io/the-limitations-of-deep-learning.html. In an interview with Kenneth Cukier in February 2021, he elaborated on how to improve "extreme generatlization," or framing: "The way you learn and adapt is by constantly making analogies with past situations and concepts. If you have a very rich and diverse bank of past situations and concepts to leverage, you will be able to make more powerful analogies."

Paris terrorism attack: This account is based on excellent reporting from: Angelique Chrisafis, "'It Looked Like a Battlefield': The Full Story of What

Happened in the Bataclan," *Guardian*, November 20, 2015, https://www.the guardian.com/world/2015/nov/20/bataclan-witnesses-recount-horror-paris -attacks; "What Happened at the Bataclan?," BBC, December 9, 2015, https:// www.bbc.co.uk/news/world-europe-34827497; Adam Nossiter and Andrew Higgins, "'Scene of Carnage' Inside Sold-Out Paris Concert Hall," *New York Times*, November 13, 2015, https://www.nytimes.com/2015/11/14/world /europe/paris-attacks.html; Andrew Higgins and Milan Schreuer, "Attackers in Paris 'Did Not Give Anybody a Chance,'" *New York Times*, November 14, 2015, https://www.nytimes.com/2015/11/15/world/europe/paris-terror -attacks-a-display-of-absolute-barbarity.html.

Quoting Gérald Bronner: Gérald Bronner, *La Pensée Extrême* (Paris: PUF, 2009). Bronner describes his experiences in attempting to deradicalize young extremists based on his approach to extreme thinking in *Déchéance de rationalité* (Paris: Grasset, 2019).

Quoting Abaaoud: David A. Graham, "The Mysterious Life and Death of Abdelhamid Abaaoud," *Atlantic*, November 19, 2015, https://www.theatlantic.com /international/archive/2015/11/who-was-abdelhamid-abaaoud-isis-paris /416739; Kersten Knipp, "'Allah Has Chosen Me': Profile of the Paris Attackers," *Deutsche Welle*, November 21, 2015, https://www.dw.com/en/allah-has -chosen-me-profile-of-the-paris-attackers/a-18865801. See also: Stacy Meichtry, Noemie Bisserbe, and Matthew Dalton, "Paris Attacks' Alleged Ringleader, Now Dead, Had Slipped into Europe Unchecked," *Wall Street Journal*, November 19, 2015, https://www.wsj.com/articles/abdelhamid-abaaoud-alleged -mastermind-of-paris-attacks-is-dead-french-prosecutor-says-1447937255.

Terrorists despise people's cognitive flexibility: Bronner, *La Pensée Extrême*.

From burning books to burning people: The sentiment is famously owed to the nineteenth-century German essayist Heinrich Heine, in "Almansor: A Tragedy" (1823): *"Dort wo man Bücher verbrennt, verbrennt man auch am Ende Menschen,"* translated as: "Where they have burned books, they will end in burning human beings."

Fitzgerald on contradictory ideas: F. Scott Fitzgerald, *The Crack-Up* (New York: New Directions Books, 1945).

"The frontiers of our imagination . . .": Inspired by Wittgenstein on the limits of language and the world. Ludwig Wittgenstein, *Tractatus Logico-Philosophicus*, prop. 5.6: (Milton Park, Abingdon, Oxon: Routledge, 1921): 150.

acknowledgments

This book has three authors but many contributors, without whom it wouldn't exist. Our collective thanks first go to our publishers, Stephen Morrow of Dutton and Jamie Joseph of Penguin UK, and our agent, Lisa Adams of the Garamond Agency, for her skilled editing. We thank Andrew Wright for editing and Phil Cain for fact-checking (though any inaccuracies remain ours). We also thank copyeditors Katherine Kinast and Erica Ferguson, proofreader Kim Lewis, text designer Nancy Resnick, US cover designer Jason Booher, and UK cover designer Steve Leard. Thanks also to Rimjhim Dey and the team at DEY, as well as Penguin and Dutton, for helping to promote the book.

Many of the people who grace the pages took the time to speak with us. We thank, in alphabetical order, Andreas Altmann, Michael Baker, Regina Barzilay, Gérald Bronner, Ronald Burt, François Chollet, Daniel Dennett, Scott Donaldson, Inez Fung, Alison Gopnik, Peter Habeler, Demis Hassabis, Alan Kay, Tania Lombrozo, Heinz Machat, Gary Marcus, Robert Merton, Alyssa Milano, Alberto Moel,

Nthabiseng Mosia, Scott Page, Judea Pearl, Sander Ruys, Peter Schwartz, Klaus Schweinsberg, Katrin Suder, Noam Tamir, Michael Tomasello, will.i.am (and Sallie Olmsted), and Apple's communications team.

In addition to our collective thanks, the authors also have individual acknowledgments.

From Kenn: My appreciation to Zanny Minton Beddoes, the editor of *The Economist*, for her support, and to my colleagues, whose ideas enriched these pages. Thank you to Peter Tufano, dean of the Saïd Business School at the University of Oxford, and to the faculty and students, for a rich intellectual environment. Likewise, I thank the team at the British think tank Chatham House, Wilton Park, and the Ditchley Foundation led by James Arroyo, for producing reports and events that improve people's framing.

Many interviews for *The Economist*'s *Babbage* podcast and *Open Future* were helpful in writing this book, including with Mustafa Suleyman of DeepMind, Patrick Collison of Stripe, Aaron Levie of Box, the entrepreneurs Elad Gil and Daniel Gross, Matt Ridley, Eric Topol, David Eagleman, Adam Grant, Howard Gardner, Daniel Levitin, Bill Janeway, Andrew McAfee, Roy Bahat, Zavain Dar, Nan Li, Benedict Evans, Azeem Azhar, David McCourt, James Field, Dan Levin, Steven Johnson, Bina Venkataraman, Sean McFate, and Shane Parrish. (And praise goes to the *Babbage* producers: Sandra Shmueli, Amica Nowlan, William Warren, Jason Hosken, Simon Jarvis, Ellie Clifford, and our boss Anne McElvoy.)

Many others fertilized my thinking, notably Helen Green, Robert Young, Daniel Fung, Niko Waesche, Tim Höttges, Michael Kleeman, Matt Hindman, John Turner, and Katia Verresen.

From Viktor: My thanks to the University of Oxford and to Keble College—great places for ideation. I also would like to thank the many individuals with whom I have had conversations about human framing large and small over the past couple of years, including my colleagues at the German Digital Council.

From Francis: My thinking has been enriched by many engaging discussions with my outstanding current and former fellow researchers at the European School of Management and Technology in Berlin. I am particularly grateful to Matt Bothner, Tamer Boyaci, Gianluca Carnabuci, Linus Dahlander, Laura Guillén, Rajshri Jayaraman, Henry Sauermann, Martin Schweinsberg, and Luc Wathieu. The diversity of their intellectual backgrounds and outlooks on a variety of research problems has considerably enhanced my repertoire of frames.

I am grateful to all my former colleagues at Duke University, from both the operations and decision science departments, for these wonderful rookie years. Working with Peng Sun, Miguel Lobo, Otis Jennings, and many others made me a better framer. The wisdom of Paul Zipkin and Bob Winkler continues to guide me to this day. I am also grateful to Joel Podolny, Ed Kaplan, and the faculty of the Yale School of Management, and in particular my former PhD student Saed Alizamir, for sharing their vision on the new curriculum.

I have greatly benefited from the excellence of INSEAD's faculty, both in France and Singapore. I am particularly in debt to Henrik Bresman, Steve Chick, Enrico Diecidue, Karan Girotra, Denis Gromb, Gilles Hilary, Serguei Netessine, Ioana Popescu, Ludo Van der Heyden, and Martin Gargiulo.

Human cooperation enables the production of things beyond a single mind, for which we are the grateful beneficiaries with this book (whose order of authorship is alphabetical).

Our final collective thanks go to our families, who put up with us during the writing process: we might have been out of the picture, but you were always in our frame.

—K.N.C., V.M.S., F.d.V.
London, Oxford/Zell am See, Berlin
November 2020

index

Abaaoud, Abdelhamid, 213–214
abstraction and generalization
  causality and, 53–54
  as defining characteristics of
    human cognition, 211
  mental models made from ability
    of, 54–55, 59
  as necessary for ambition and
    transcendence, 55
  pattern recognition and, 56
  relationship between, 64
accountability, 64, 65–66
Adair, John, 46
Adichie, Chimamanda Ngozi, 84
agency
  causality and, 65
  counterfactuals and, 91
  explainability as foundation of, 64
  framing as empowering, 27
  framing as ideal for efficiently
    preparing for, 208–209
  mental models and, 9
  mutability and, 107
  number of constraints and, 118, 141
  privileging human inaction and, 110
  responsibility and, 65–66
  social structures and, 66

agility of mind, 215–218
airplanes, development of, 36–38
All Quiet on the Western Front
  (Remarque), 83–84
AlphaZero system, 17–18
alternative realities
  constraints and shaping, 100–103
  contradictions in, 110–111
  counterfactuals and, 12–13, 79,
    82–86, 94
  envisioning, and shaping future,
    94–95
  existence of more than one, 159
  framing and envisioning, 9, 79,
    90, 94
  minimal-change principle and, 108
  monocultures and, 186
Amazon business model, 133–134
ambition and abstraction and
  generalization, 55
Americanah (Adichie), 84
Ansari, Anousheh, 194
antibiotics, ineffectiveness of, 1–2
Apple
  framing by teams at, 164–165
  inspiration for computer
    system, 159

index

Apple *(cont.)*
   leadership of, ability to frame
      differently, 149, 150–151
   Nokia versus, 6–7
Ardern, Jacinda, 32
Arendt, Hannah, 173–174, 180–181,
   197, 198
Aristotle, 84–85
Armstrong, Neil, 34
artificial intelligence (AI)
   cannot conjure constraints, 118
   e-sports, 69–70
   failure to see causality, 45
   generated music, 118–119
   human element in, 93, 211
   hyper-rationalists' reliance on, to
      solve problems, 15–16
   inability of, to frame, 44, 45–46
   lack of imagination, 119
   as reinforcing significance of
      framing, 211
   self-driving cars, 92–93
arts
   AI-generated music, 118–119
   business model for music
      industry, 120
   constraints and, 100–103, 111–113
   as constructed counterfactual
      realities, 82–85
   imagination and, 82–85
   mental models and, 11
Austrian wine industry, 108–109

Bach, Johann Sebastian, 118–119
Barzilay, Regina, 2–3, 4–5, 19, 211
Bay of Pigs invasion, 89, 234
Bernanke, Ben "Helicopter Ben,"
   49–51, 101
Bezos, Jeff, 134
Black-Scholes theory, 39–40
Blue Ocean Strategy, 35
Branscomb, Lewis, 161
Brin, Sergey, 194
Bronner, Gérald, 213, 214
Brunelleschi, Filippo, 11
Burt, Ronald, 157
Bush, George W., 49
business and management
   Amazon, 133–134
   benefits of mental diversity within,
      161–166, 241–242

case study method of education, 86,
   87–88, 155
difficulties changing corporate
   culture, 170–171
mental models and, 35
monocultures and death of, 182–183
music industry model, 120
reform of traditional pedagogical
   method in schools, 149–150
Silicon Valley versus East Coast
   technology titans, 183, 185–186
"thinking outside the box," 46
Byrne, Ruth, 90, 110

Camden, New Jersey, police force,
   134–136
Cappelli, Louis, Jr., 135
carbon dioxide and climate,
   74–76, 168
"carbon sinks," 76
Carcraft, 93
Carter, Jimmy, 116
Cassandras, 167–168
Cassirer, Ernst, 25
Catmull, Ed, 167–168
"causal determinism," 88–89
causality
   ability to abstract from direct
      observation and, 53–54
   agency and, 65
   AI's failure to see, 45
   children and, 80–82
   coincidence and, 66–67
   correlation and, 68
   counterfactuals and, 77, 79, 90
   enables comprehension and
      explainability of reality, 52, 60
   as foundation of human
      cognition, 12
   in framing, 88–90
   input of humans needed for
      technology to outperform
      humans, 70
   needed for application of mental
      models, 62
   predictability with, 52
   reactions resulting from, 53
   as result of being part of society, 58
   scientific methodology prevents
      wrong inferences made from, 12
   skepticism about, 68

statisticians and, 68
ultra-emotionalists and, 68–69
causal reasoning, 55
Cerf, Bennett, 101–102
Charging Bull statue, 198–199
Charpentier, Emmanuelle, 137
Chollet, François, 211
Churchill, Winston, 41
"Circumstances Affecting the Heat of
the Sun's Rays" (Foote), 73–74
clean-slate strategy, 158–160, 241
climate and carbon dioxide,
74–76, 168
Coconet, 118–119
cognitive complexity, 161
"cognitive effort," 110
"cognitive foraging," 156–158, 160
cognitive niche, 57, 58, 59, 230
"Cognitive Wheels" (Dennett), 44–45
coincidence and causality, 66–67
Collins, Jim, 2–3
Collison, Patrick, 185
Computers as Theatre (Laurel), 85
consistency principle, 110–114
constraints
agency and number of, 118, 141
application method, 120–121
application of too many, 45
as boundaries on alternative
realities, 100–103
changing, 201–202
consistency of, 104, 110–114
current reality as impacted by,
117–118
enable identification of viable
options, 117
goal of, 114
hard, described, 104
imagination and, 47, 220
importance to counterfactuals of,
13, 115
increase agency, 118
as liberating, 100–103
minimal, 104
minimal-change principle and,
108–110
mutability of, 104–107, 110
space exploration and, 105
technology cannot conjure, 118
control, 64, 65–66
Cook, Tim, 151

Cooper, Sarah, 201–202
correlation and causality, 68
counterfactuals
agency and, 91
alternative realities and, 12–13, 79,
82–86, 94
causality and, 77, 79, 90
causal link between carbon dioxide
and climate and, 74–75
children and, 80–82
cognitive homogeneity as
death of, 207
as counterbalance to "causal
determinism," 88–89
as crucial to progress by enabling
what-if questions, 12–13
described, 12
in education, 86–88
finding relevant, 45
focused and goal-oriented
nature of, 76
as form of evolution, 93–94
functionality of, 94
imagination and, 76, 79, 90
implicit knowledge and,
90–91
literature and art, 82–85
minimal-change principle and,
109–110
mutable constraints and, 106
omitting versus adding mutable
action and, 110
thinking in, as natural for
humans, 77
Coupland, Douglas, 112
Covid-19, framing of, 31–33
Craik, Kenneth, 226
creativity. *See* imagination
Crick, Francis, 132
CRISPR, 137
Cuban missile crisis,
89–90
"cultural niche," 58
Cuusoo, 165–166
"Cyclopedia of Puzzles," 46

Dabiq, 213
Darwin, Charles, 7, 131
data, effect of frame applied to, 6
Days of Destruction, Days of Revolt
(Hedges and Sacco), 135

decision-making
  framing as fundamental to, 5, 8
  influence of different
    characterizations of outcomes, 10
  mental models reduce cognitive
    load by focusing mind, 11–12
  values in, 39–40
"deep reinforcement learning," 70
Defense of the Ancients 2 (Dota 2), 69–70
Dennett, Daniel, 44–45
Descartes, René, 16
DeVore, Irven, 230
Diamond, Jared, 183–184
Dick, Philip K., 111
"diversity dividend," 161–166
Donham, Wallace, 87, 156, 240
Doudna, Jennifer, 137

Earhart, Amelia, 160
Easy Solar, 203–204
Ebola, misframing of, 30–31, 32
economy. *See also* financial markets
  classical models of, 130
  death of business monocultures,
    182–183
  essence of market, 176–177
  financial crisis of 2008, 49–51, 101
Edison, Thomas, 10, 117
efficiency
  of choosing and applying mental
    models, 153, 208–209
  framing and, 110, 144
  human processing and, 110
  in reframing, 129–131, 144
Einstein, Albert, 8, 35, 78, 131–132,
    138–139
electric cars, 142
The End of History and the Last Man
    (Fukuyama), 20
Entebbe raid, 97–100, 101, 107,
    115, 235
e-sports, 69–70
evolution, theory of, 7
explainability
  causality enables, of reality, 60
  as essential to success of mental
    model, 62
  as foundation of human agency,
    responsibility, and control, 64
  helps learning, 63–64
  as human need, 65

Fasciculus Medicinae, 6
Fearless Girl statue, 198–199
Fermat's Last Theorem, 137
financial markets
  Charging Bull and *Fearless Girl*
    statues, 198–199
  free flow of information and, 215
  historical mental models for, 50
  mental models for financial crisis of
    2008, 50–51
  options pricing in, 39–40
  quantitative easing, 51
Fitzgerald, F. Scott, 216
Flipkart, 119
Florida, Richard, 192
Foote, Eunice, 73–74, 168, 232
framing. *See also* causality;
      constraints; counterfactuals;
      mental models
  agility of mind as undergirding, 217
  AI as reinforcing significance of, 211
  AI's inability to do, 44, 45–46
  to allow adaptation and survival, 21
  attention to agency and, 107
  being open-minded and, 204
  conditions for, 221
  dangers of poor, 214–215
  described, 4–5, 36–38
  efficiency and, 110, 144
  emotionalists as poor at, 210
  as empowering agency, 27
  as enabling creativity and
    imagination, 26, 33
  envisioning alternative realities
    and, 9, 79, 90, 94
  as fundamental to
    decision-making, 5, 8
  as fundamental to human
    cognition, 5, 25
  governments, 29–30
  homophily and, 89, 162, 234
  humans cannot stop, 46
  as liberating, 27
  magnification of certain elements
    and minimization of others, 6
  need for flexibility in, 214
  oppression and, 175–176
  other terms for, 25
  as process, 39
  processes involved in, 208–209
  as subconscious action, 8

technology's inability to do, 17–18,
    44, 45–46
terrorists and, 213–214
uniformity as end of successful, 207
"framing effect," 10
Francis I (king of France), 169
Freud, Sigmund, 25, 80
Frisch, Otto, 133
Fukuyama, Francis, 20, 181
Fung, Inez, 75–76, 168

Gabriel, Peter, 112
Gazzaniga, Michael, 62–63
Gehry, Frank, 102–103
Geisel, Theodor Seuss, 101–102, 103
gene editing, 137
generalization. See abstraction and
    generalization
"global optimum," 166–167, 243
Google, 194
Google DeepMind, 17–18
Gopnik, Alison, 80–82
Graham, Martha, 102, 103
Great Depression, 50
Green Eggs and Ham (Seuss), 101–102
Griezmann, Antoine, 77–78
groupthink, 89, 162, 234
Grove, Andy, 167, 194

Habeler, Peter, 123–126, 127
Habermas, Jürgen, 195–196
Hahn, Otto, 132–133
halicin, process of finding, 2–3
Hansen, James, 75
Harari, Yuval Noah, 20, 79, 205
Harvard Business Review, 156, 240
Hedges, Chris, 135
Henry, Joseph, 73
Heytea shops, 202–203
Higgs boson, 35
Hillary, Sir Edmund, 123
Hofstadter, Douglas, 230
Homo Deus (Harari), 20
homophily, framing and tendency
    toward, 89, 162, 234
Huang, Cheng-Zhi Anna, 118–119
Huang, Jen-Hsun, 194
human cognition. See also entries
    beginning with cognitive
adhering to well-honed mental
    models as default of, 127, 179, 207
agility of mind, 215–218
causality as foundation of, 12
of children, 80–82
counterfactuals as form of evolution
    of, 93–94
counterfactuals as natural to, 77
creating model of world as main
    purpose of, 226
defining characteristics of, 211
dimensions of, 13
dissonance of reframing, 140
as essence of humanness, 180
fundamental nature of framing to, 5
homogeneity of, as death of
    counterfactuals, 207
hyper-rationalists and
    ultra-emotionalists and
    uniqueness of, 18
importance of pluralism to, 181
mental models as fundamental to,
    5, 11, 25, 26, 208
mental models reduce load on, by
    focusing, 11–12
mutability and, 106–107
preference for processing
    efficiently, 110
restrictions on, 175–176
science and understanding, 206
as simulation of reality, 26
social structure's belief in validity of
    dominant mental model and, 179
terrrorists' consistency, 213
human progress, 19–21
Hume, David, 68
hyper-rationalists
scientific management theory, 17
technology as answer to problems,
    15–16, 69, 210–211

IBM, 182
IKEA, 129–130
imagination
advantages and disadvantages of
    lively, 38
agility of mind and, 218
AI lacks, 119
constraints and, 47, 220
counterfactuals and, 76,
    79, 90
enabled by frames, 26, 33
literature and, 82–85

index

imagination *(cont.)*
  tolerance and, 192–193
  values and, 39
immigration, 191–194
implicit knowledge and
    counterfactuals, 90–91
information, free flow of, 215
"insight problems," 152
instinct, 16–17, 69
Internet Protocol, 132
inventions, changing frames for, 10
irrationality and humanness, 16
Israel, 97–100, 101, 107, 115

Jobs, Steve, 149, 150–151, 159, 194
Johnson-Laird, Philip, 226
Joy, Bill, 165

Kaepernick, Colin, 6
Kahneman, Daniel, 10, 90
Kamprad, Ingvar, 129
Kaplan, Craig, 152
Kay, Alan, 158–159, 241
Kennedy, John F., 89–90, 234
Kim, W. Chan, 35
King, Martin Luther, Jr., 41
Kleiner, Eugene, 42
Kodak, 182
Kuhn, Thomas, 10

Langdell, Christopher Columbus,
    86–87
Langley, Samuel, 37
language, grammatical, 57, 58
Lanier, Jaron, 112
"latticework of models," 129
Laurel, Brenda, 85
learning and explainability, 63–64
learning as disruptive, 152–154
"Lego Ideas," 165–166
Leopold the Pious, 169
Lilienthal, Otto, 36
Lister, Joseph, 61–62
Lo, Andrew, 130
"local optimum," 166–167, 243
Lombrozo, Tania, 63–64
Lysenko, Trofim, and Lysenkoism, 7

MacGyver (television program), 91
Mandžukić, Mario, 77–78
maps, 27–28

Mauborgne, Renée, 35
McCarthy, John, 44
McDowell, Alex, 114
Meitner, Lise, 133
mental diversity
  advantages of, when identifying
    solutions, 166–167, 176
  broadening range of frames,
    155–156, 160–161, 241
  business monocultures and, 183
  clean-slate strategy for increasing,
    158–160, 241
  "cognitive foraging" for increasing,
    156–158, 160
  conceptual leaps necessary for,
    152–153
  friction resulting from, 194–195
  ideological silos and, 207
  importance of, when reframing,
    162–163
  as mind-set, not method, 151–154
  within organizations, 161–166,
    241–242
  Podolny and, 150–151
  rise and fall of social structures and,
    183–185
  social structure's belief in validity of
    dominant mental model and, 179
  variation not volume as
    important, 154
mental models
  art and, 11
  banning certain, 186–187
  broadness of, and ability to work in
    different circumstances, 144–146
  building real models to support,
    115–117
  business and management and, 35
  causal, from ability to abstract from
    direct observation and, 54–55, 59
  choosing new, 40–44
  coexistence of competing,
    198–199
  coexistence of new and old, 134
  cognitive dexterity necessary to
    entertain many different, 168
  convincing causal explanations
    needed for application of, 62
  dangers of exclusion of alternative,
    179–182
  defined, 226

efficiency of choosing, 153, 208–209
emotionalists and, 69
employed affect options, 5
end of history and liberal, market democracy as only, 181–182
everyday use of, 9, 25
explainability as essential to success of, 62
for financial crisis of 2008, 50–51
flawed causal, 66–67
as foundation of human cognition, 5, 25, 26, 208
hard constraints and, 104
harnessing, 139–140, 219
historical, for financial markets, 50
importance of diversity of, when reframing, 162–163
invention of new, 7–8
keep world manageable and thus actionable, 9
learning enabled by, 64
maps as physical representations of, 27–28
as means of finding solutions, 4–5, 8, 38–39
need for diversity of, 151–152, 186
nine-dot test and, 46
as operationalizing values, 39
other terms for, 25
pluralism as flourishing of many clashing, 177–178
pluralism of, versus uniformity of, 14–15
poor, 6–7, 60–61, 178–179, 186
reapplication of same successful, 127, 179, 207
reduce cognitive load by focusing mind, 11–12
as shaping worldview, 39–40
single, as truth, 179
social structure's belief in validity of dominant, 179
space exploration and, 33–35
technology's need for human input of causal, to outperform humans, 70
as templates for human cognition, 11
tendency toward homophily and, 89, 162, 234
tension between, 160–161
use and validation of, 40

Messner, Reinhold, 123–126, 127
metaphors, importance of, 57
MeToo movement, 24
migration and mobility, 191–194
Milano, Alyssa, 23–24
minimal-change principle, 108–110
Minority Report (film), 111–114
misframing, 6–7, 10, 30–31
Mokyr, Joel, 183–184
monocultures, 179–183
monolithic thinking, 20, 180
Monument Valley, 85–86
moon landing, 33–34
Morris, Jan (formerly James), 160
Mosia, Nthabiseng, 203–204
mountain climbing, 123–126, 127
Mount Everest, 123–126, 127
Munger, Charlie, 129
Murdoch, Rupert, 194
Musk, Elon, 105–106, 194
mutability, 104–107, 110
mutilated checkerboard problem, 152–153

Nadella, Satya, 194
Neptune, prediction of existence of, 35
Netanyahu, Jonathan "Yoni," 100
Newton, 7–8, 78, 131
New York Times, 34, 170–171
Nie Yunchen, 202–203
nine-dot test, 46, 47
Nix, Kevin, 189
Nokia versus Apple, 6–7
Norgay, Tenzing, 123
Norway, 163

Occam's razor, 108
Ono, Koichi, 65
OpenAI, 70
options
    AI's failure to conjure restraints creates too many, 118
    constraints enable identification of viable, 117
    counterfactuals and, 90
    framing as ideal for efficiently identifying valuable, 208
    mental models employed affect, 5
    reframing provides new, 126
"Our World in Data" project, 19

Page, Scott, 166–167, 243
paradigm shifts, 10–11
"paradox of tolerance," 178, 244
Parker, Robert, 109
Pasteur, Louis, 61
pattern recognition, 56
Pauling, Linus, 132
Pearl, Judea, 68
Perec, Georges, 103, 236
Perfume (Süskind), 83
Piaget, Jean, 80
Pichai, Sundar, 194
Pinker, Steven, 56, 57
Plato, 77
play, 80–82
pluralism
  banning certain mental models,
    186–187
  benefits of, 176
  Chinese versus European societies,
    183–185
  coexistence of competing mental
    models,
    198–199
  cultural diversity and, 193
  debate in "public sphere,"
    195–197
  in economic and political spheres,
    176–177
  education and childhood
    socialization to foster, 190–191
  embracing variation to foster,
    188–190
  expansion and restriction of,
    173–176
  flourishing of multiplicity of
    clashing mental models, 177–178
  as fostering and celebrating
    differences, 14–15
  friction resulting from, 194–195
  goal of, 186
  importance of, 151–152,
    179–181, 186
  as means to end, 177
  migration and mobility to foster,
    191–194
  as necessary for societal survival,
    177–178
  reapplication of same mental
    models and, 179
  social pressure to censor and, 186
  versus uniformity of mental
    models, 14–15
  as unnatural state for humans,
    187–188
Podolny, Joel, 149–151, 164–165
Poetics (Aristotle), 84–85
Popper, Karl, 178, 244
Porat, Ruth, 194
possibilities. *See* options
Pozo, Susan, 154
pretending/pretend play, 80–82
problem-solving. *See* solutions
"problem space," 166–167
progress, counterfactuals as crucial to,
  12–13

quantitative easing, 51

racial discrimination and
  color-blindness, 191
Rand, Ayn, 194
reading, silently or aloud, 42–44
reality/realities. *See also* alternative
  realities
  causality enables comprehension
    and explainability of, 52, 60
  constraints as impacting current,
    117–118
  frames simplify, 9
  human cognition as
    simulation of, 26
  human comprehension of, through
    analogies, 230
  order in, 71
  of terrorists, 214
Redd, Dana, 135
reframing
  characteristics of individuals
    involved in, 136–137
  circumstances surrounding,
    140–141
  difficulty of repeatedly, 138–139
  difficulty of unlearning, 140
  efficiently, 129–131, 144
  effort demanded by, 139–140
  examples of, 123–126, 202–203
  failure and, 132–133
  frequency of, 11, 143
  impacts of inventions on, 10
  importance of mental diversity
    when, 162–163

paradigm shifts and, 10–11
provides new options, 126
by reinvention, 131–132, 220
by repertoire riffling, 13–14,
    128–129, 220
by repurposing, 129–131,
    203–204, 220
as revolutionary act, 133
as riskier and potentially more
    rewarding than staying with
    existing mental models, 209
tendency to coalesce around
    consensus position when, 164
timing of, 141–142
Regional Advantage (Saxenian), 183
Remarque, Erich Maria, 83–84
The Republic (Plato), 77
responsibility, 64, 65–66
right-wing populists, governance by
    innate sense of rightness of one's
    beliefs, 16
The Rise of the Creative Class
    (Florida), 192
Rorschach tests, 6
Rousseau, Jean-Jacques, 16–17, 80, 132

Sacco, Joe, 135
same-sex marriage campaign (US),
    188–190
Sapiens (Harari), 79
SARS, 31, 32
Saxenian, AnnaLee, 183
Schwartz, Peter, 111–113
Science, 163–164
sciences
    broadening range of frames,
        160–161, 241
    China versus Europe,
        184–185
    development of drugs, 2–3
    free flow of information and, 215
    invention of new frames and
        physics, 7–8
    reframing in, 131–132, 137
    tension between mental
        models in, 160
    understanding human cognition
        and, 206
scientific management theory, 17
scientific method, 67
self-driving cars, 92–93

Semmelweis, Ignaz, 60–61, 62
Seuss, Dr. (Geisel), 101–102, 103
sexual harassment in Hollywood,
    23–24
Shklar, Judith, 197–198
Shomron, Dan, 97, 98, 99, 107
Simon, Herbert, 152
simulations, importance of, 115–117
Singapore, 144–145
"singularity," 15
Smalltalk, 159, 241
social coordination
    human understanding of need for,
        57–58
    individual and, 221
    as marker apex of our past and elixir
        of our future, 205–206, 208
social structures
    agency and, 66
    belief in validity of dominant
        mental models, 179
    benefits from pluralism to, 176
    Camden, New Jersey, police force,
        134–136
    constraints as impacting, 117–118
    friction resulting from pluralism,
        194–195
    mutability and, 107
    pluralism and survival of,
        177–178
    rise and fall of, and mental
        diversity, 183–185
    role of "loyal opposition"/court
        jester, 168–169
    tendency toward homophily, 89,
        162, 234
solutions
    advantages of variation when
        identifying, 166–167, 176
    from faulty mental models,
        60–61
    framing need for efficient, 144
    hyper-rationalists' reliance on
        technology, 15–16, 69
    mental models as means of finding,
        4–5, 8, 38–39
    Occam's razor, 108
"Some Philosophical Problems from
    the Standpoint of Artificial
    Intelligence" (McCarthy), 44
Soviet Union, Lysenkoism, 7

space exploration
    mental models and, 33–35
    mutability principle applied to,
        105–106
SpaceX, 105–106, 107
Spielberg, Steven, 111–113
Spotify, 145–146
statisticians and causality, 68
Stern, Johanna, 173–174
stimuli, reacting to, 52
Stockfish program, 18
Strassmann, Fritz, 132–133
"structural holes," 157
subconscious, development
    of frames, 8
Süskind, Patrick, 83

Tamir, Noam, 99, 100
Taylor, Frederick, 17
technology. *See also* artificial
    intelligence (AI)
    cannot conjure constraints, 118
    computer programming,
        158–159, 241
    as hyper-rationalists' answer to
        problems, 15–16, 69, 210–211
    inability of, to frame, 17–18,
        44, 45–46
    lack of counterfactuals, 76
    need of, for human input of causal
        mental modes to outperform
        humans, 70
    object-oriented programming of
        computers, 159, 241
    as product of accumulation of
        improvements across time, 58–59
    transformation of immutable to
        mutable constraints, 106
terrorism, 212–214
"theory theory," 81
Thiel, Peter, 194
Thomson, Scott, 135, 136
tolerance, paradox of, 178, 244
tolerance and imagination,
    192–193
Tomasello, Michael, 56, 57–58
Tooby, John, 230
transcendence, abstraction and
    generalization as necessary for, 55

Triboulet (court jester), 169
truth, 20, 180
Tversky, Amos, 10
Tyndall, John, 74, 232

ultra-emotionalists
    as bad framers, 210
    causality and, 68–69
    as impulse followers,
        209–210
    mental models and, 69
    reliance on gut and instinct,
        16–17
    uniqueness of human cognition
        and, 18
Unger, Roberto, 196–197
unitary versus variety, 179–182
US Constitution, framers of, 29

values, 39
    imagination and, 39
    mental models as
        operationalizing, 39
Vavilov, Nikolai, 7, 11
video games, 69–70, 85–86
"visualizations," 94

Walt Disney Company, 46
Watson, James, 132
Waymo, 92–93
Weinstock, Peter, 117
Weiss, Bari, 170–171
Welch, Jack, 17
wheel, development of, 58, 59
Wiles, Andrew, 137–138
will.i.am, 120
William of Ockham, 108
Willis, Bruce, 194
Wittgenstein, Ludwig, 25
"world building," 114
worldview, mental models as shaping,
    39–40
Wright, Orville and Wilbur, 36–38
Wysocki, Joseph, 36

Xerox PARC, 158–159, 182

"zando test," 81–82
Zuckerberg, Mark, 205

about the authors

KENNETH CUKIER is a senior editor at *The Economist* and host of its weekly podcast on technology, *Babbage*. He is also an associate fellow at Saïd Business School at the University of Oxford.

VIKTOR MAYER-SCHÖNBERGER is professor of internet governance and regulation at the Oxford Internet Institute at the University of Oxford. He is also a faculty affiliate of the Belfer Center of Science and International Affairs at Harvard University.

FRANCIS DE VÉRICOURT is professor of management science and the director of the Center for Decisions, Models, and Data at the European School of Management and Technology (ESMT) in Berlin.